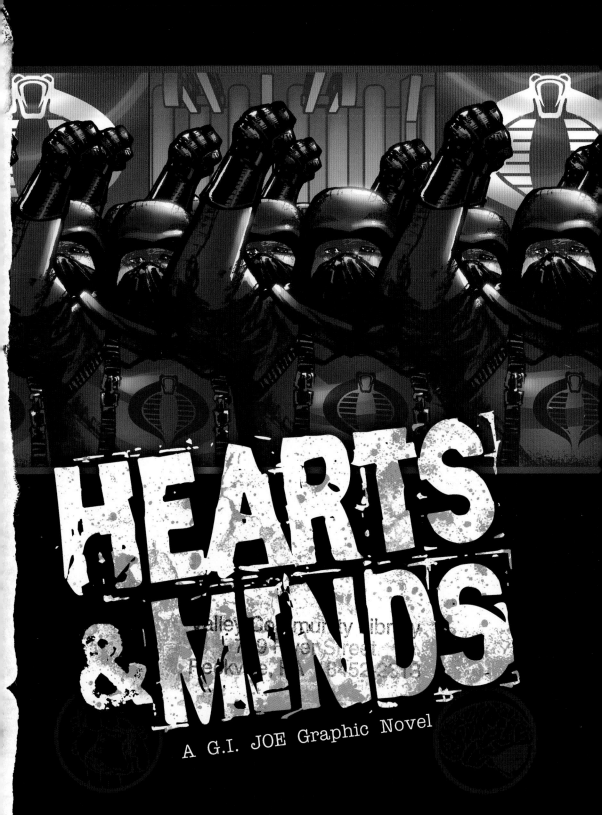

HEARTS & MINDS

A G.I. JOE Graphic Novel

ASSISTANT EDITOR:
CARLOS GUZMAN

COLLECTION EDITOR:
JUSTIN EISINGER

COLLECTION DESIGNER:
NEIL UYETAKE

COVER DESIGN:
BILL TORTOLINI

Licensed By:

Special thanks to Hasbro's Aaron Archer, Michael Kelly, Amie Lozanski, Joe Furfaro, Ed Lane, Michael Provost, Erin Hillman, Samantha Lomow, and Michael Verrecchia for their invaluable assistance.

www.**IDWPUBLISHING**.com   ISBN: 978-1-60010-776-4   13 12 11 10   1 2 3 4

IDW Publishing is: Operations: Ted Adams, CEO & Publisher • Greg Goldstein, Chief Operating Officer • Matthew Ruzicka, CPA, Chief Financial Officer • Alan Payne, VP of Sales • Lorelei Bunjes, Director of Digital Services • Jeff Webber, Director of ePublishing • AnnaMaria White, Dir., Marketing and Public Relations • Dirk Wood, Dir., Retail Marketing • Marci Hubbard, Executive Assistant • Alonzo Simon, Shipping Manager • Angela Loggins, Staff Accountant • Cherrie Go, Assistant Web Designer • Editorial: Chris Ryall, Chief Creative Officer, Editor-In-Chief • Scott Dunbier, Senior Editor, Special Projects • Andy Schmidt, Senior Editor • Bob Schreck, Senior Editor • Justin Eisinger, Senior Editor, Books • Kris Oprisko, Editor/Foreign Lic. • Denton J. Tipton, Editor • Tom Waltz, Editor • Mariah Huehner, Editor • Carlos Guzman, Assistant Editor • Bobby Curnow, Assistant Editor • Design: Robbie Robbins, EVP/Sr. Graphic Artist • Neil Uyetake, Senior Art Director • Chris Mowry, Senior Graphic Artist • Amauri Osorio, Graphic Artist • Gilberto Lazcano, Production Assistant • Shawn Lee, Graphic Artist

FOREWORD

"We have no alternative, call in G.I. JOE!" Those words came from the first animated TV commercial to announce the launch of a new line of Marvel comic books. I can't remember how old I was, or what was happening in my life, but I remember that commercial, as I did the next one that advertised a new line of action figures. They began with "Infantry Trooper—Code Name: Grunt" and ended with "Commando—Code Name: Snake Eyes." I remember the first time I saw those action figures, sitting on display at a friend's house. They seemed to be light-years ahead of the other 3¾-inch action figures (from a franchise that shall remain nameless); their detail, their weapons, even their ability to bend at the knees and elbows. This was, of course, before the earth-shattering invention of the "kung-fu grip." They say you never forget your first love. Mine was Scarlett. She was beautiful and smart and had a small semiautomatic pistol on the inside of her forearm. What more could any man ask?

They also say you never forget your first G.I. JOE comic. Mine was issue number 34: "Shakedown" by Sensei Larry Hama. It was the story of a dogfight between Ace and Lady J in a Skystriker, and Wild Weasel and Baroness in a Rattler. It was thrilling and intelligent and, I believe, as Eisner-worthy as anything out there. I still keep that worn yellow issue on the shelf next to my desk. I still smile when I re-read the last few panels, as both Ace and Wild Weasel, after trading missile and gunfire, end their duel by trading mutual salutes.

A big thanks to Christos Gage for introducing me to the crew at IDW (incidentally, his graphic novel *Area 10* will blow you away!). And thanks to everyone at IDW, especially Andy Schmidt. Being allowed to write for G.I. JOE is one of those childhood fantasies that can't be rivaled. The initial concept for *Hearts and Minds* as a series came directly from Andy Schmidt. After reading my first writing sample, a day in the life of Firefly, he suggested I expand it into a five-issue, ten-story miniseries. He thought it would be great to just read about some of the characters' backstories, their methods and motivations, their "hearts" and "minds." If, after reading this, you agree, then feel free to direct your praise directly at Andy.

My deepest gratitude goes to, of course, my partners in this creative endeavor, Howard Chaykin and Antonio Fuso. To me, comic books will always be a visual medium and comic artists will always be the stars. I'm just the guy who does the scribbling, and, incidentally, not all of my scribbling is even my own. The narration part of the "Doc" story... probably the best writing in the whole project... that's not me, that's the Hippocratic Oath. Howard and Antonio are both masters in their field and this newb feels especially privileged to share the same cover credits with them.

Hearts and Minds was a labor of love, a chance to revisit with some of the heroes of my youth. Hopefully I've managed to impart some of that passion in these pages. **YO JOE!**

Max Brooks
September 2010

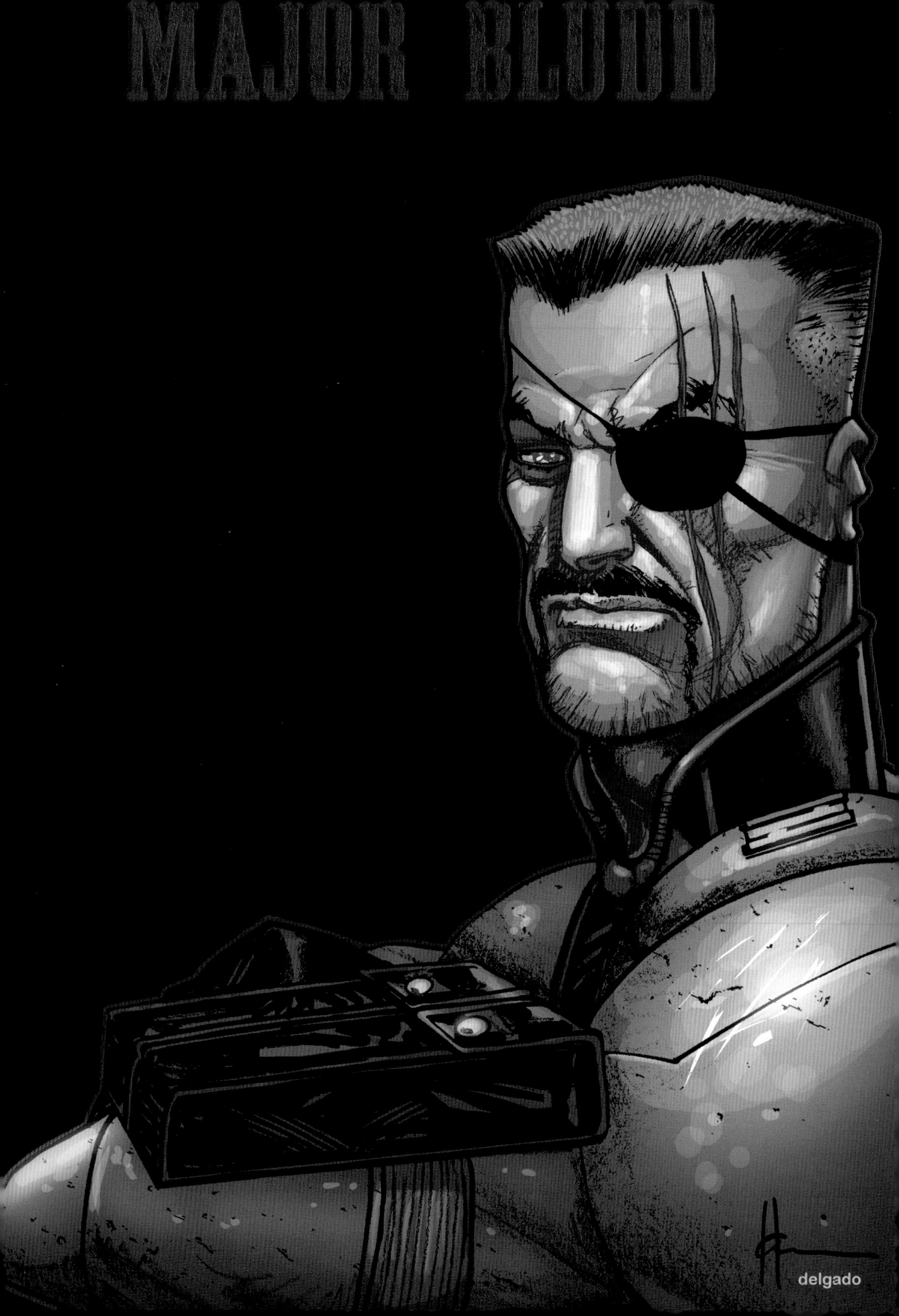
MAJOR BLUDD
delgado

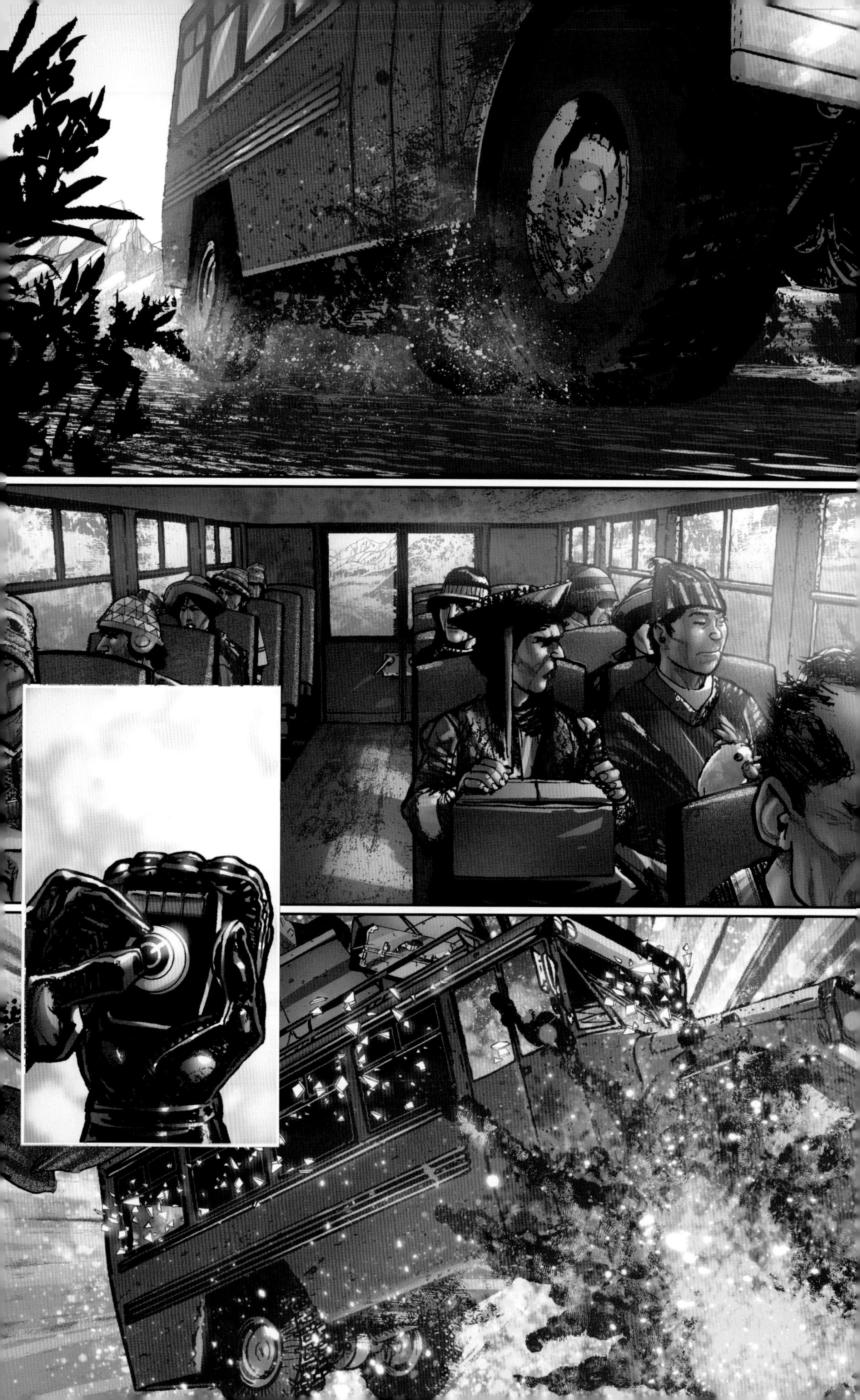

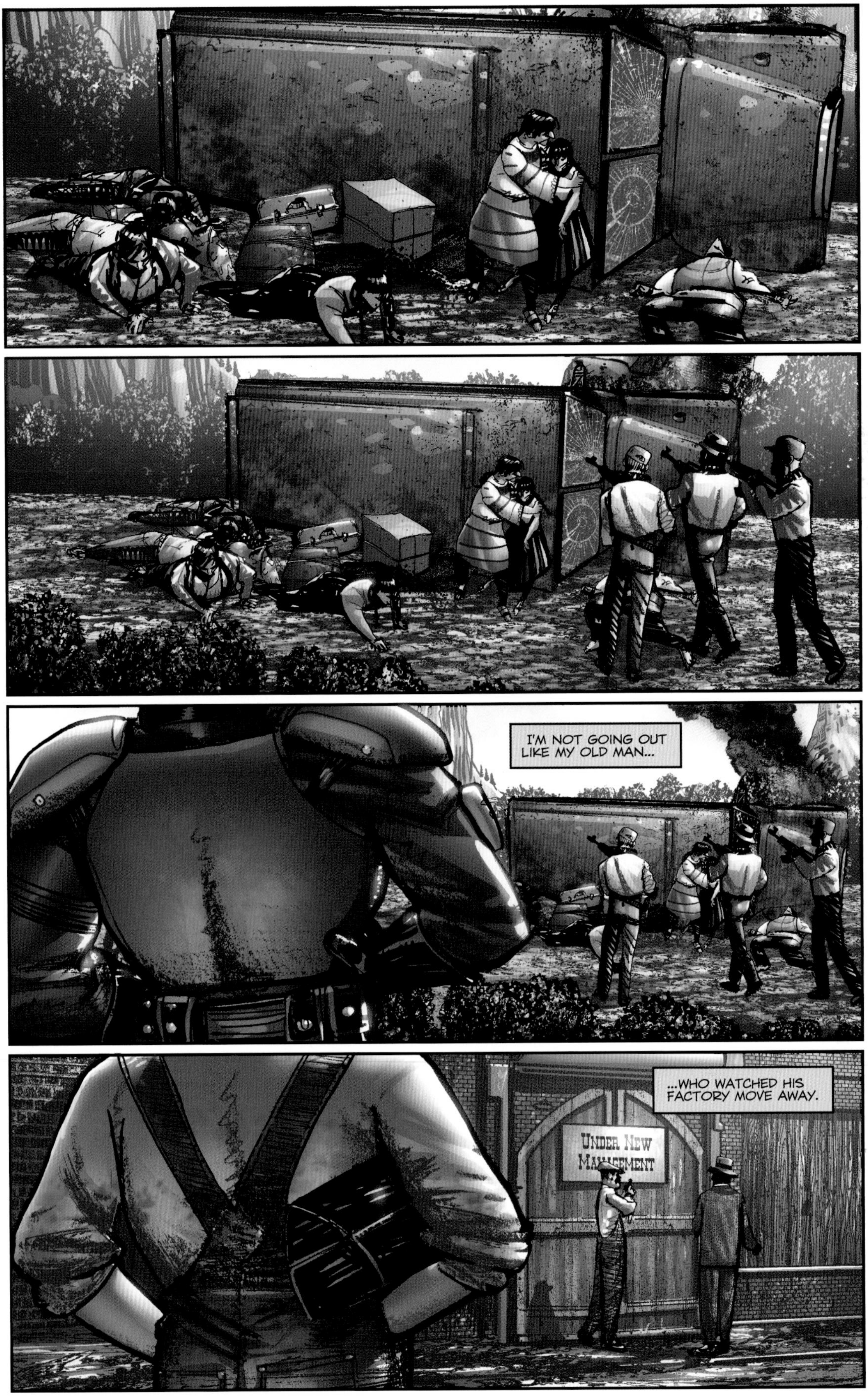
I'M NOT GOING OUT LIKE MY OLD MAN...
...WHO WATCHED HIS FACTORY MOVE AWAY.
UNDER NEW MANAGEMENT

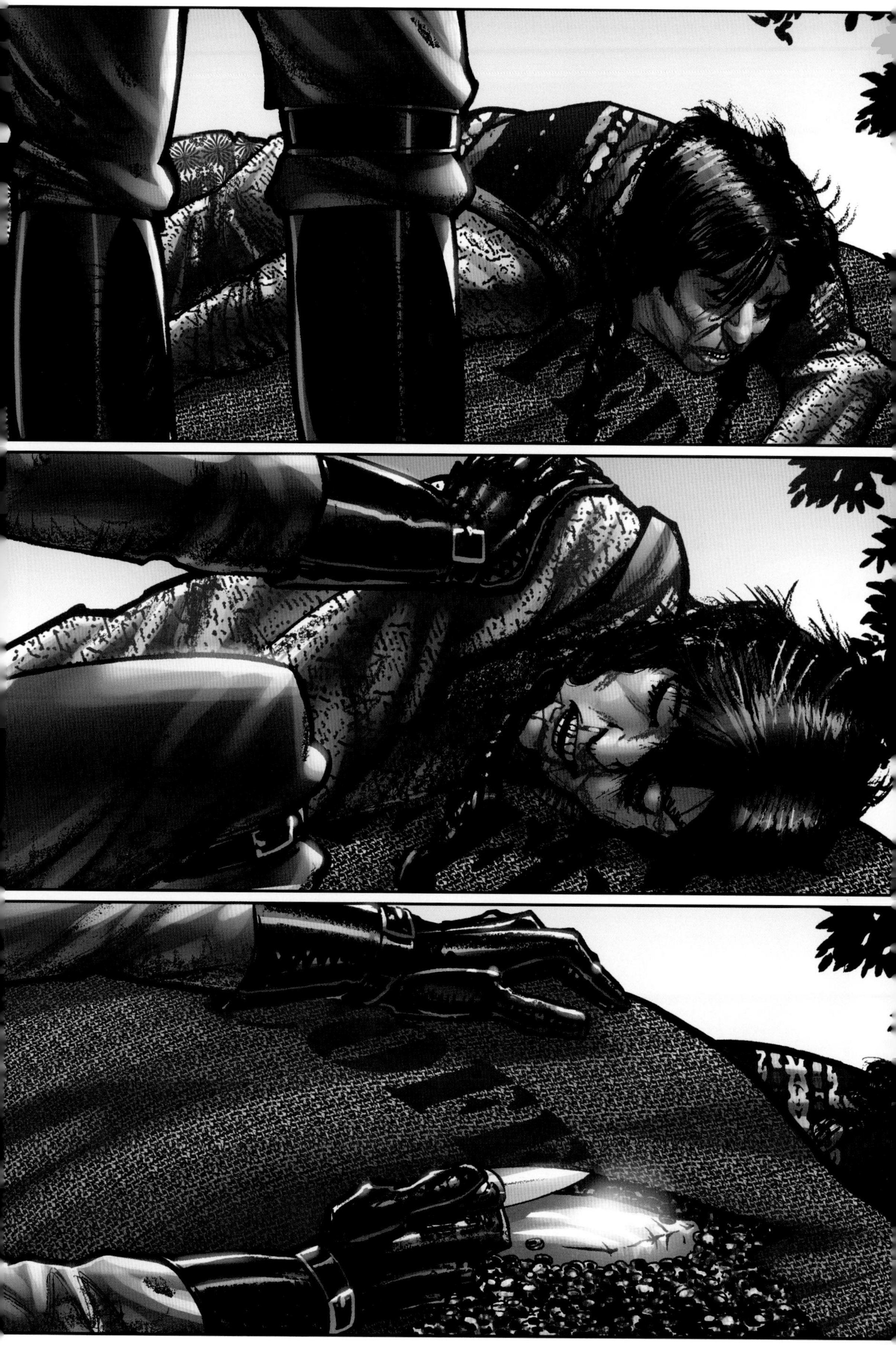

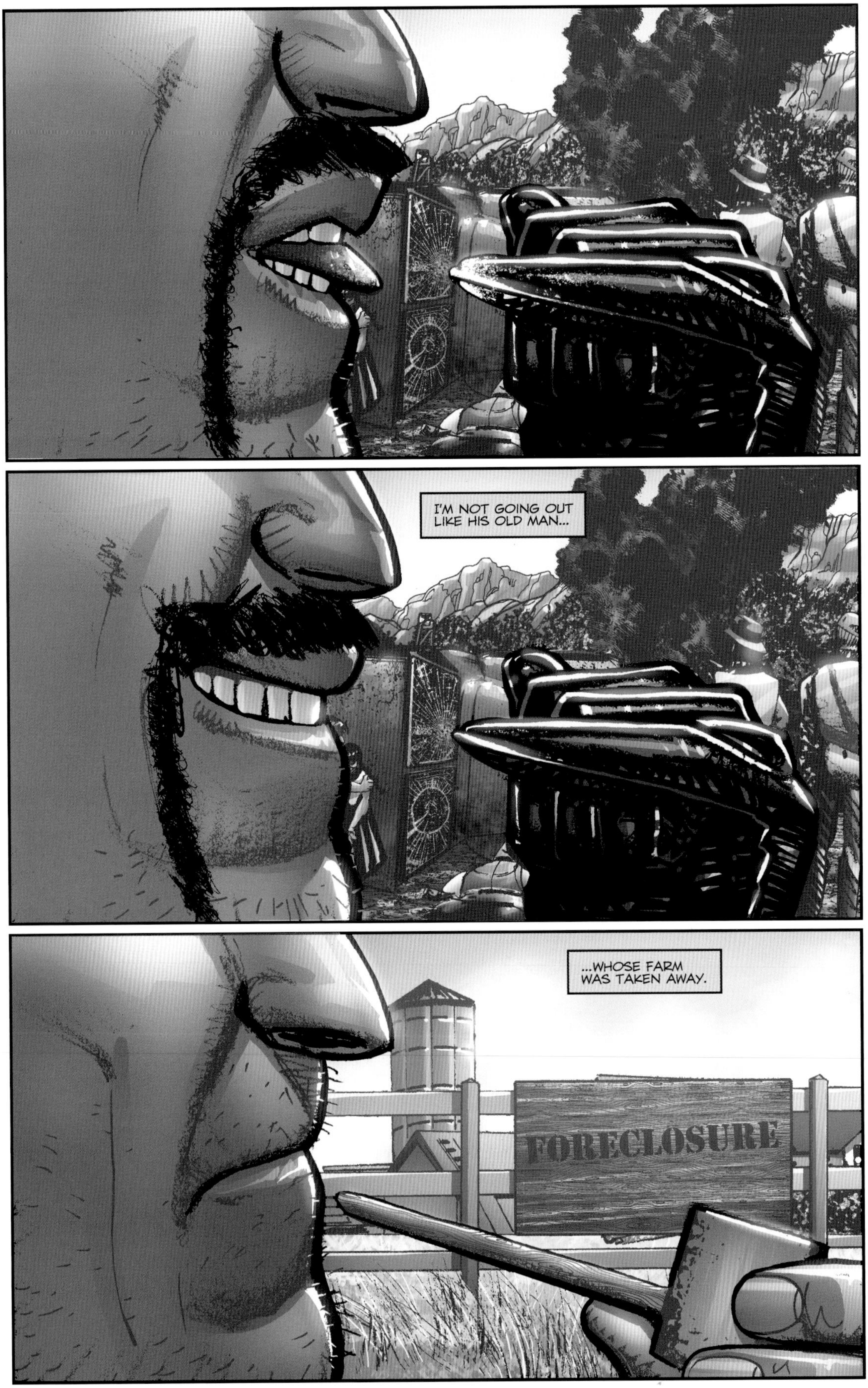
I'M NOT GOING OUT LIKE HIS OLD MAN...
...WHOSE FARM WAS TAKEN AWAY.
FORECLOSURE

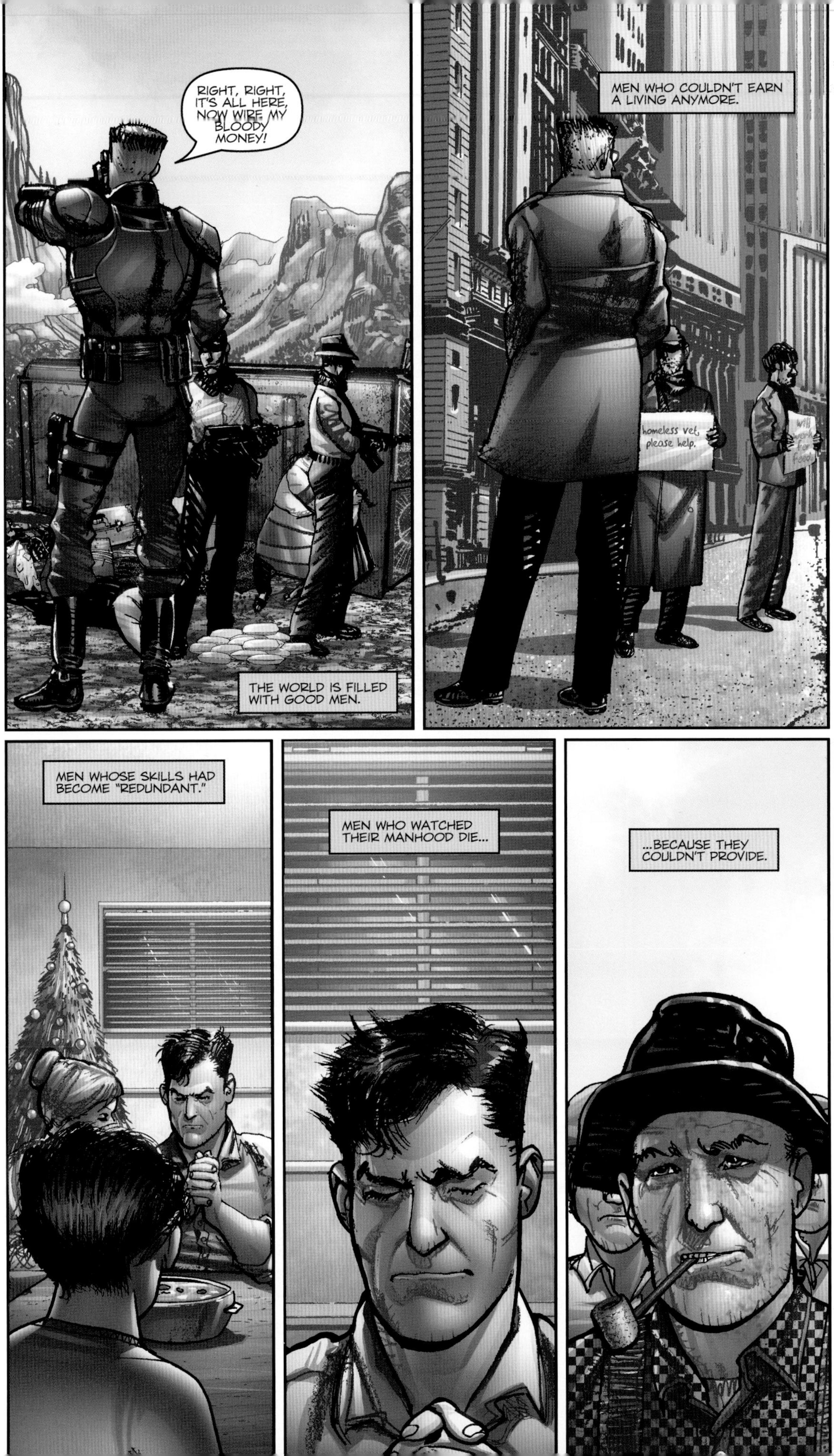
RIGHT, RIGHT, IT'S ALL HERE, NOW WIRE MY BLOODY MONEY!
THE WORLD IS FILLED WITH GOOD MEN.
MEN WHO COULDN'T EARN A LIVING ANYMORE.
homeless vet, please help.
MEN WHOSE SKILLS HAD BECOME "REDUNDANT."
MEN WHO WATCHED THEIR MANHOOD DIE...
...BECAUSE THEY COULDN'T PROVIDE.

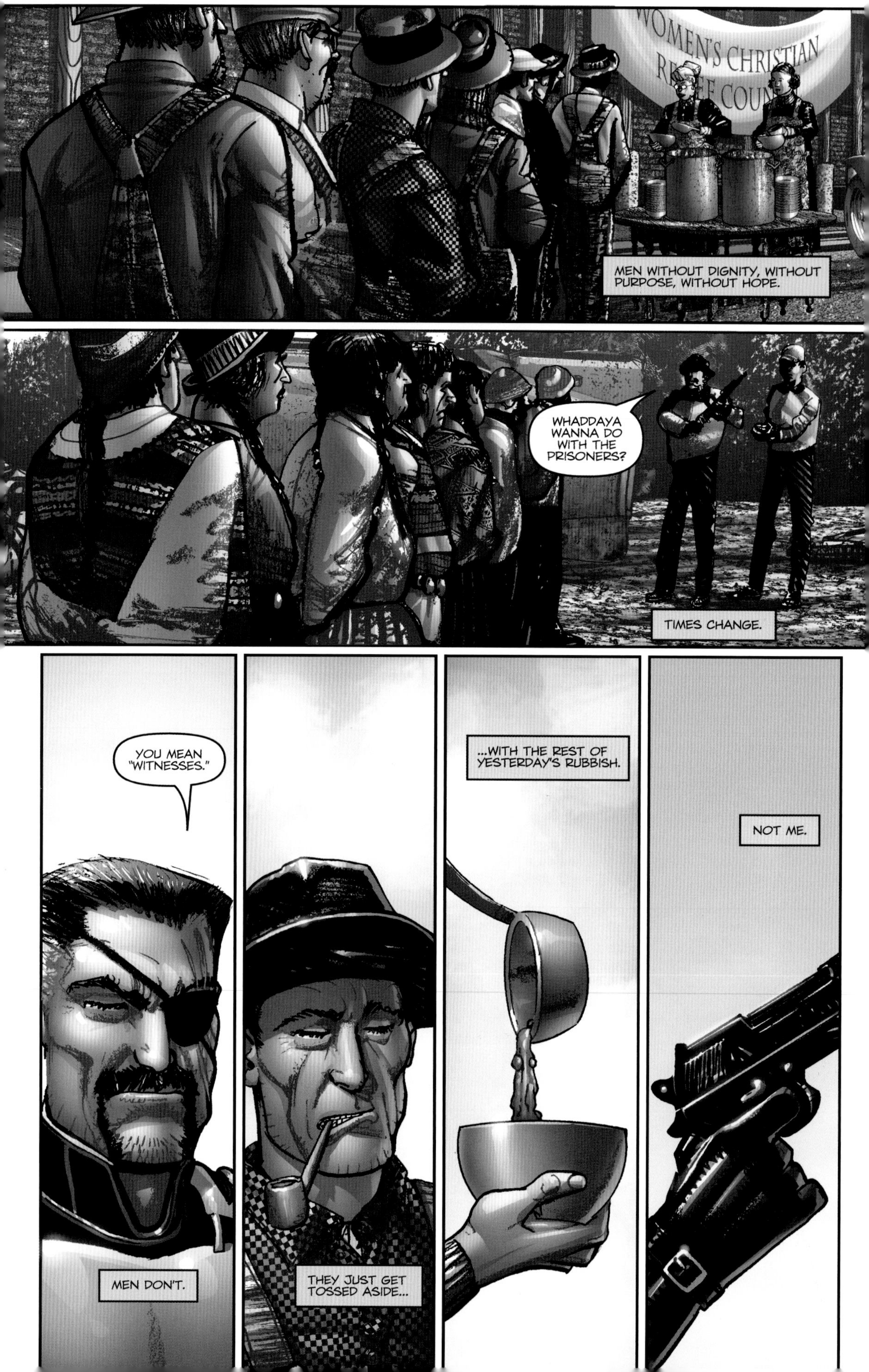
WOMEN'S CHRISTIAN
MEN WITHOUT DIGNITY, WITHOUT PURPOSE, WITHOUT HOPE.
WHADDAYA WANNA DO WITH THE PRISONERS?
TIMES CHANGE.
YOU MEAN "WITNESSES."
MEN DON'T.
THEY JUST GET TOSSED ASIDE...
...WITH THE REST OF YESTERDAY'S RUBBISH.
NOT ME.

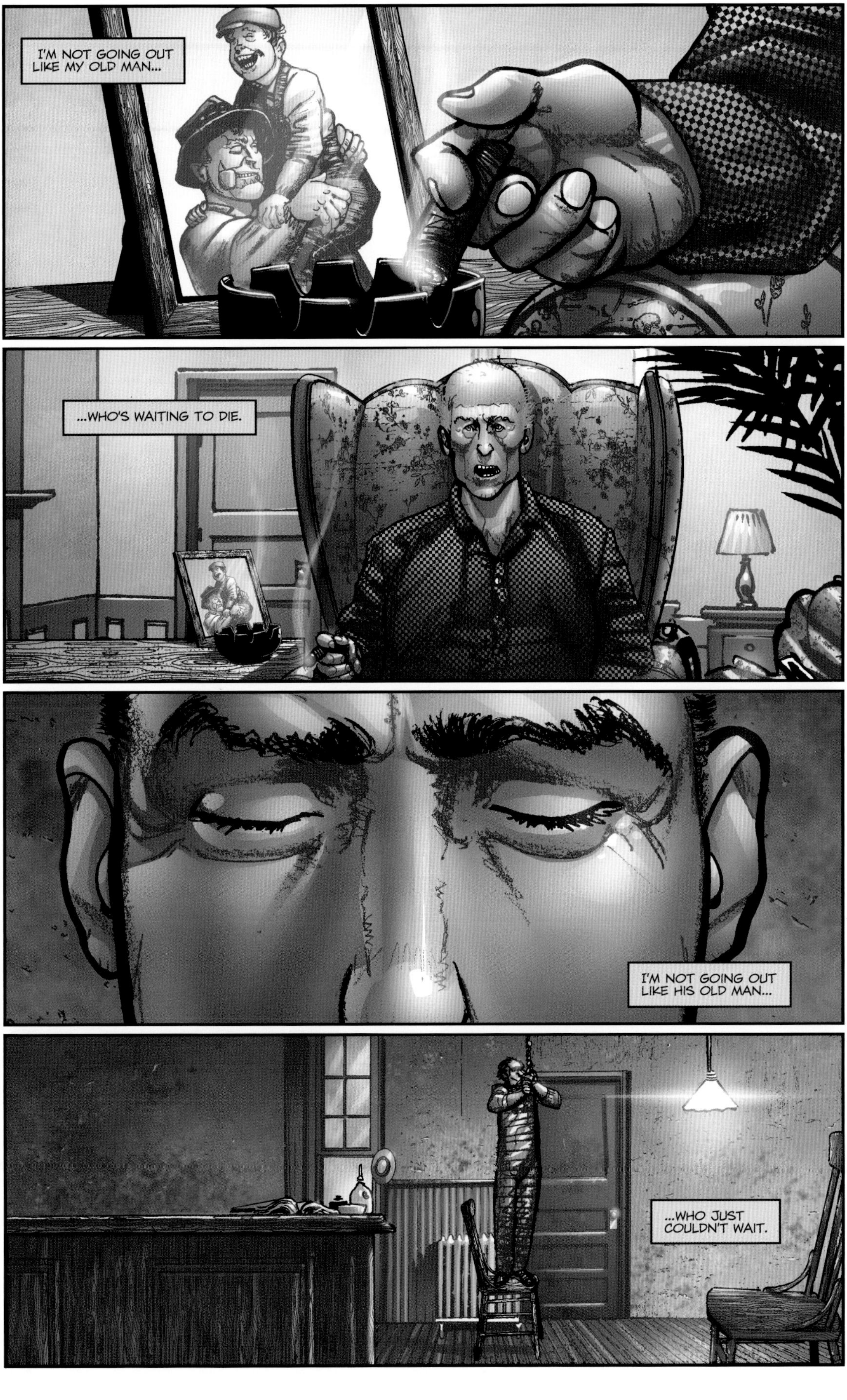
I'M NOT GOING OUT LIKE MY OLD MAN...
...WHO'S WAITING TO DIE.
I'M NOT GOING OUT LIKE HIS OLD MAN...
...WHO JUST COULDN'T WAIT.

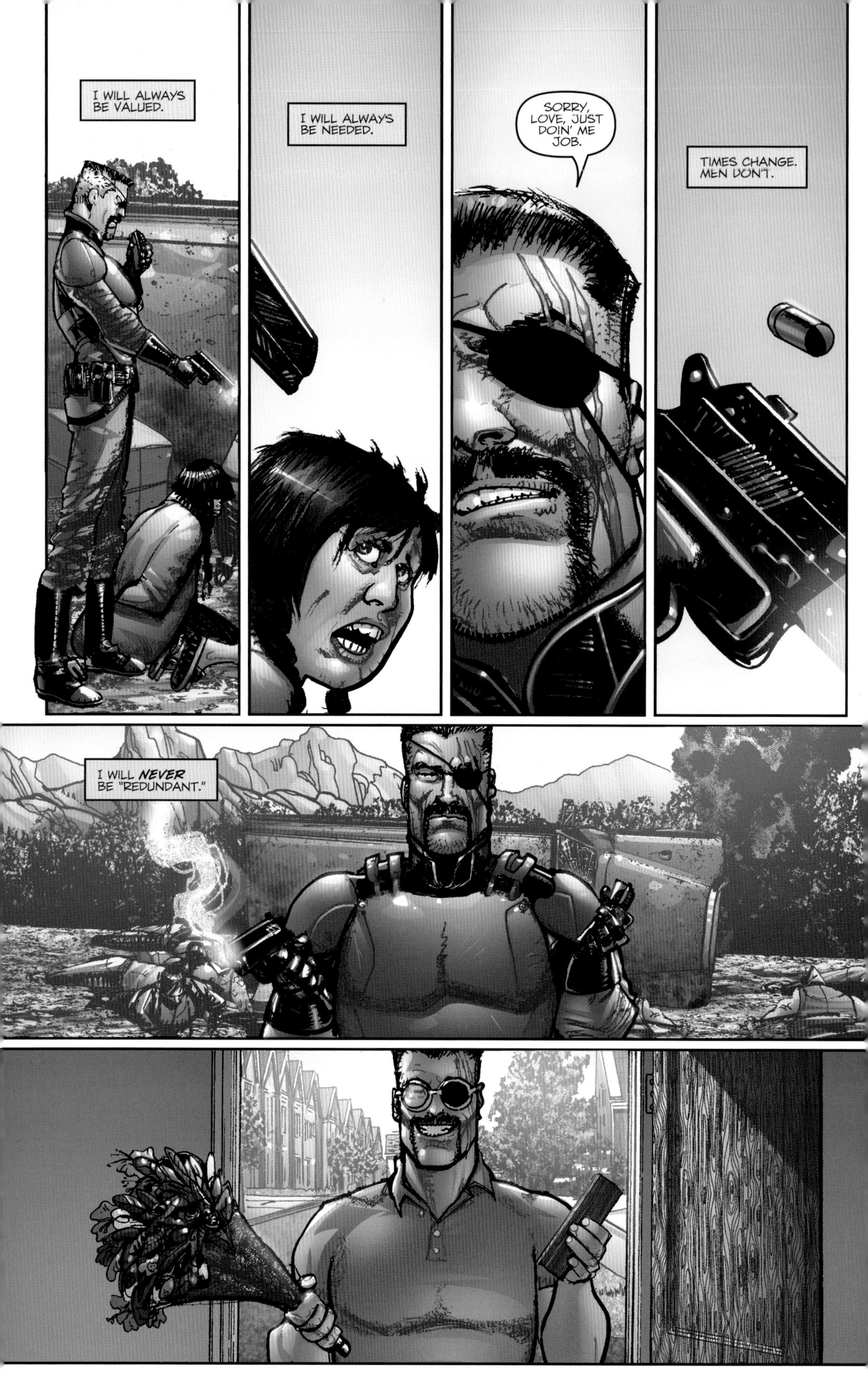
I WILL ALWAYS BE VALUED.
I WILL ALWAYS BE NEEDED.
SORRY, LOVE, JUST DOIN' ME JOB.
TIMES CHANGE. MEN DON'T.
I WILL *NEVER* BE "REDUNDANT."

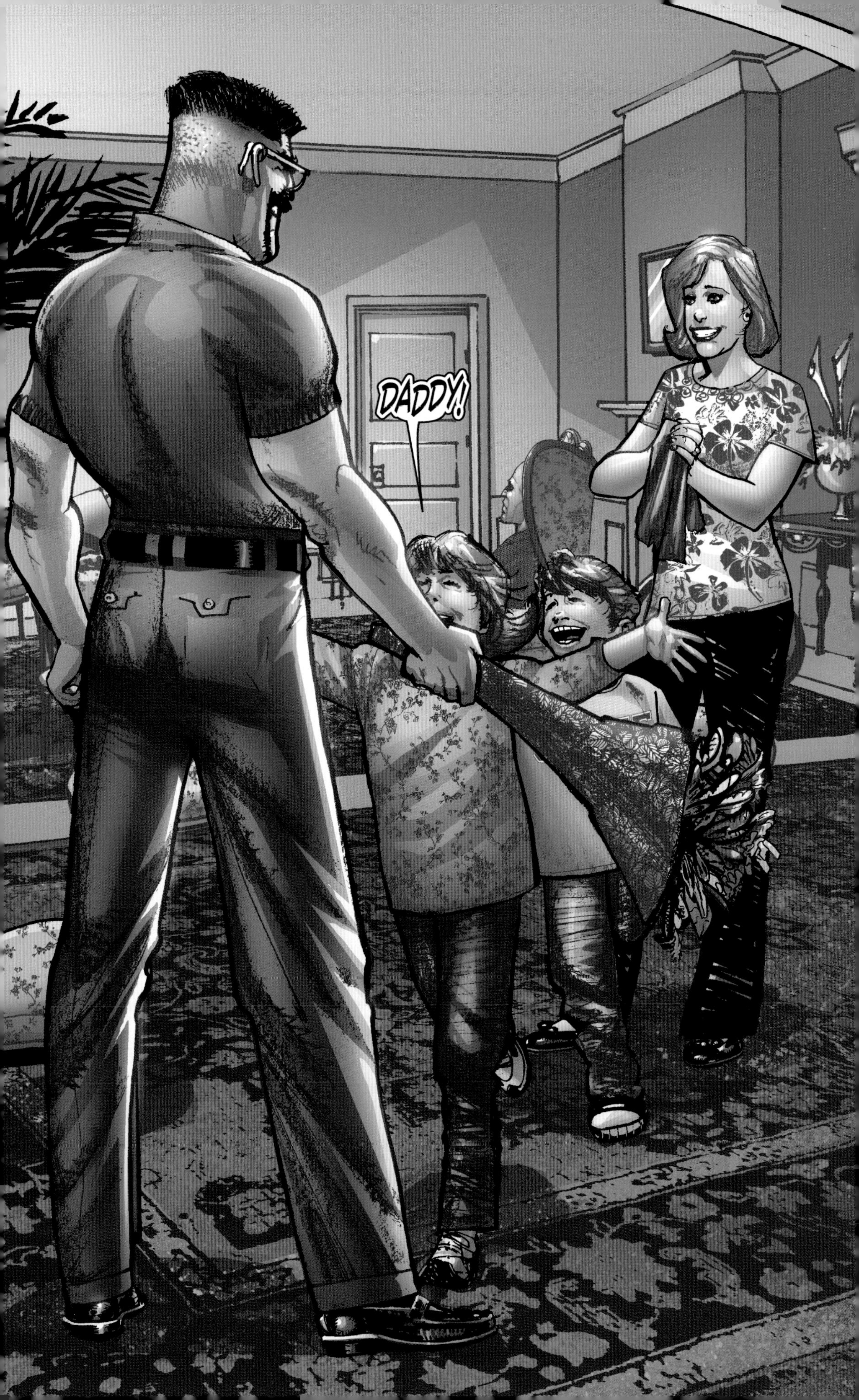
DADDY!

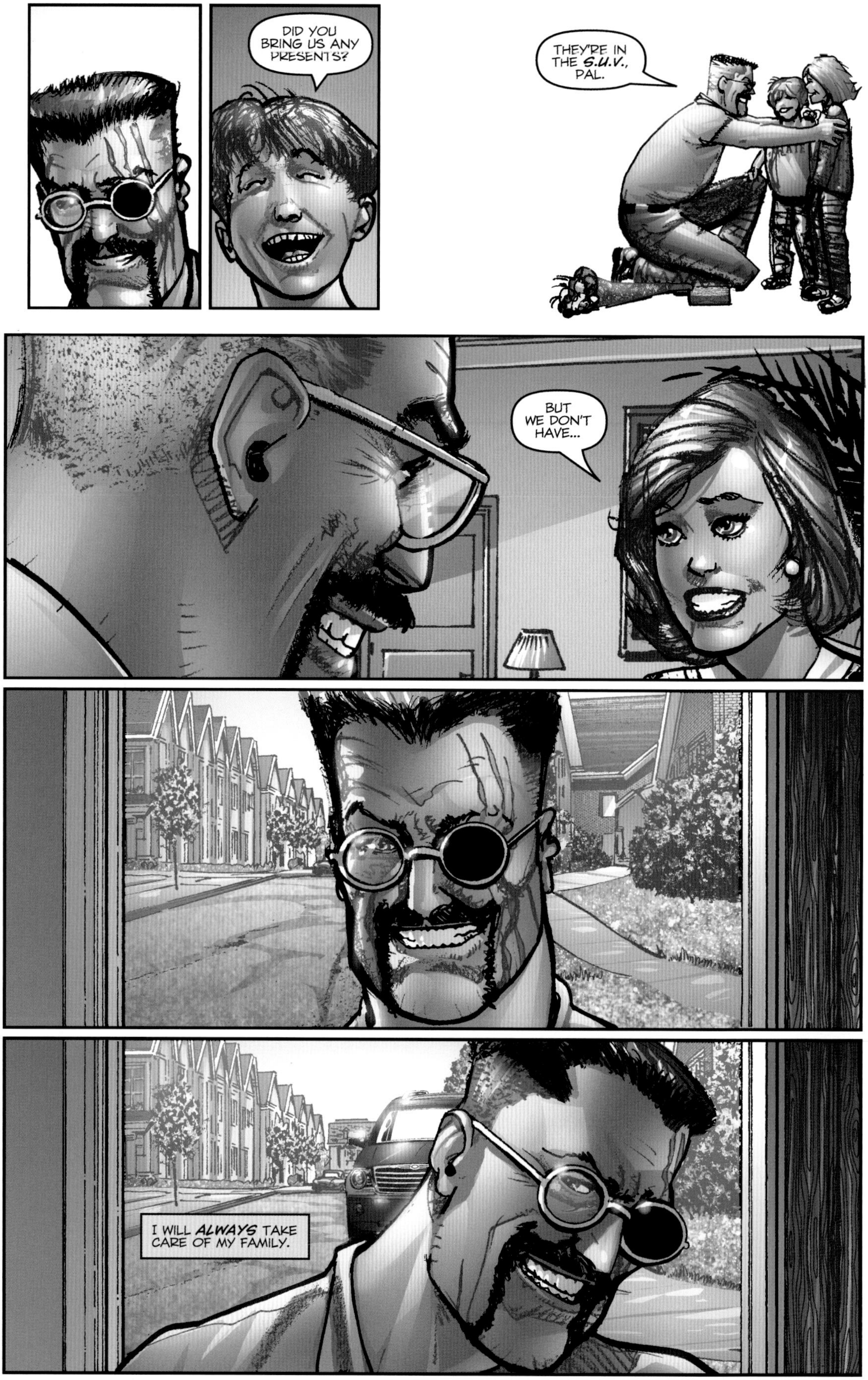
DID YOU BRING US ANY PRESENTS?
THEY'RE IN THE S.U.V., PAL.
BUT WE DON'T HAVE...
I WILL ALWAYS TAKE CARE OF MY FAMILY.

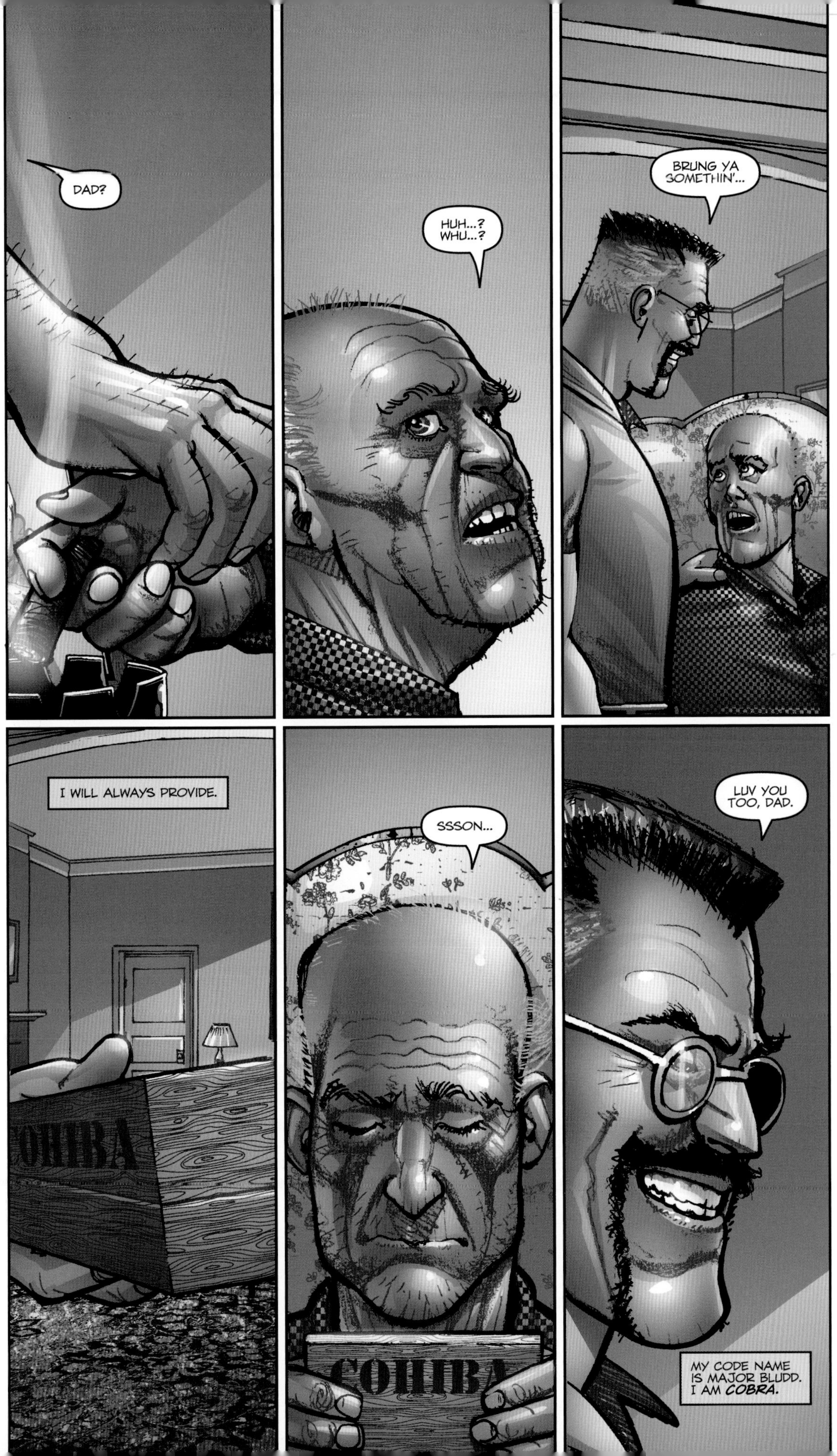
DAD?
HUH...? WHU...?
BRUNG YA SOMETHIN'...
I WILL ALWAYS PROVIDE.
COHIBA
SSSON...
COHIBA
LUV YOU TOO, DAD.
MY CODE NAME IS MAJOR BLUDD. I AM COBRA.

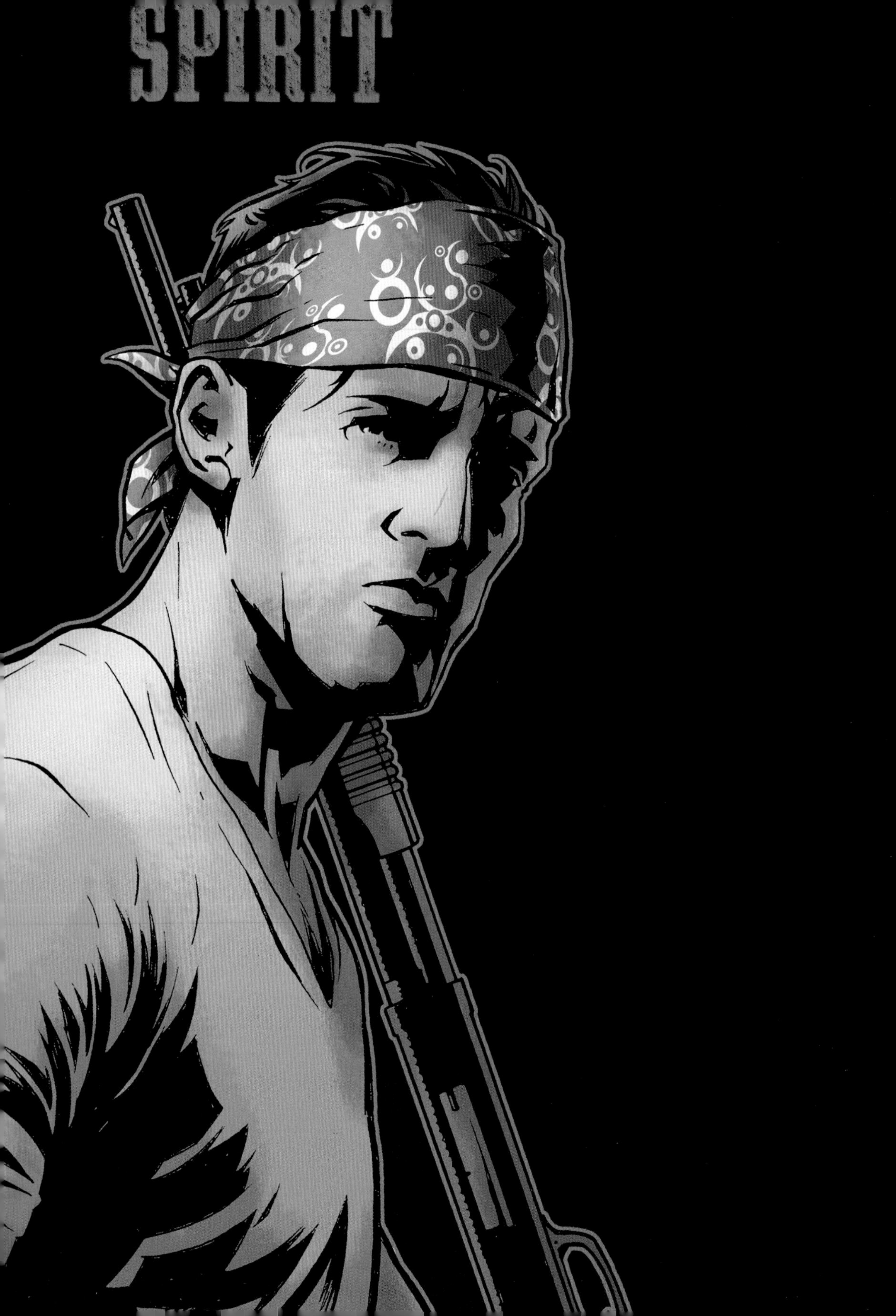
SPIRIT

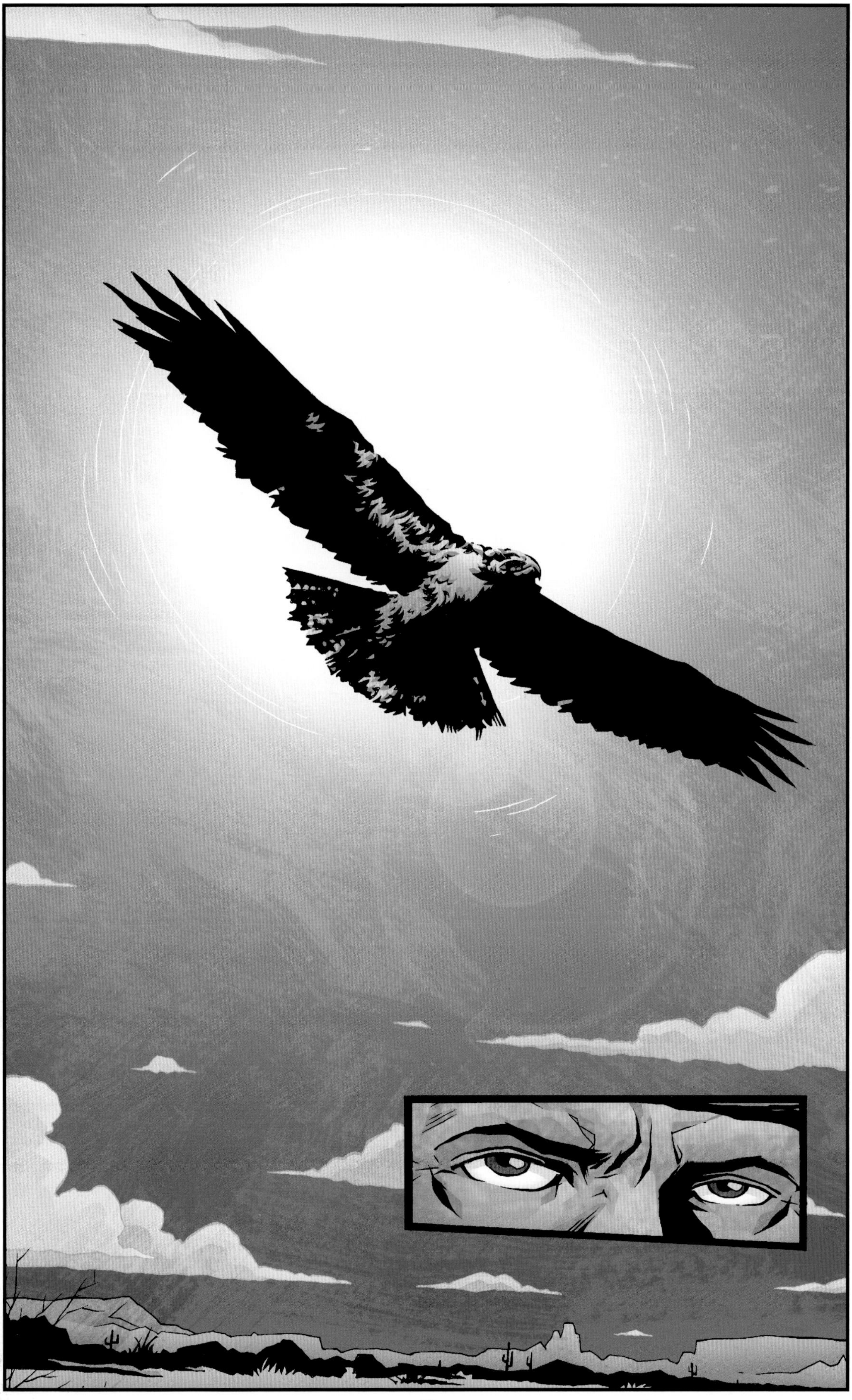

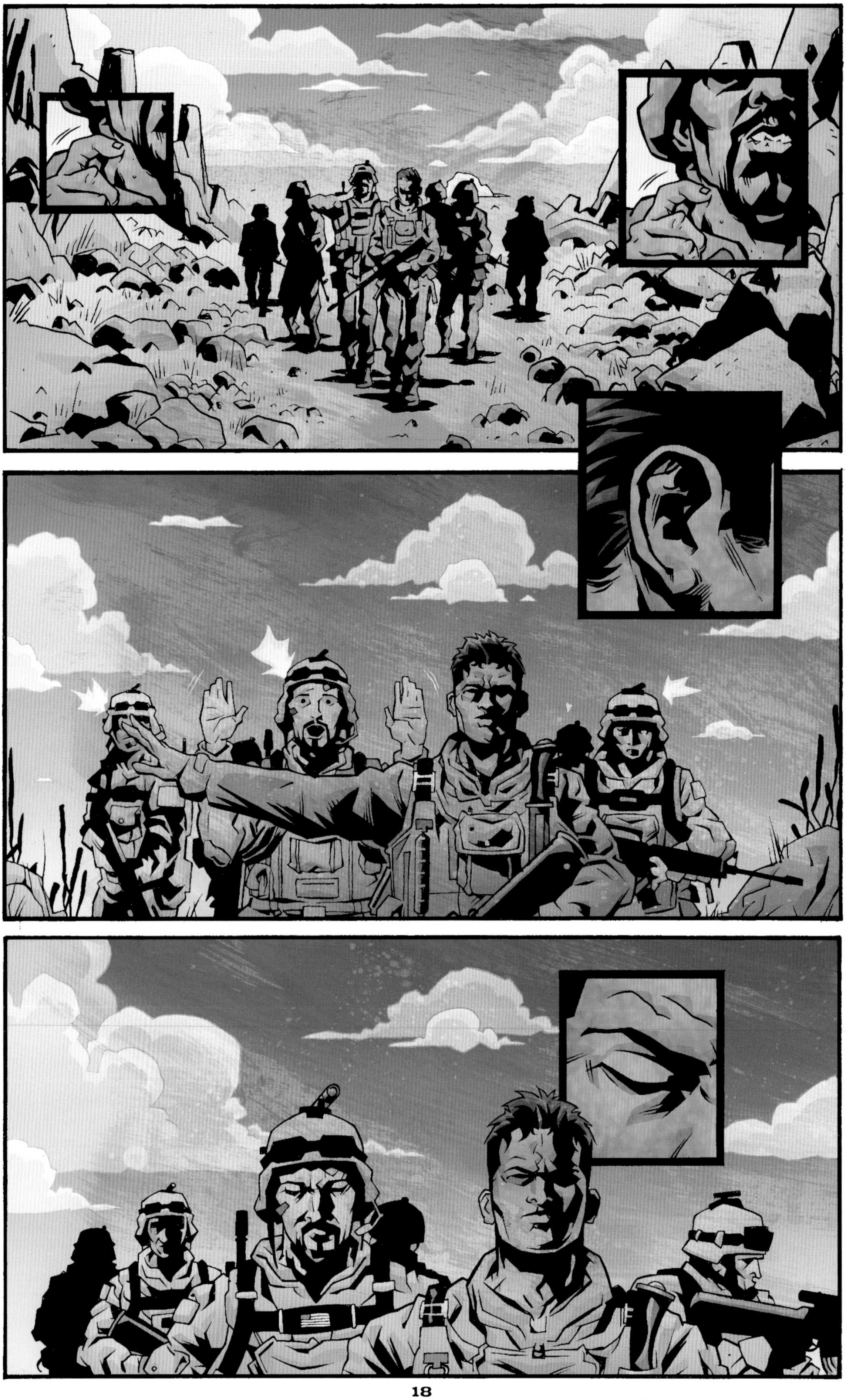

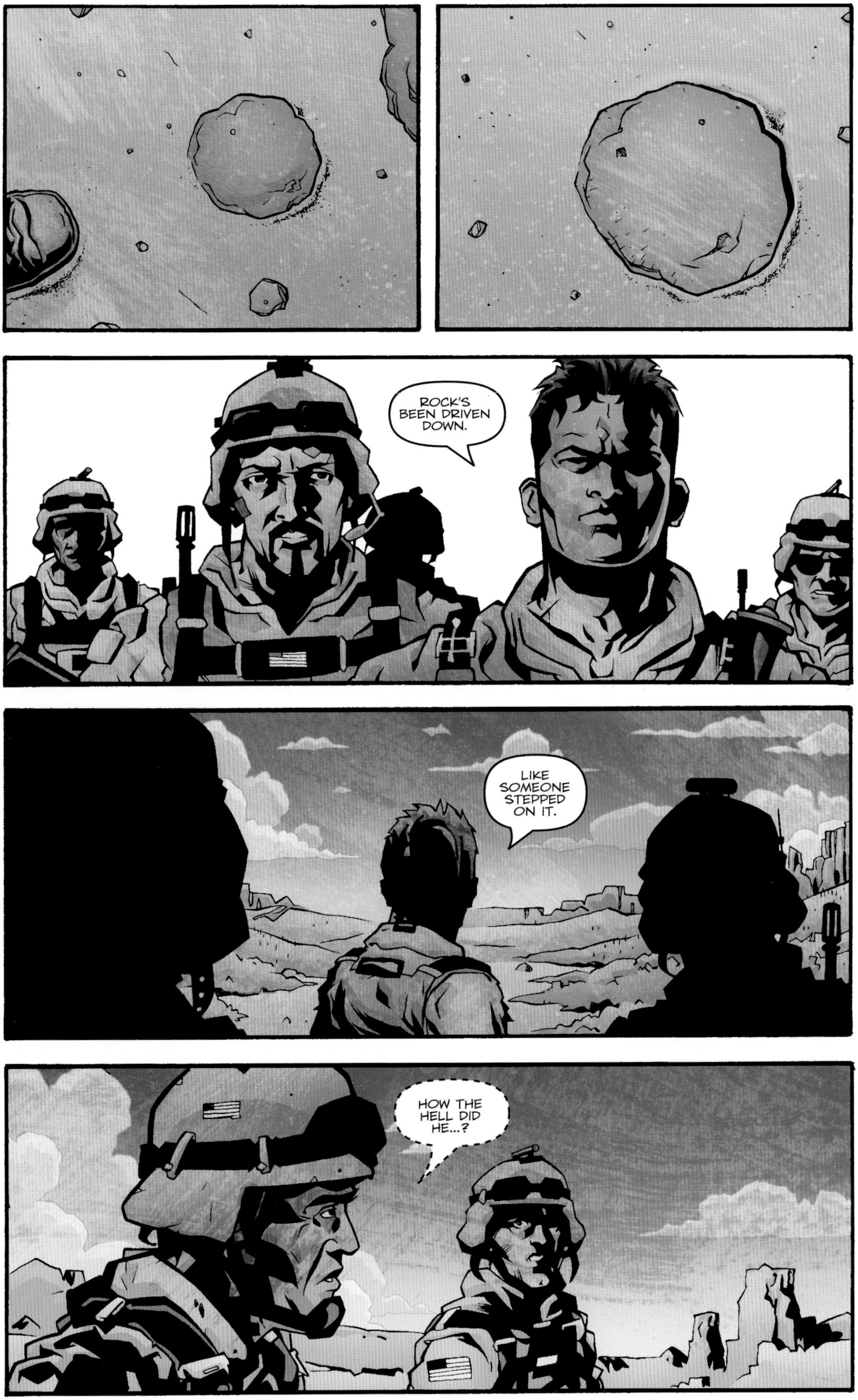
ROCK'S BEEN DRIVEN DOWN.
LIKE SOMEONE STEPPED ON IT.
HOW THE HELL DID HE...?

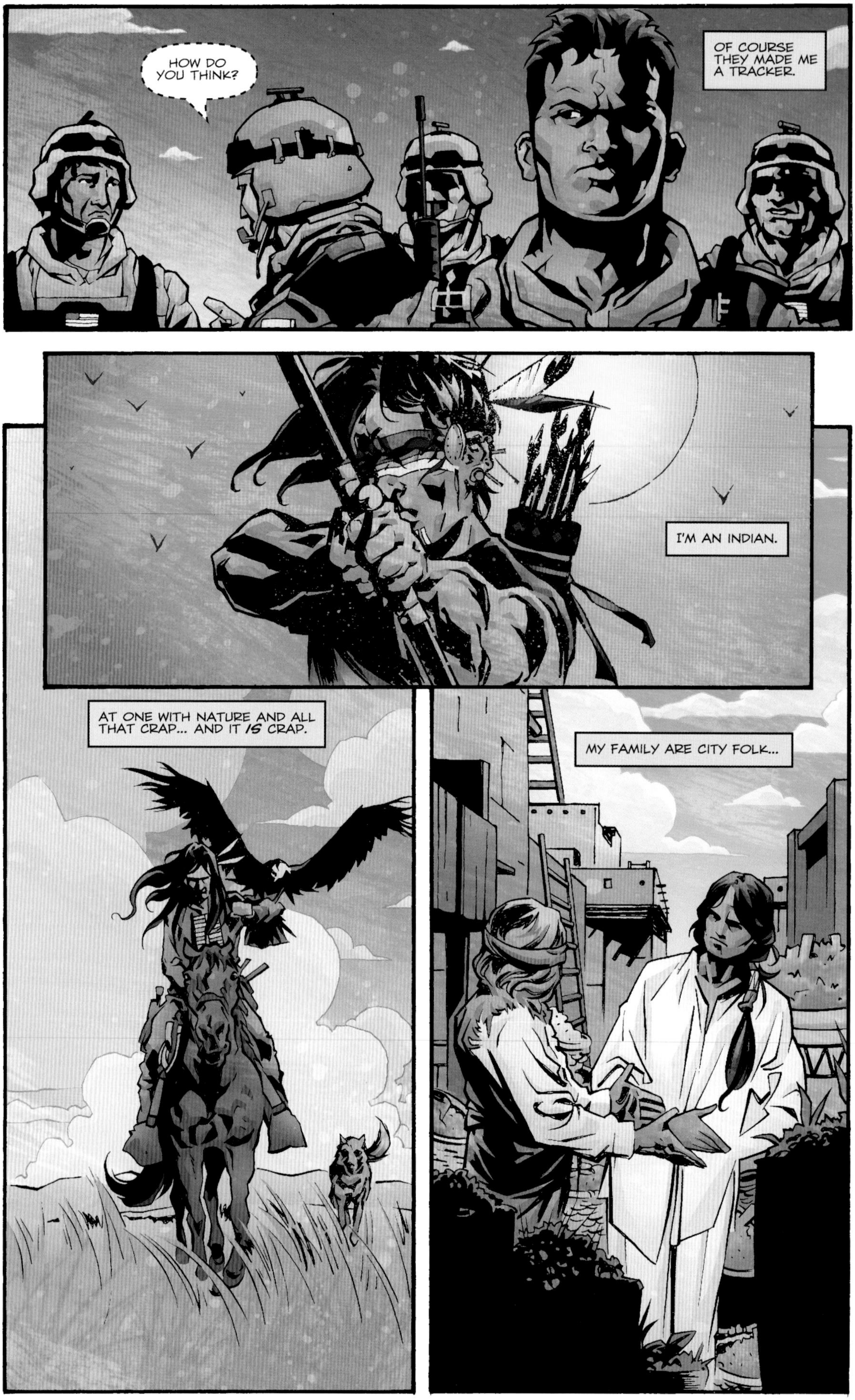
HOW DO YOU THINK?
OF COURSE THEY MADE ME A TRACKER.
I'M AN INDIAN.
AT ONE WITH NATURE AND ALL THAT CRAP... AND IT *IS* CRAP.
MY FAMILY ARE CITY FOLK...

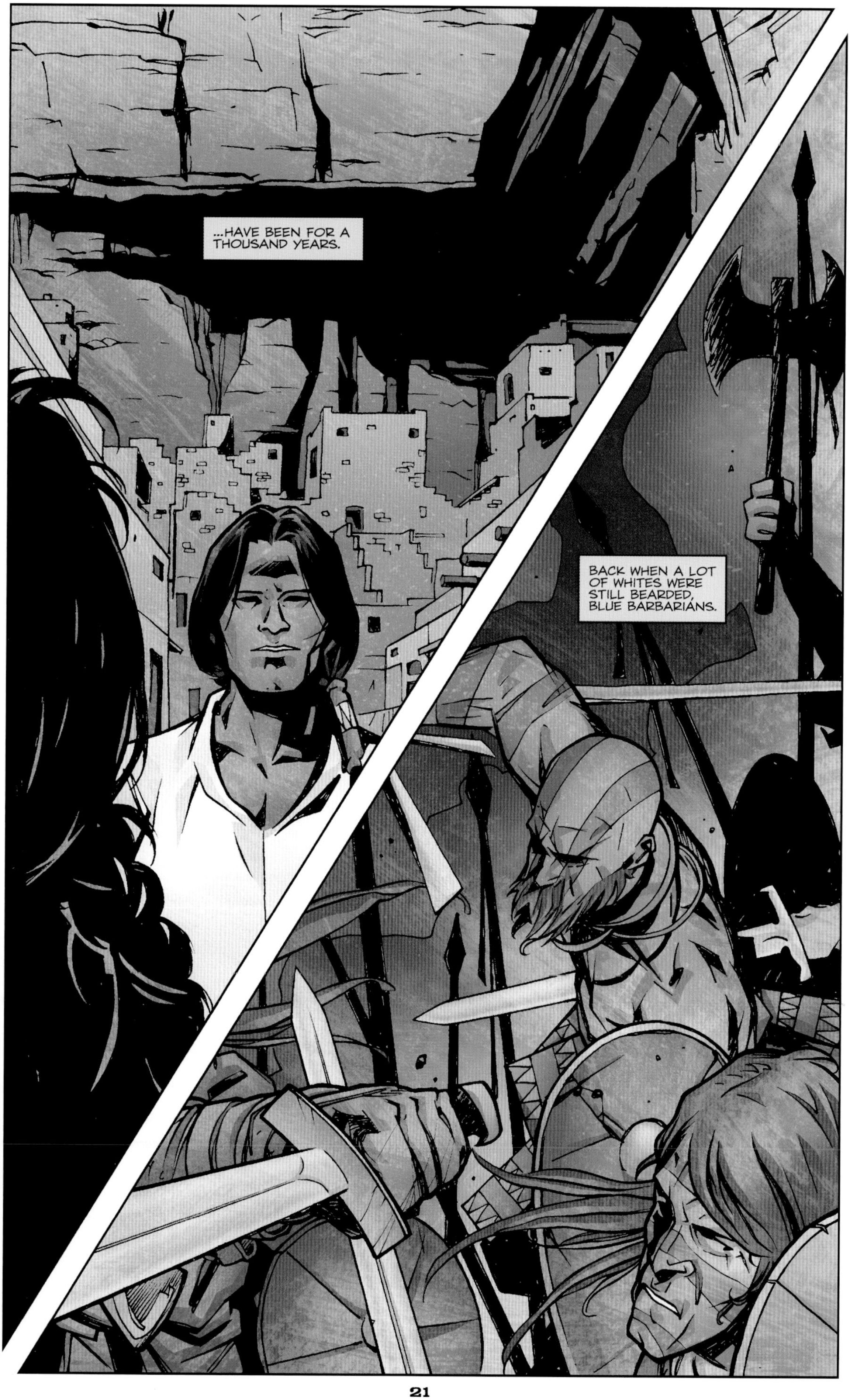
...HAVE BEEN FOR A
THOUSAND YEARS.
BACK WHEN A LOT
OF WHITES WERE
STILL BEARDED,
BLUE BARBARIANS.

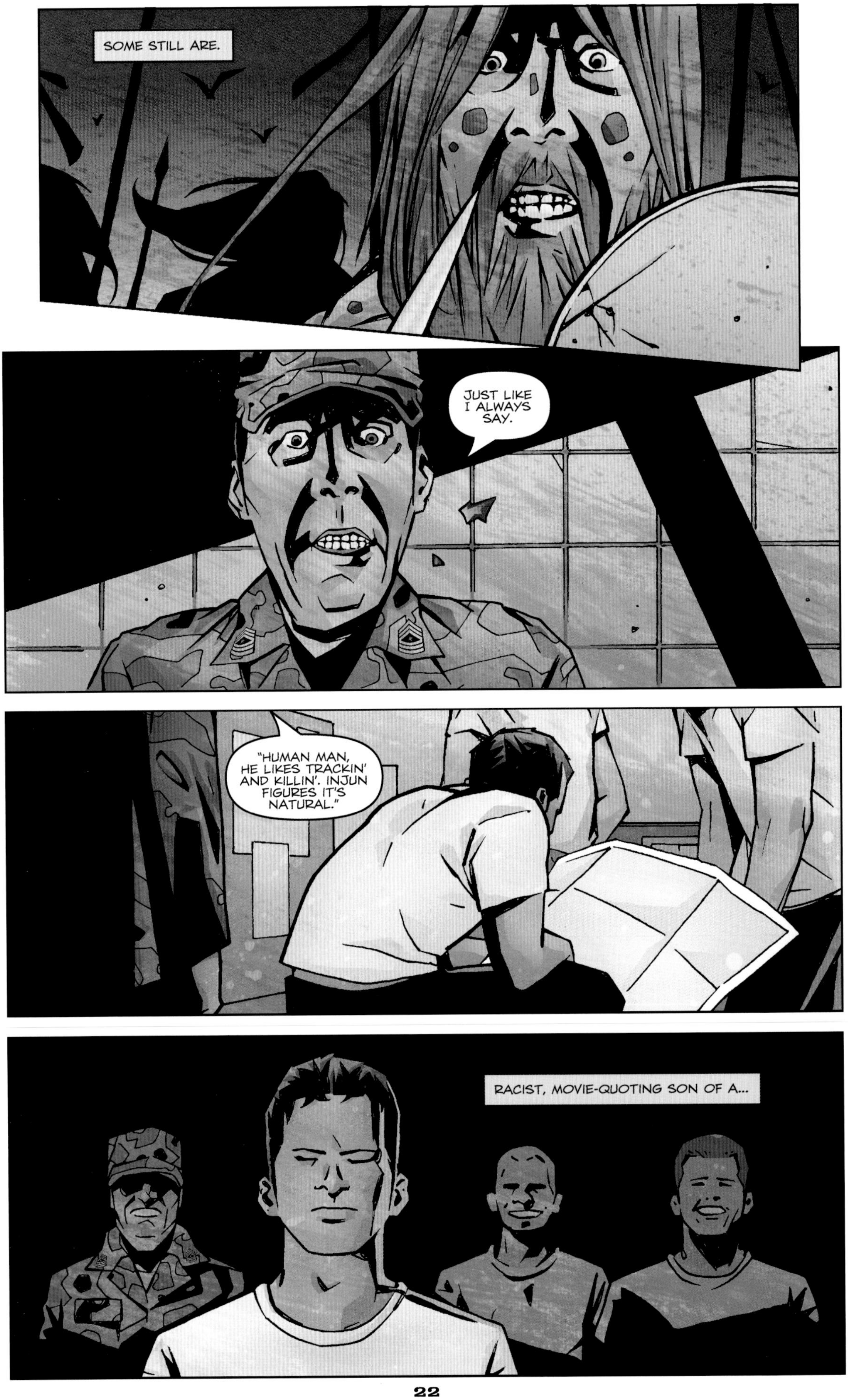
SOME STILL ARE.
JUST LIKE I ALWAYS SAY.
"HUMAN MAN, HE LIKES TRACKIN' AND KILLIN'. INJUN FIGURES IT'S NATURAL."
RACIST, MOVIE-QUOTING SON OF A...

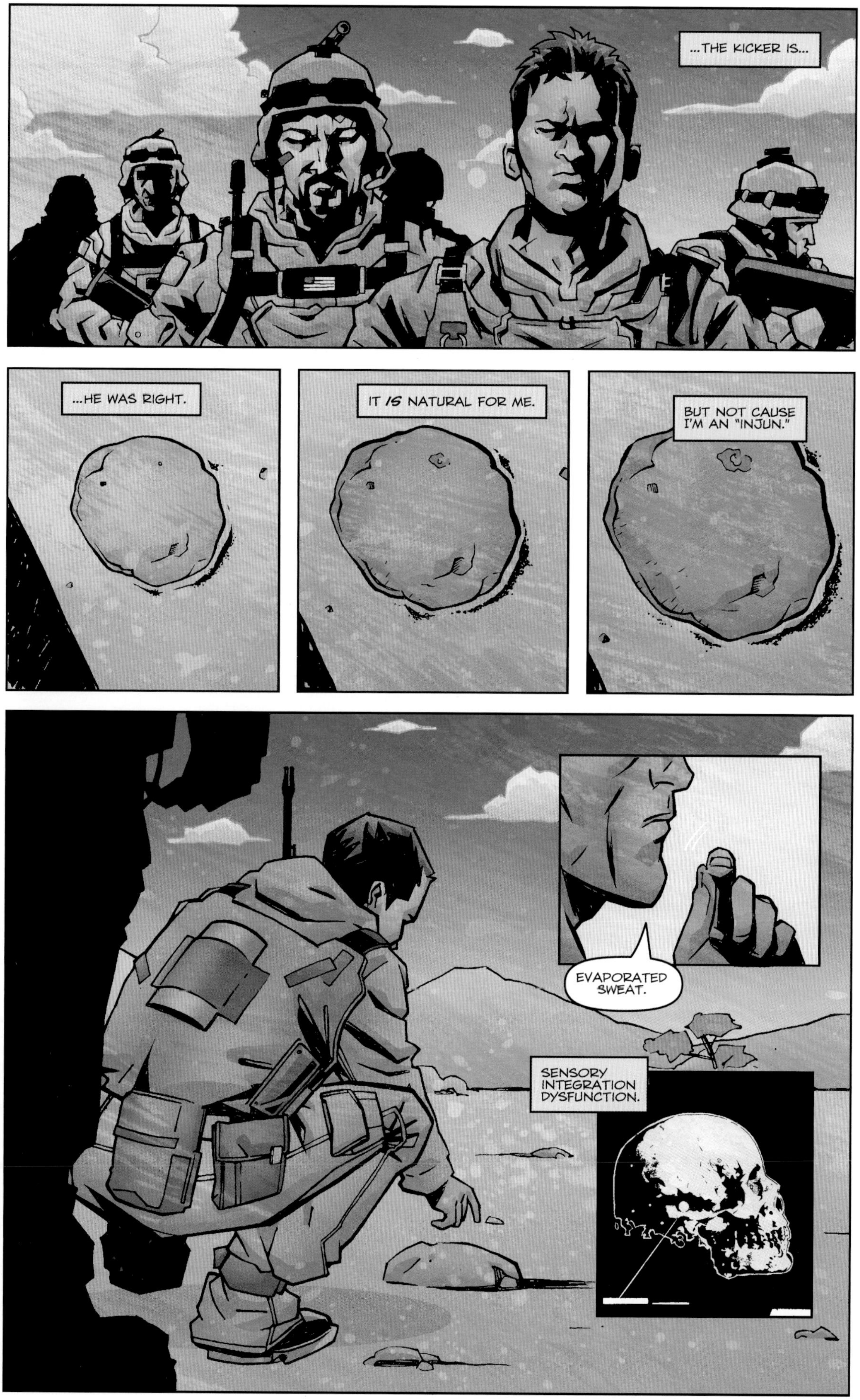
...THE KICKER IS...
...HE WAS RIGHT.
IT IS NATURAL FOR ME.
BUT NOT CAUSE I'M AN "INJUN."
EVAPORATED SWEAT.
SENSORY INTEGRATION DYSFUNCTION.

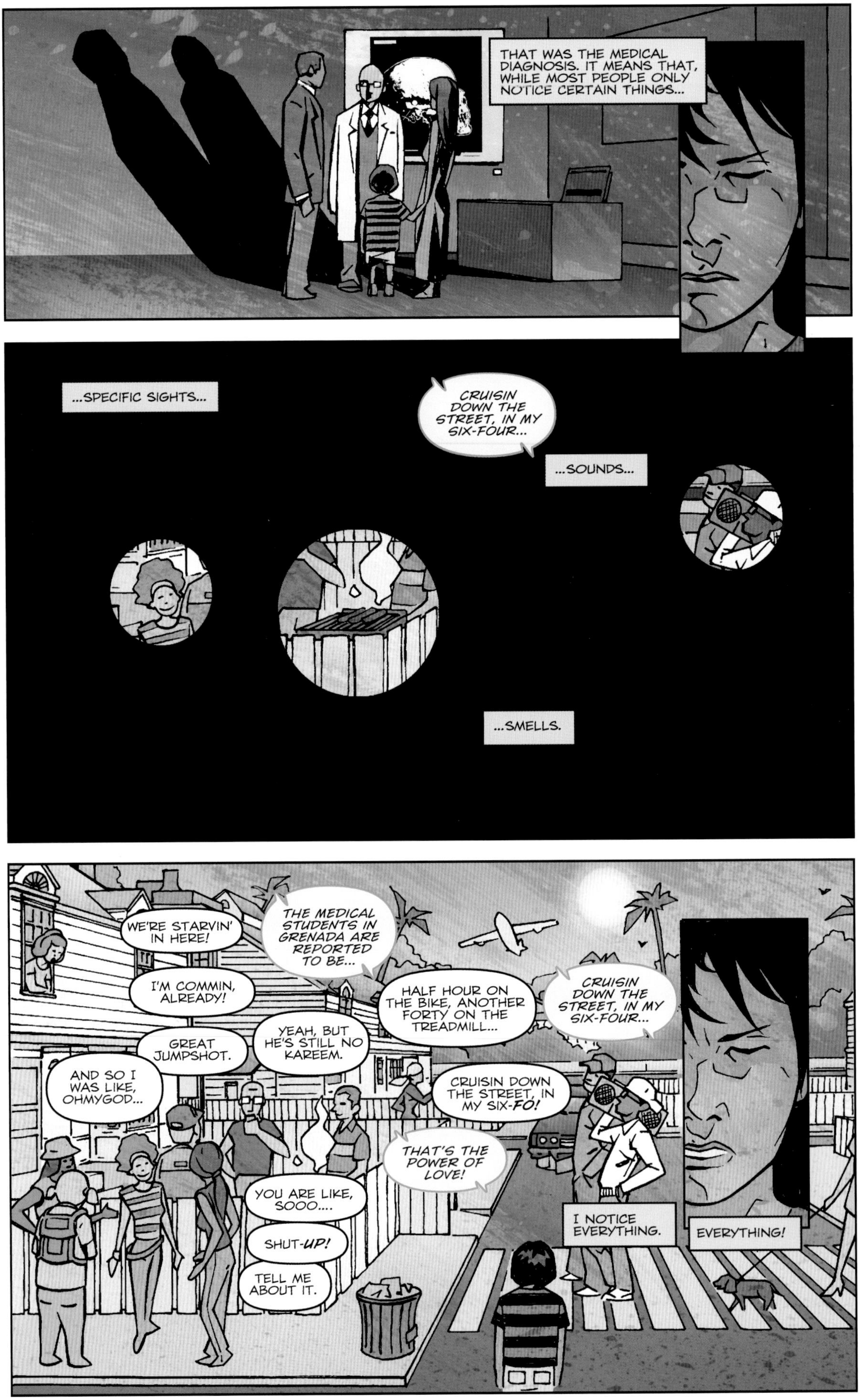

THAT WAS THE MEDICAL DIAGNOSIS. IT MEANS THAT, WHILE MOST PEOPLE ONLY NOTICE CERTAIN THINGS...
...SPECIFIC SIGHTS...
CRUISIN DOWN THE STREET, IN MY SIX-FOUR...
...SOUNDS...
...SMELLS.
WE'RE STARVIN' IN HERE!
THE MEDICAL STUDENTS IN GRENADA ARE REPORTED TO BE...
I'M COMMIN, ALREADY!
HALF HOUR ON THE BIKE, ANOTHER FORTY ON THE TREADMILL...
CRUISIN DOWN THE STREET, IN MY SIX-FOUR...
GREAT JUMPSHOT.
YEAH, BUT HE'S STILL NO KAREEM.
AND SO I WAS LIKE, OHMYGOD...
CRUISIN DOWN THE STREET, IN MY SIX-FO!
THAT'S THE POWER OF LOVE!
YOU ARE LIKE, SOOO....
SHUT-UP!
TELL ME ABOUT IT.
I NOTICE EVERYTHING.
EVERYTHING!

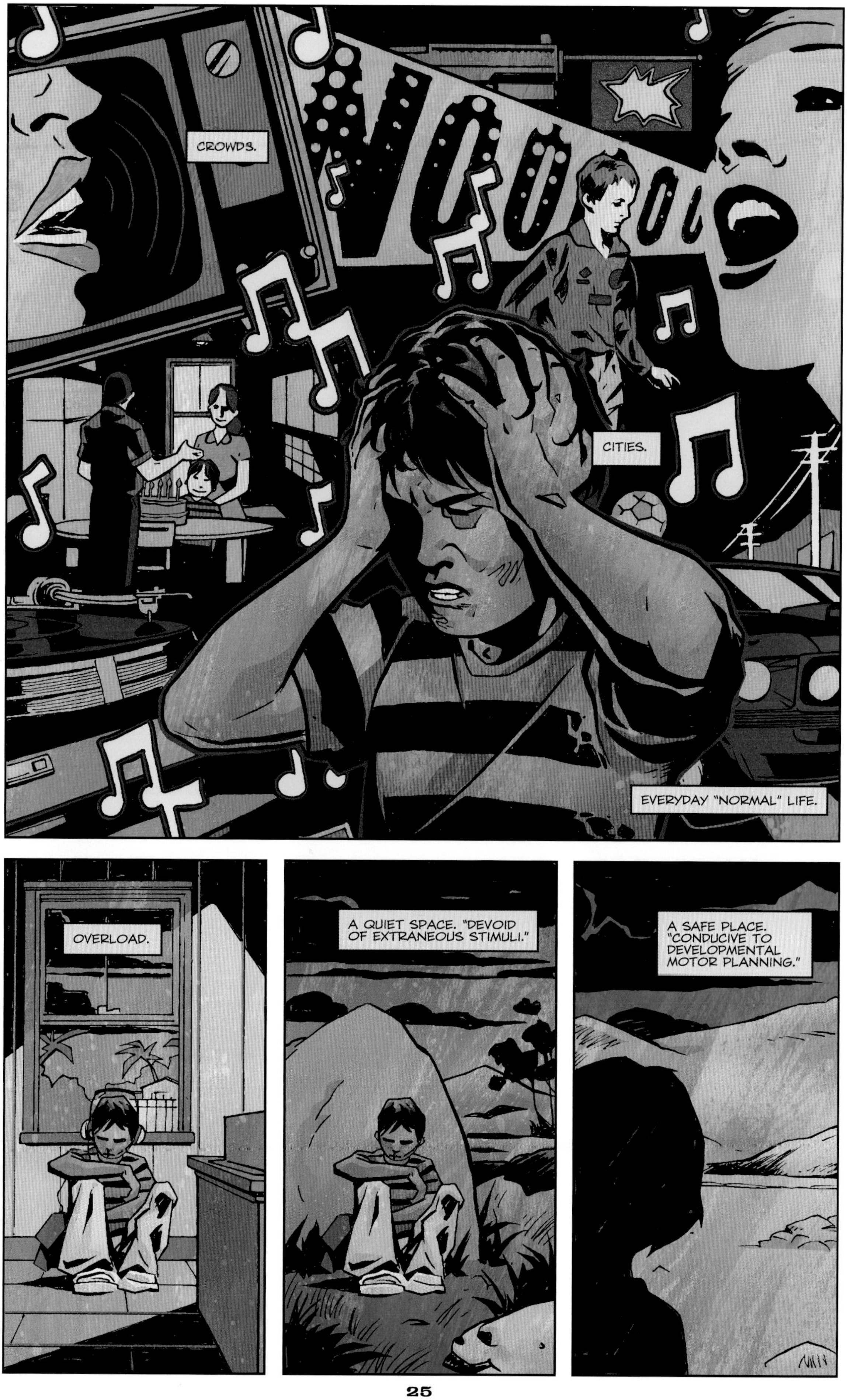
CROWDS.
CITIES.
EVERYDAY "NORMAL" LIFE.
OVERLOAD.
A QUIET SPACE. "DEVOID OF EXTRANEOUS STIMULI."
A SAFE PLACE. "CONDUCIVE TO DEVELOPMENTAL MOTOR PLANNING."

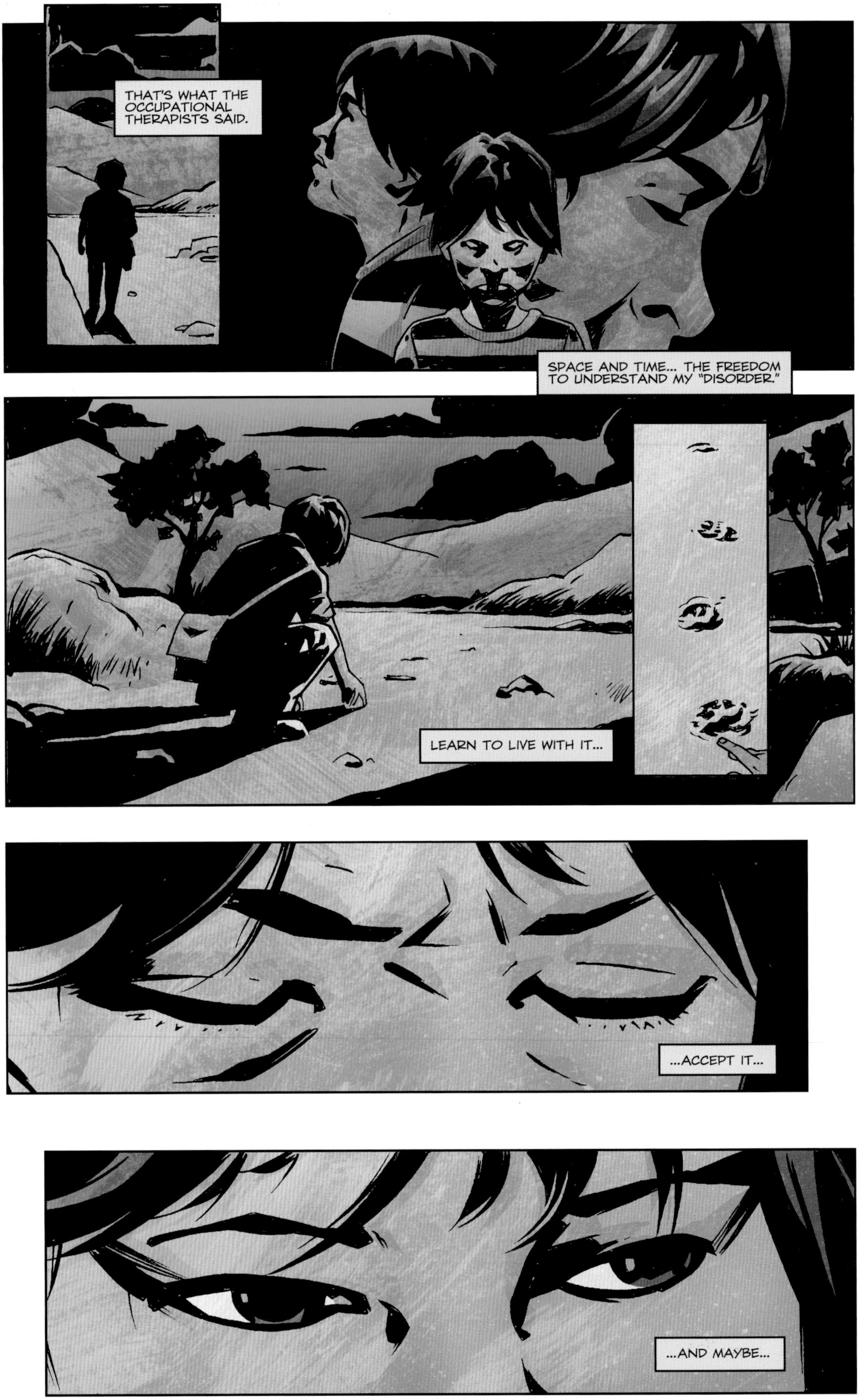
THAT'S WHAT THE OCCUPATIONAL THERAPISTS SAID.
SPACE AND TIME... THE FREEDOM TO UNDERSTAND MY "DISORDER."
LEARN TO LIVE WITH IT...
...ACCEPT IT...
...AND MAYBE...

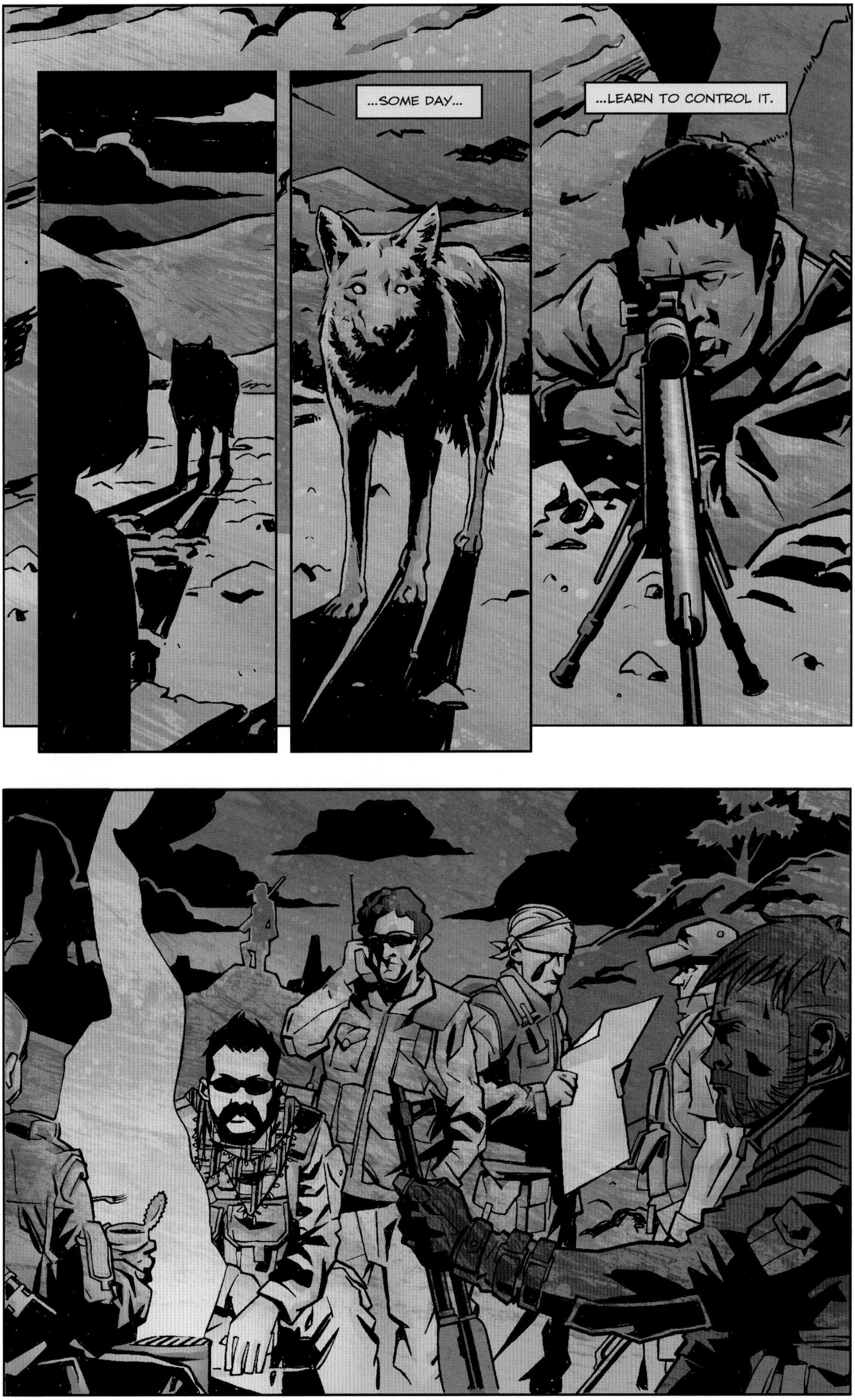
...SOME DAY...
...LEARN TO CONTROL IT.

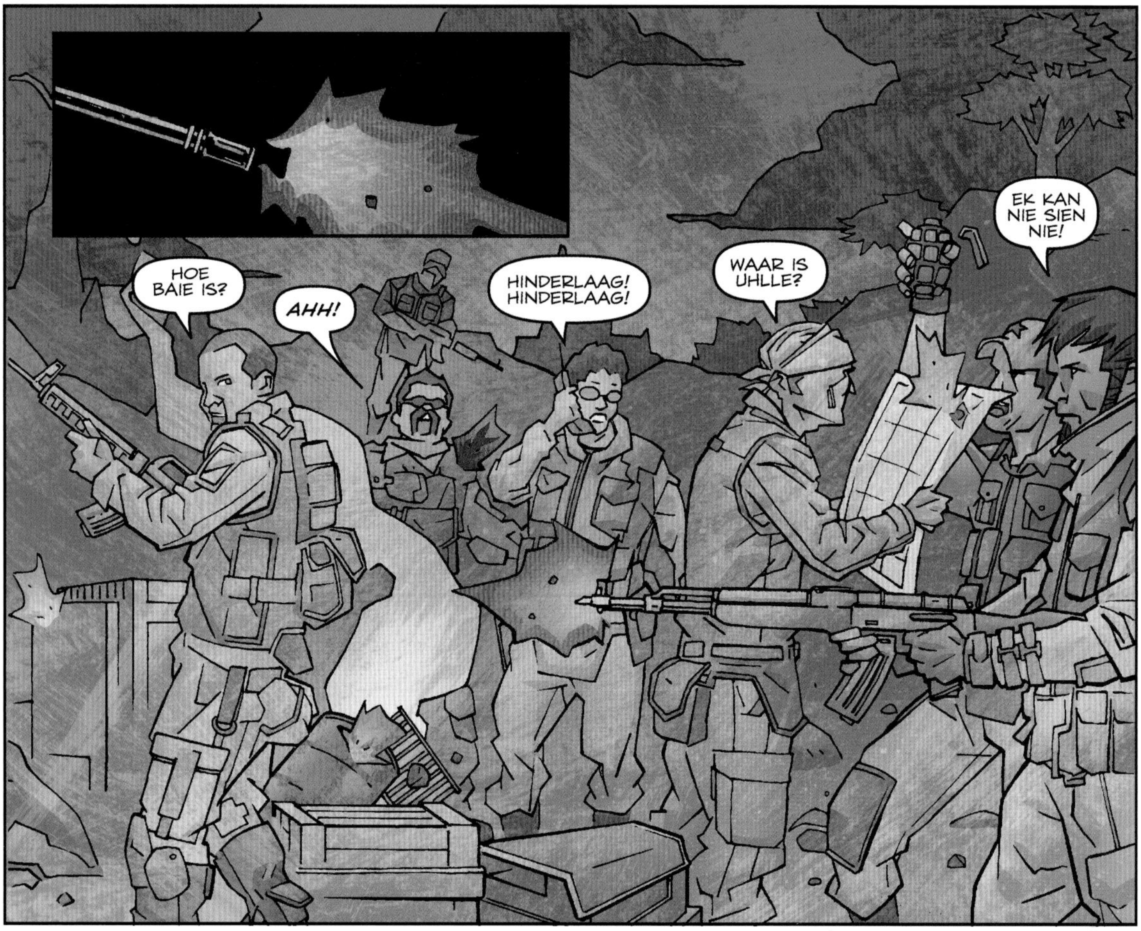
HOE BAIE IS?
AHH!
HINDERLAAG! HINDERLAAG!
WAAR IS UHLLE?
EK KAN NIE SIEN NIE!

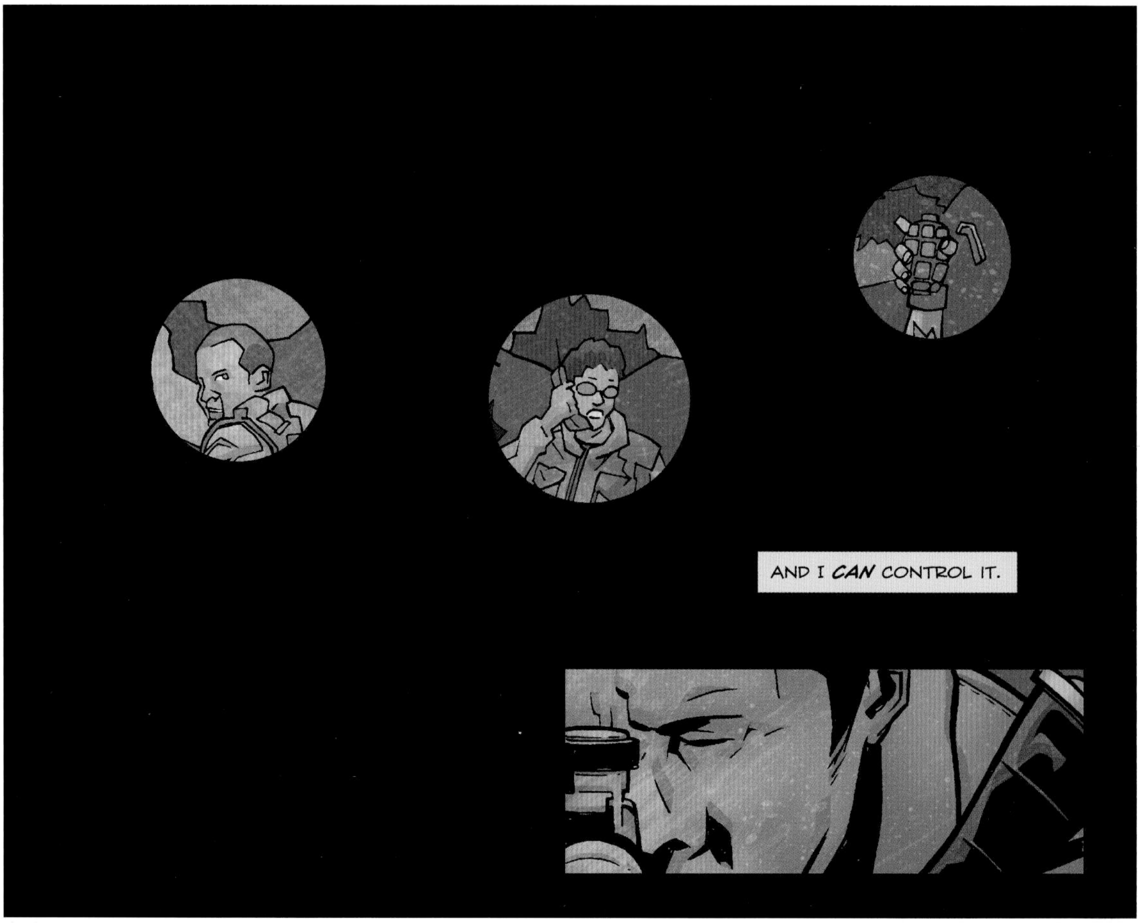
AND I *CAN* CONTROL IT.

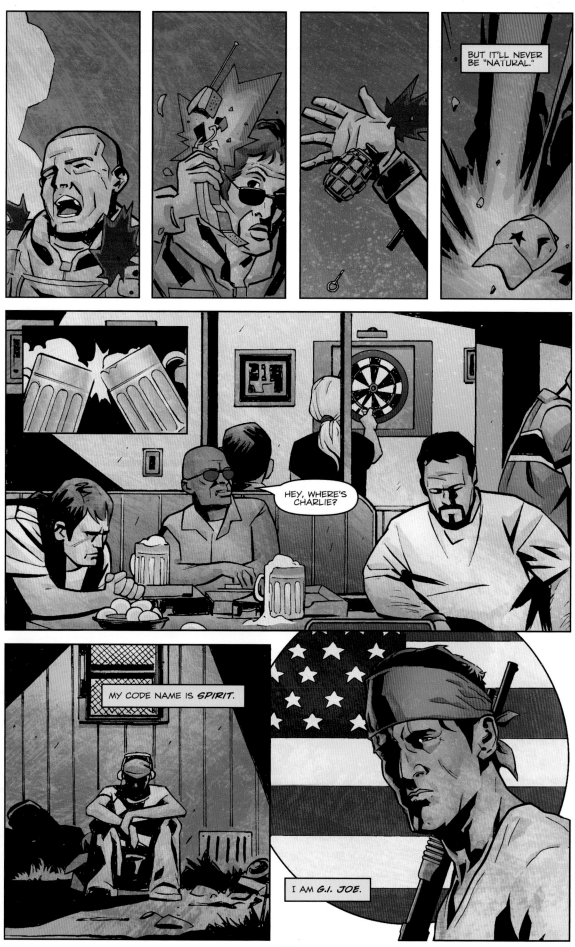

BUT IT'LL NEVER BE "NATURAL."

HEY, WHERE'S CHARLIE?

MY CODE NAME IS *SPIRIT*.

I AM *G.I. JOE*.

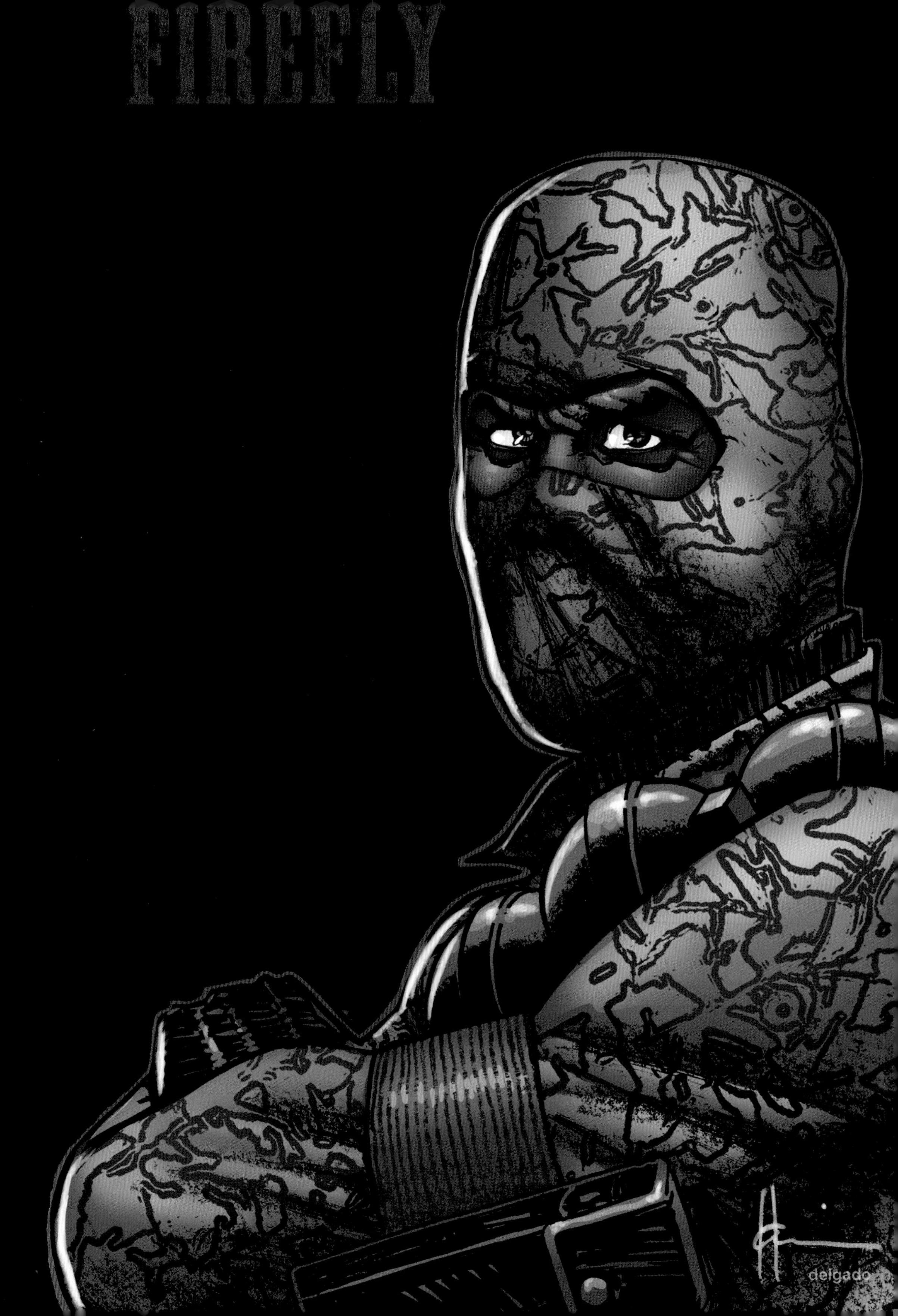
FIREFLY
delgado

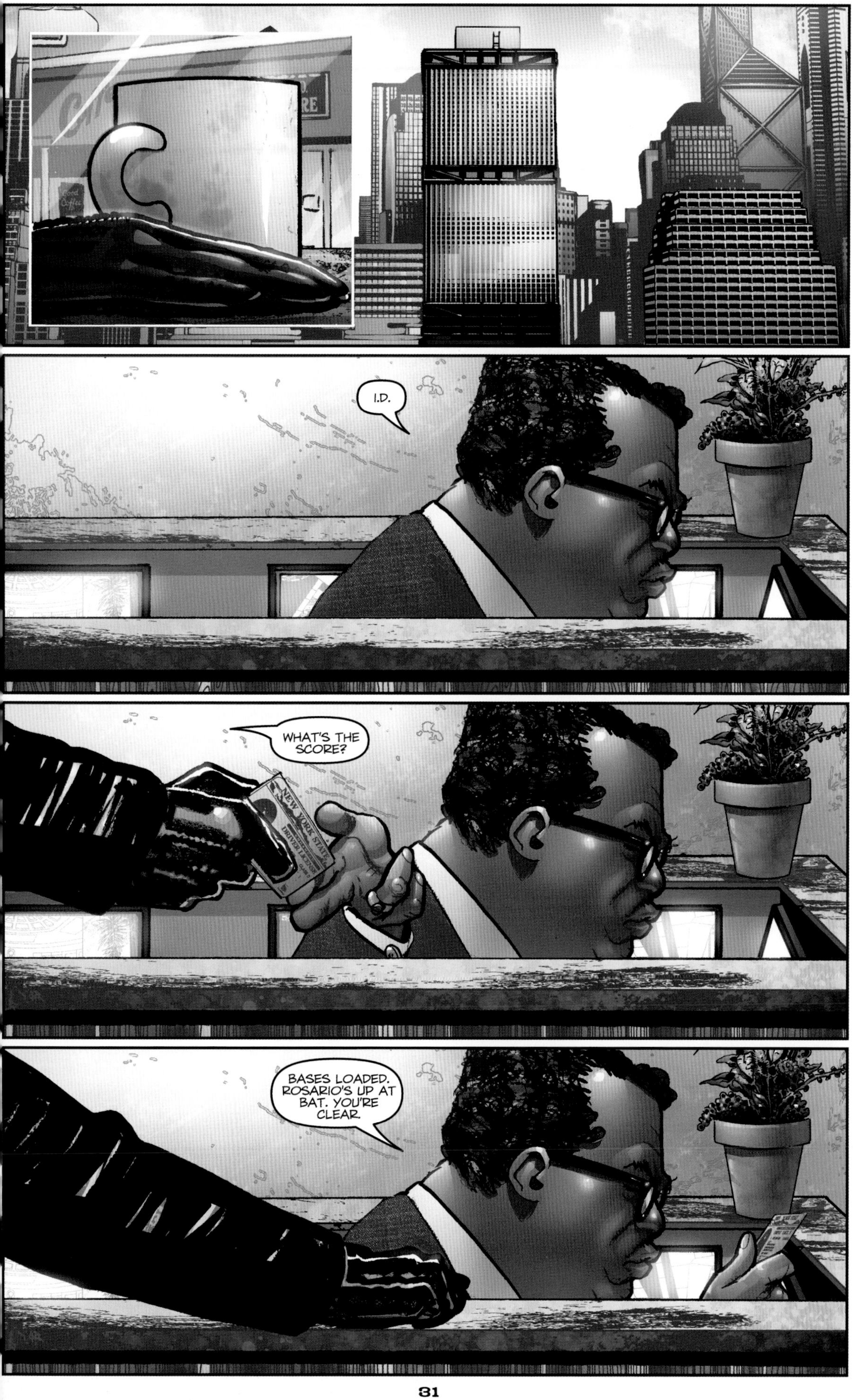
I.D.
WHAT'S THE SCORE?
NEW YORK STATE
DRIVER LICENSE
BASES LOADED. ROSARIO'S UP AT BAT. YOU'RE CLEAR.

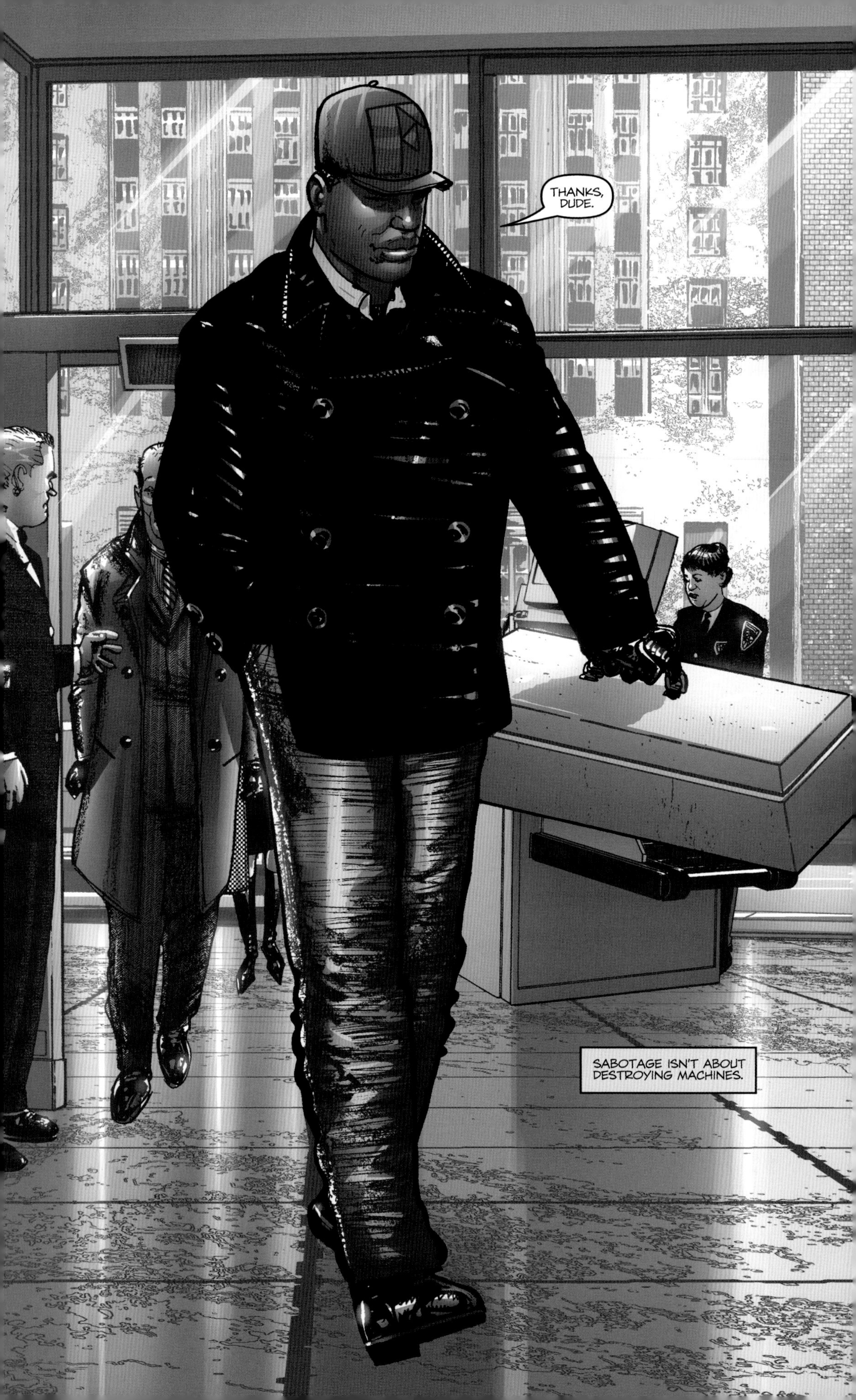
THANKS, DUDE.
SABOTAGE ISN'T ABOUT DESTROYING MACHINES.

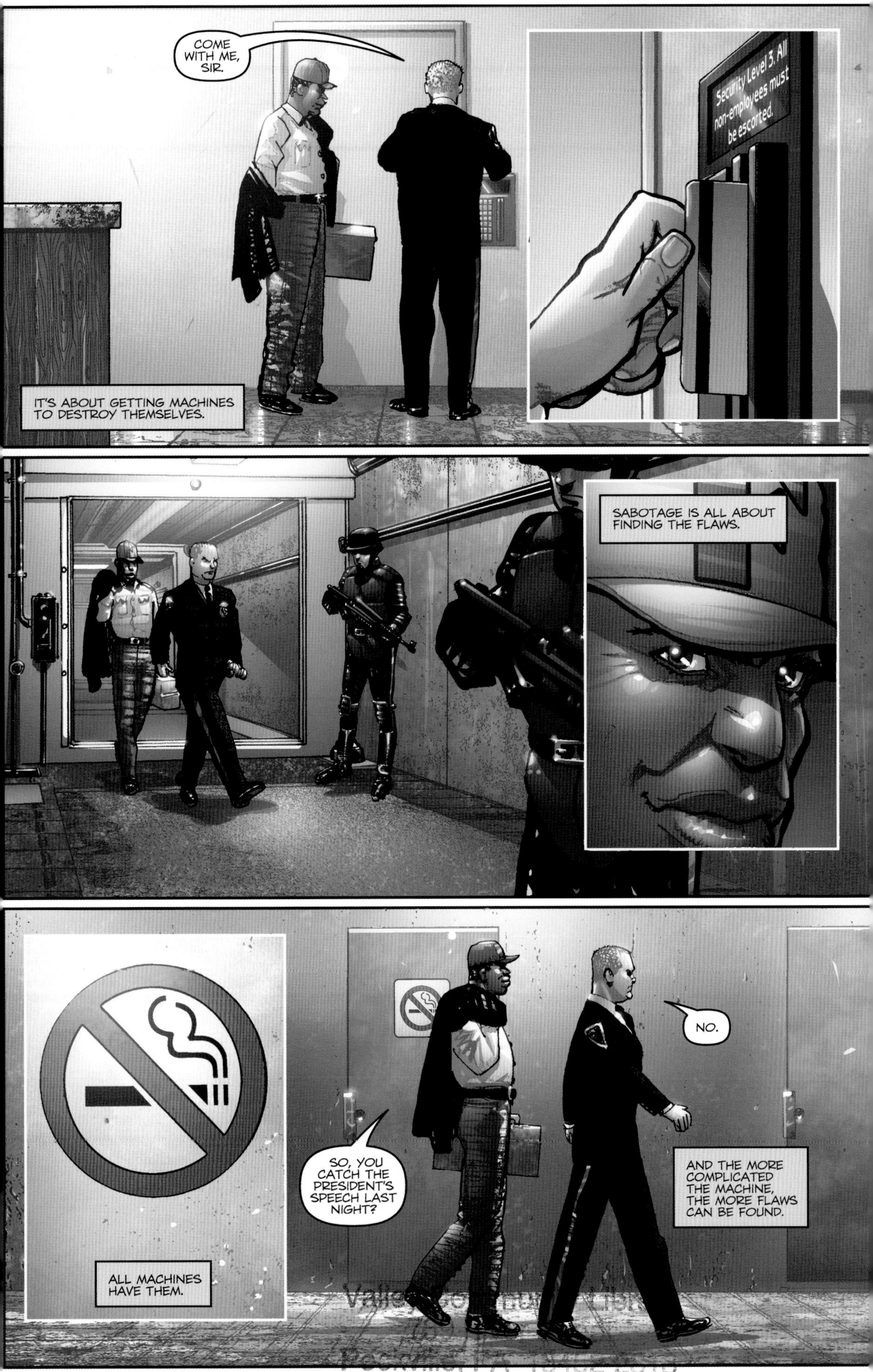
COME WITH ME, SIR.
IT'S ABOUT GETTING MACHINES TO DESTROY THEMSELVES.
Security Level 3. All non-employees must be escorted.
SABOTAGE IS ALL ABOUT FINDING THE FLAWS.
ALL MACHINES HAVE THEM.
SO, YOU CATCH THE PRESIDENT'S SPEECH LAST NIGHT?
NO.
AND THE MORE COMPLICATED THE MACHINE, THE MORE FLAWS CAN BE FOUND.

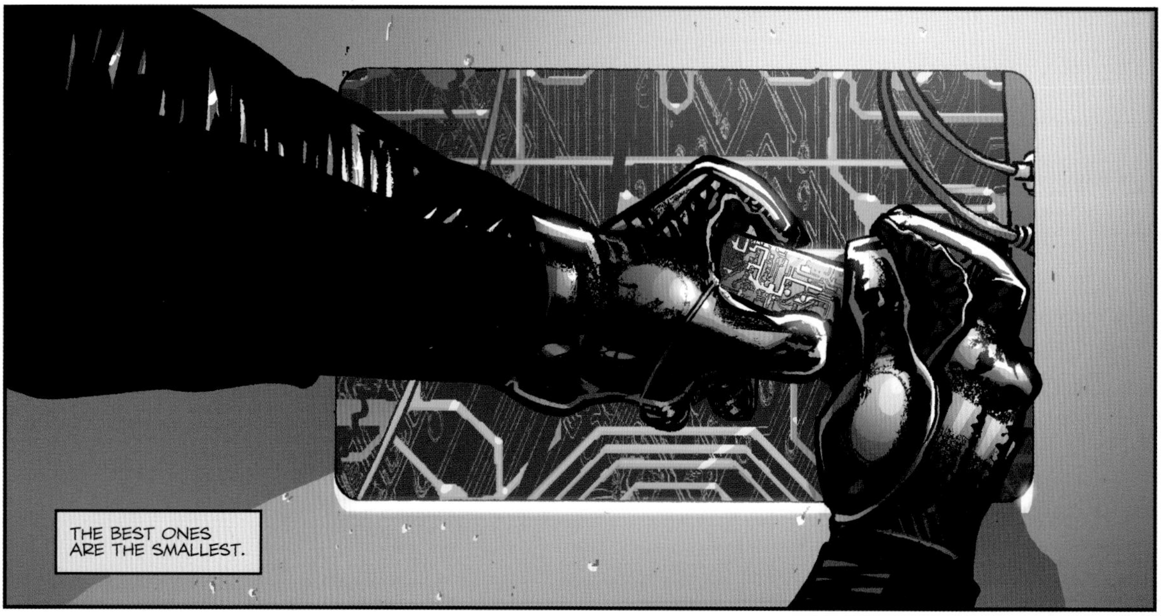
THE BEST ONES ARE THE SMALLEST.

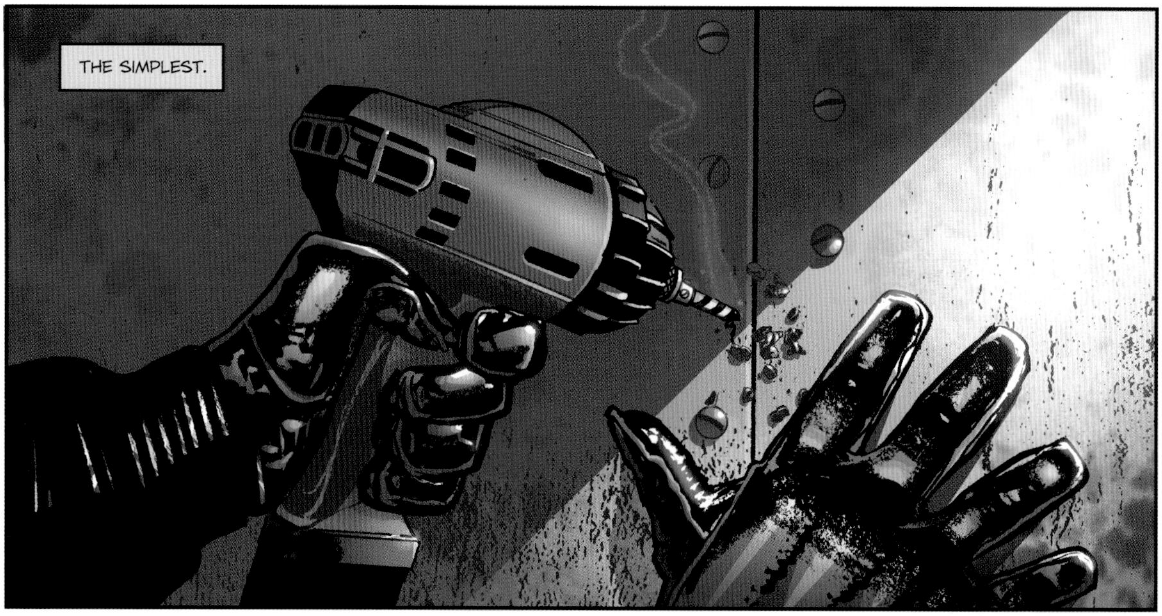
THE SIMPLEST.

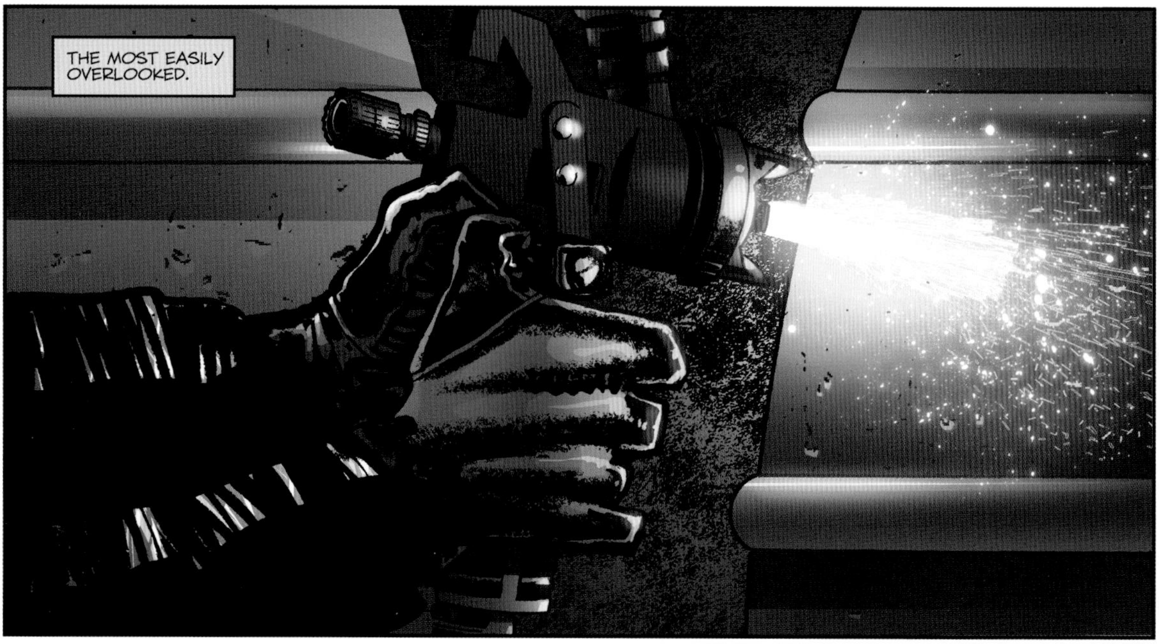
THE MOST EASILY OVERLOOKED.

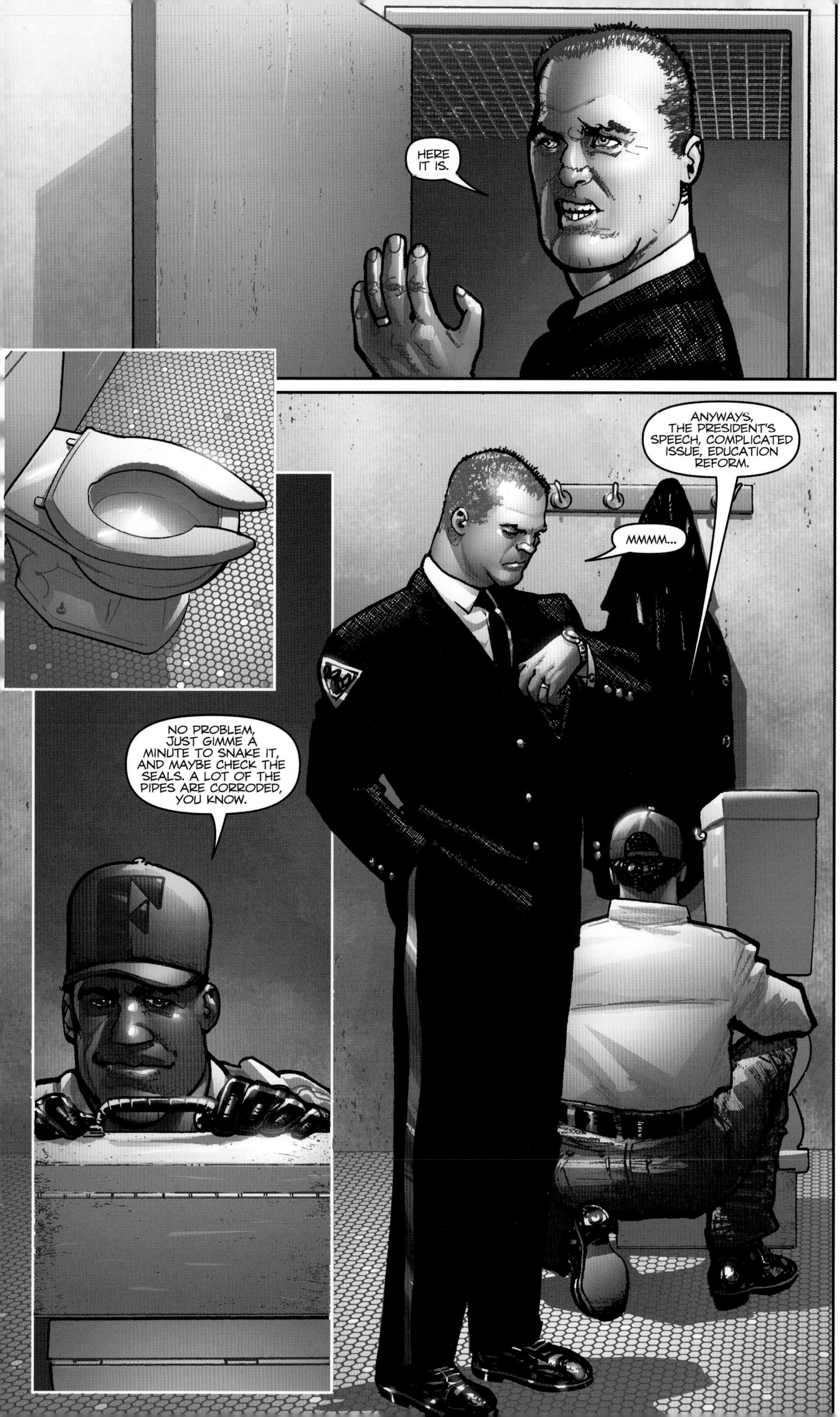
HERE IT IS.
ANYWAYS, THE PRESIDENT'S SPEECH, COMPLICATED ISSUE, EDUCATION REFORM.
MMMM...
NO PROBLEM, JUST GIMME A MINUTE TO SNAKE IT, AND MAYBE CHECK THE SEALS. A LOT OF THE PIPES ARE CORRODED, YOU KNOW.

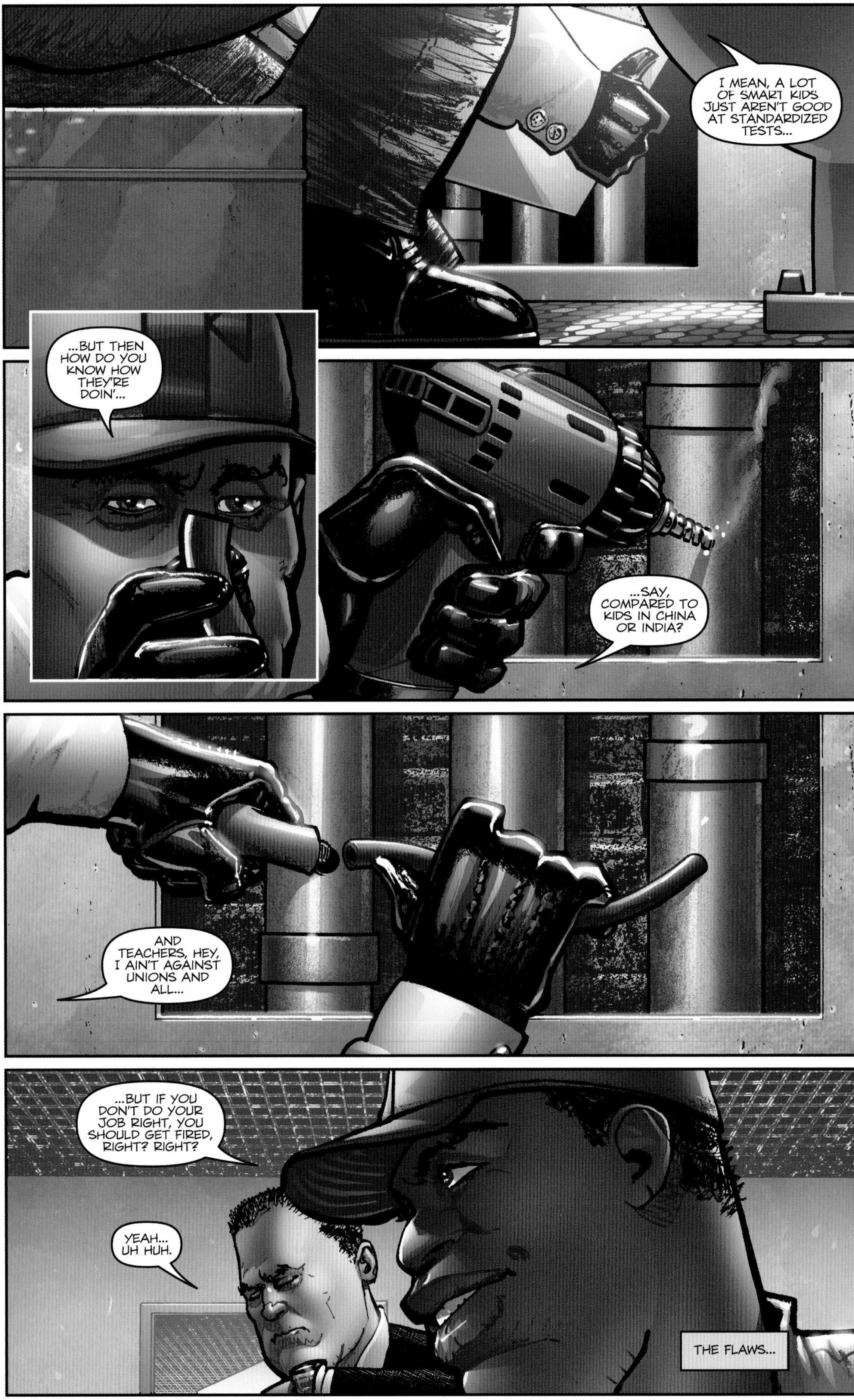
I MEAN, A LOT OF SMART KIDS JUST AREN'T GOOD AT STANDARDIZED TESTS...
...BUT THEN HOW DO YOU KNOW HOW THEY'RE DOIN'...
...SAY, COMPARED TO KIDS IN CHINA OR INDIA?
AND TEACHERS, HEY, I AIN'T AGAINST UNIONS AND ALL...
...BUT IF YOU DON'T DO YOUR JOB RIGHT, YOU SHOULD GET FIRED, RIGHT? RIGHT?
YEAH... UH HUH.
THE FLAWS...

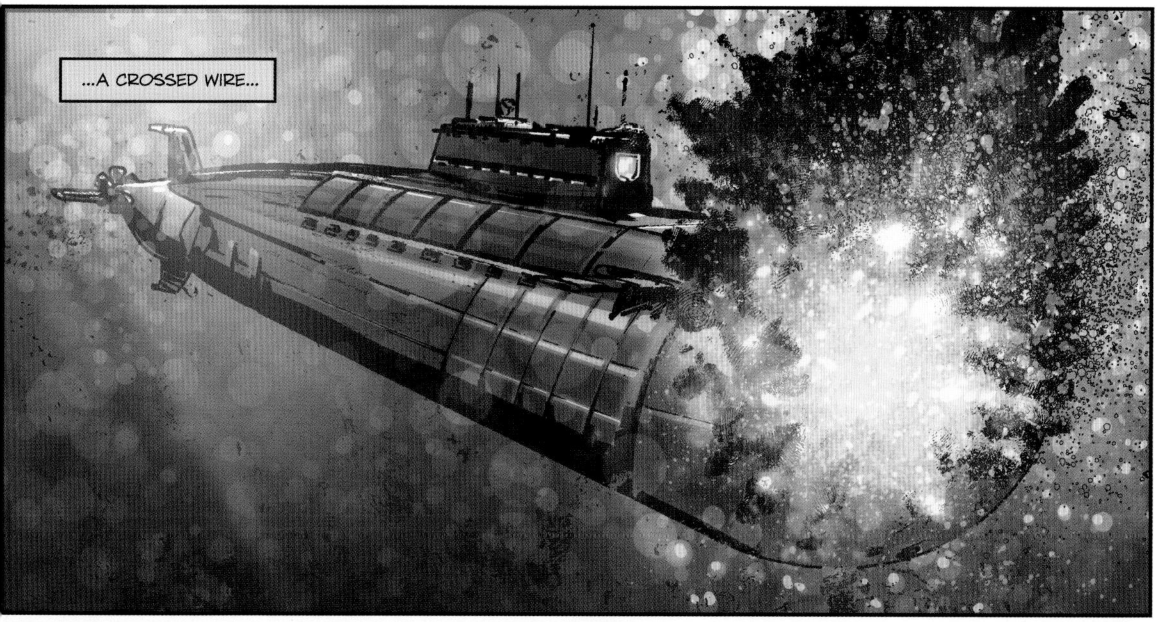
...A CROSSED WIRE...

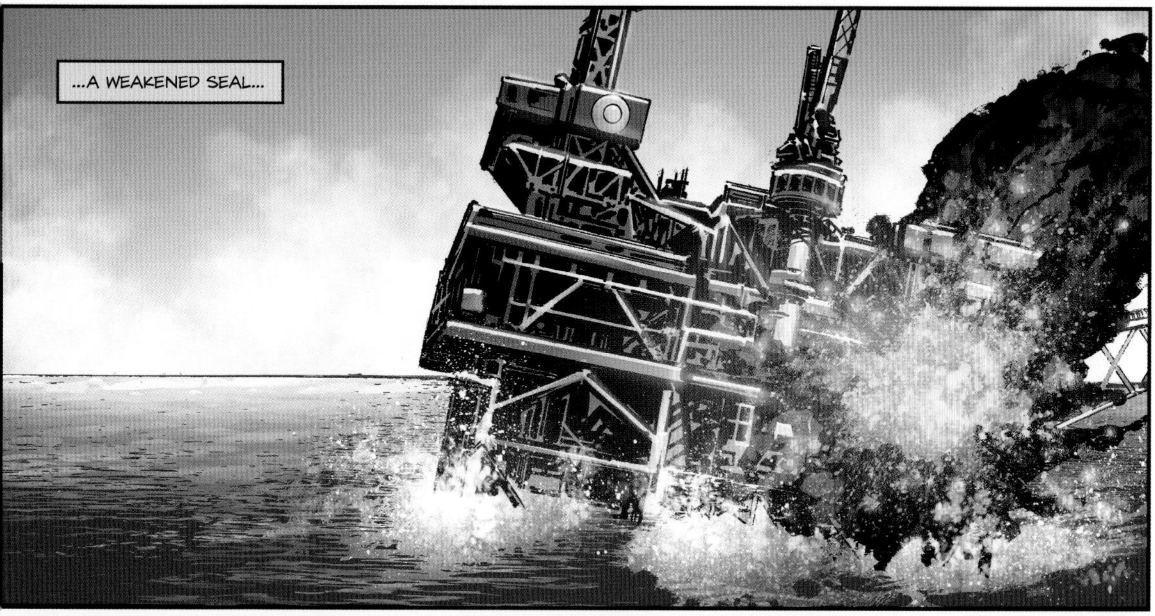
...A WEAKENED SEAL...

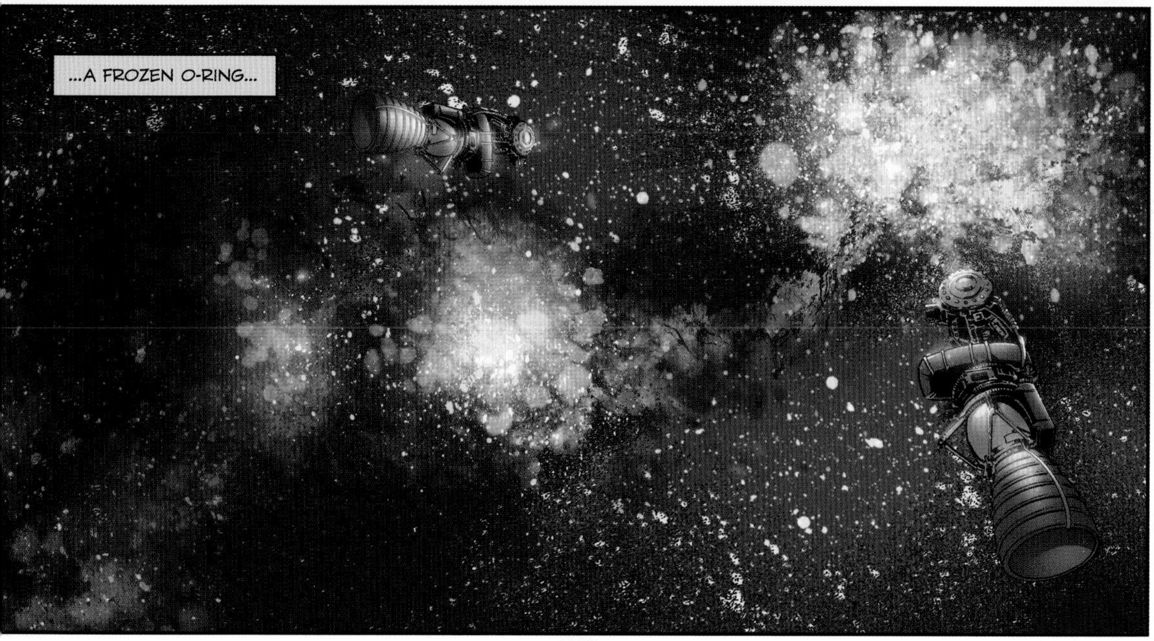
...A FROZEN O-RING...

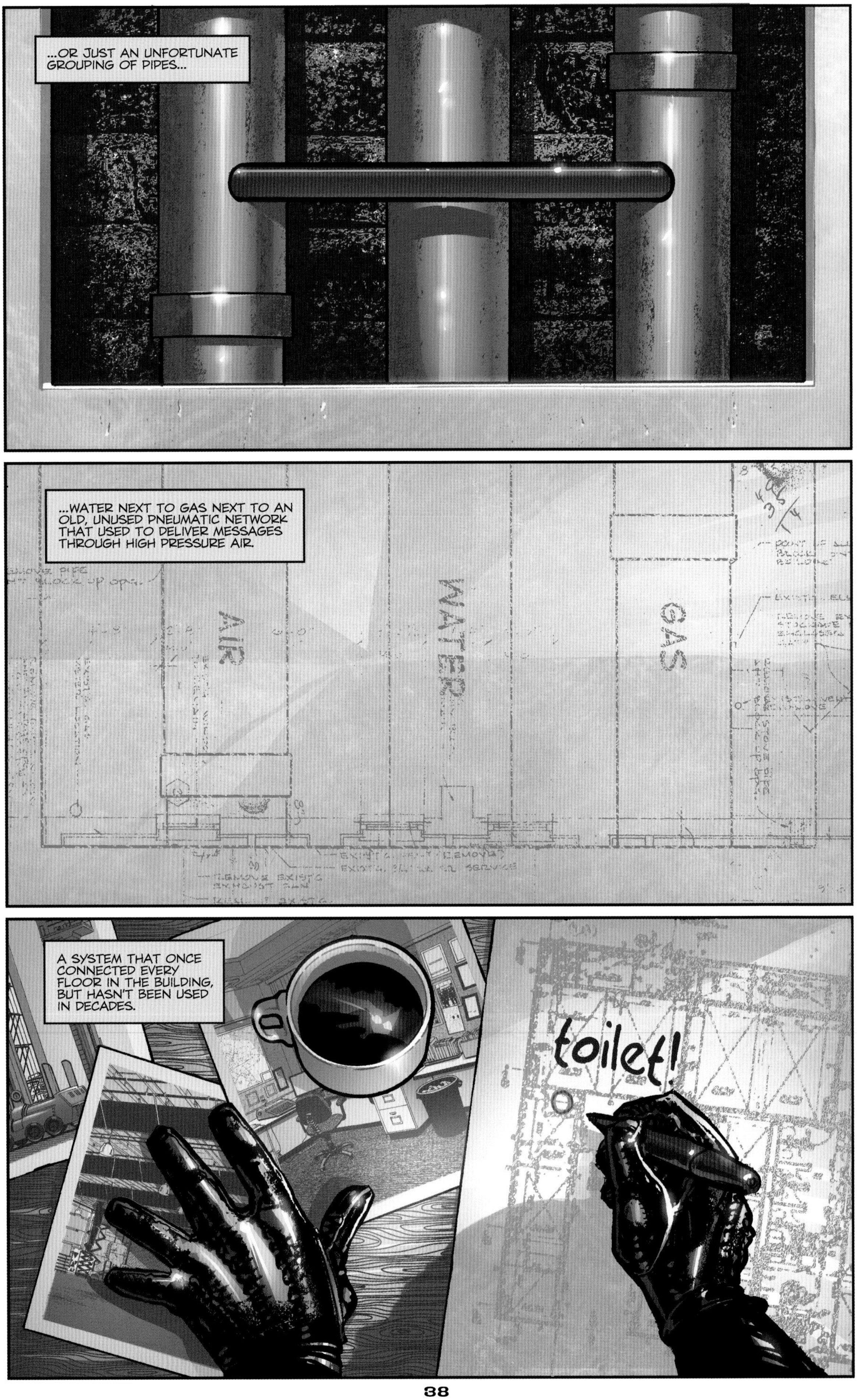
...OR JUST AN UNFORTUNATE GROUPING OF PIPES...
...WATER NEXT TO GAS NEXT TO AN OLD, UNUSED PNEUMATIC NETWORK THAT USED TO DELIVER MESSAGES THROUGH HIGH PRESSURE AIR.
AIR
WATER
GAS
A SYSTEM THAT ONCE CONNECTED EVERY FLOOR IN THE BUILDING, BUT HASN'T BEEN USED IN DECADES.
toilet!

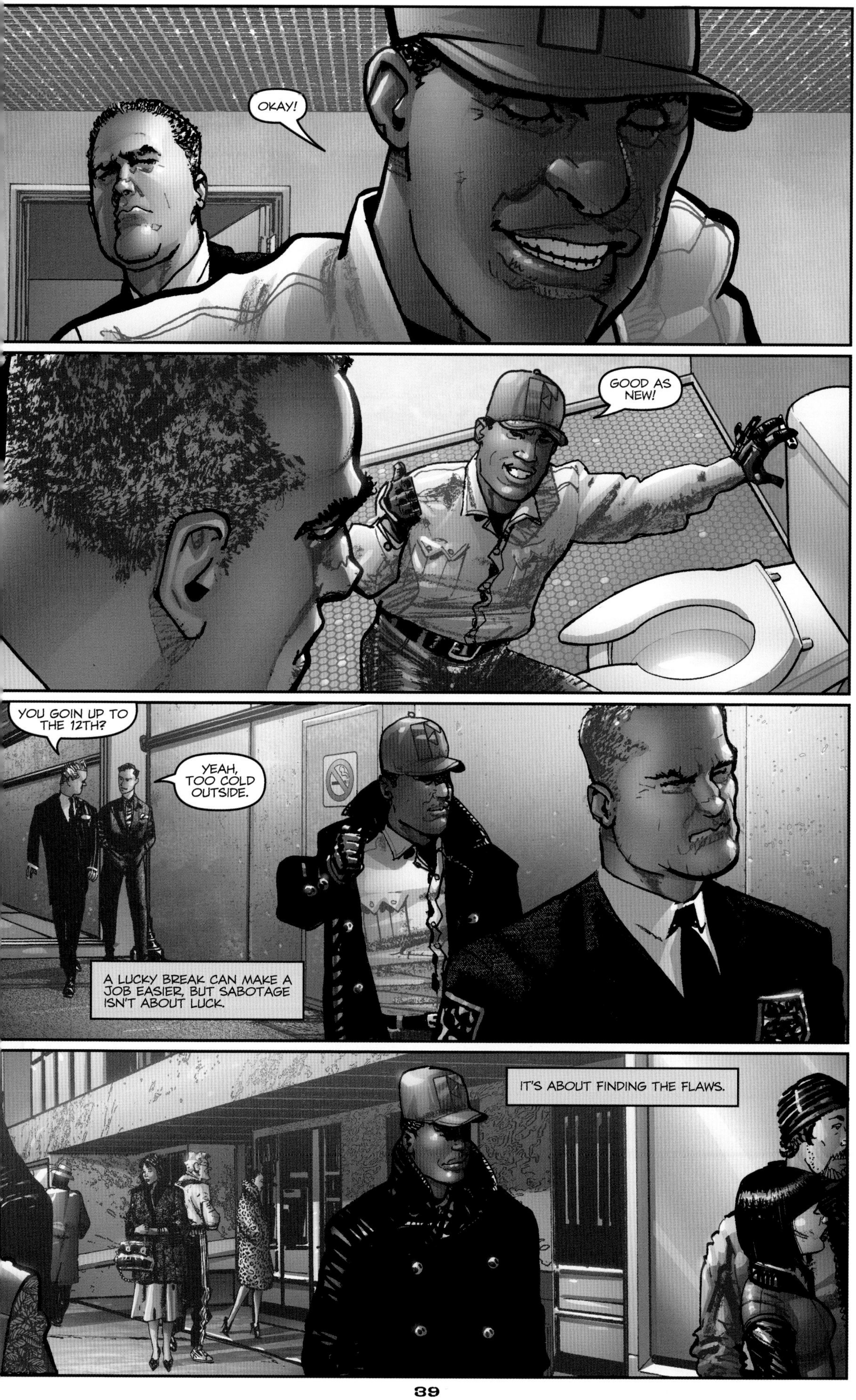
OKAY!
GOOD AS NEW!
YOU GOIN UP TO THE 12TH?
YEAH, TOO COLD OUTSIDE.
A LUCKY BREAK CAN MAKE A JOB EASIER, BUT SABOTAGE ISN'T ABOUT LUCK.
IT'S ABOUT FINDING THE FLAWS.

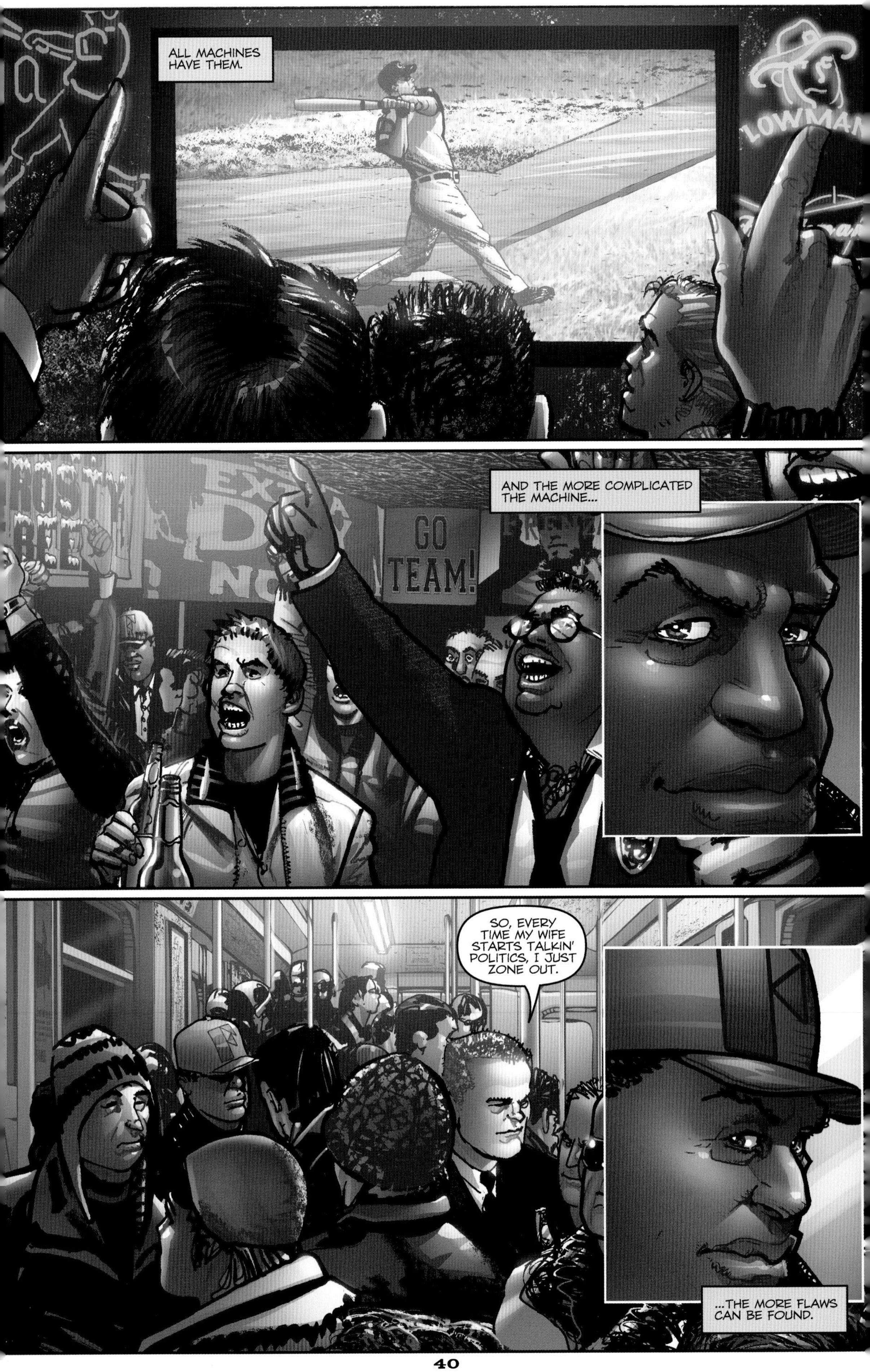
ALL MACHINES HAVE THEM.
AND THE MORE COMPLICATED THE MACHINE...
GO TEAM!
SO, EVERY TIME MY WIFE STARTS TALKIN' POLITICS, I JUST ZONE OUT.
...THE MORE FLAWS CAN BE FOUND.

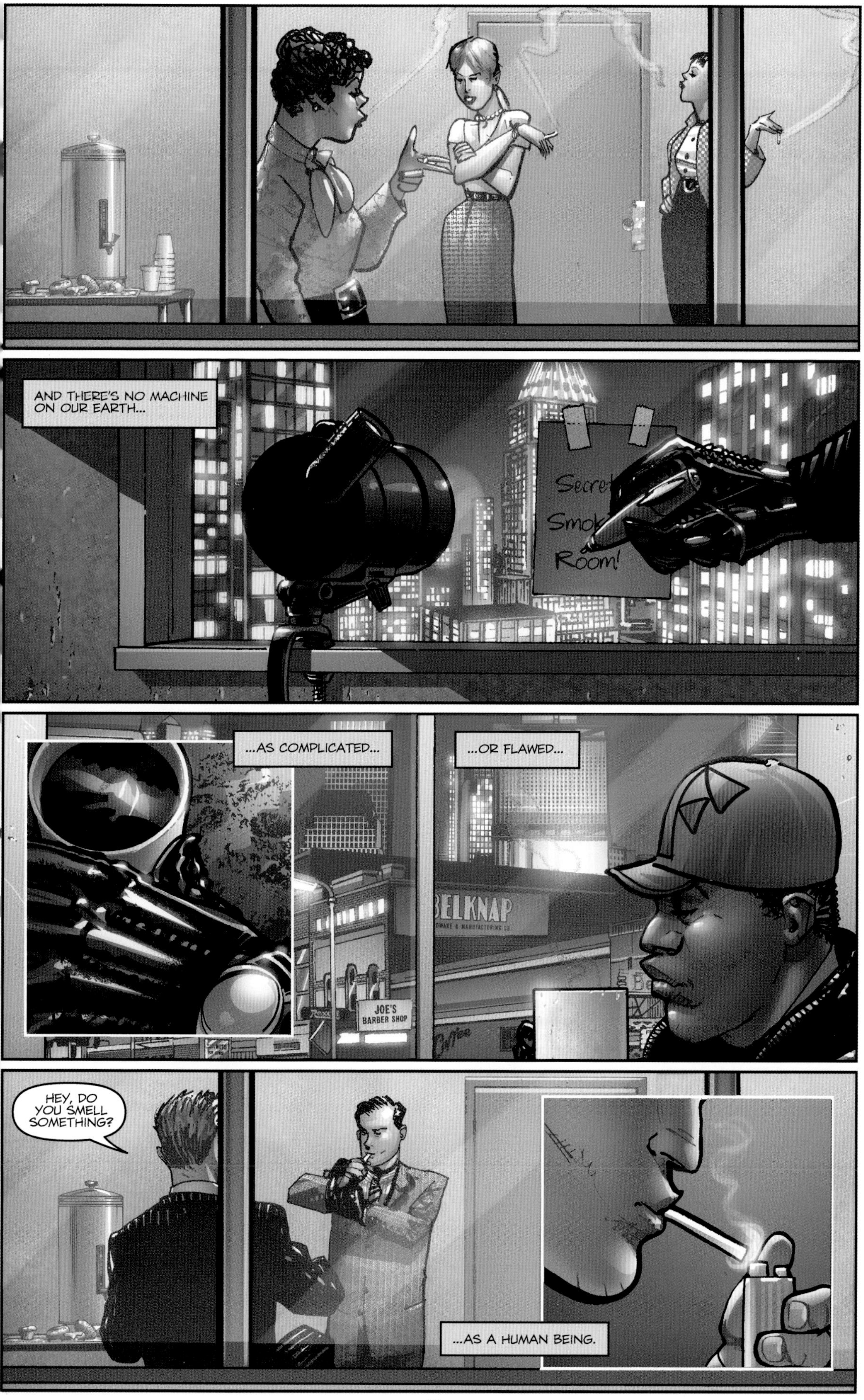
AND THERE'S NO MACHINE ON OUR EARTH...
Secret
Smok
Room!
...AS COMPLICATED...
...OR FLAWED...
BELKNAP
JOE'S
BARBER SHOP
HEY, DO YOU SMELL SOMETHING?
...AS A HUMAN BEING.

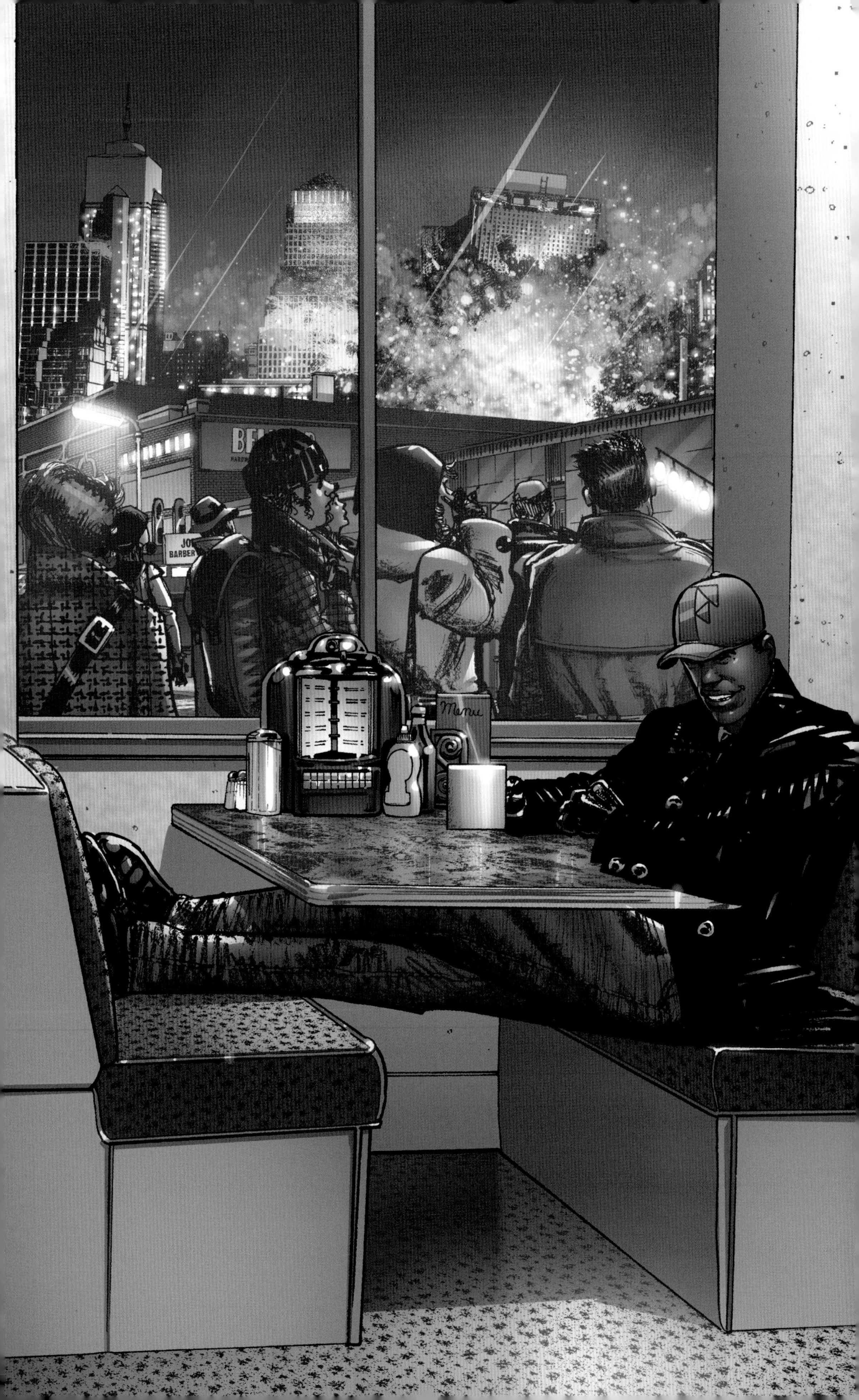
BARBER
Menu

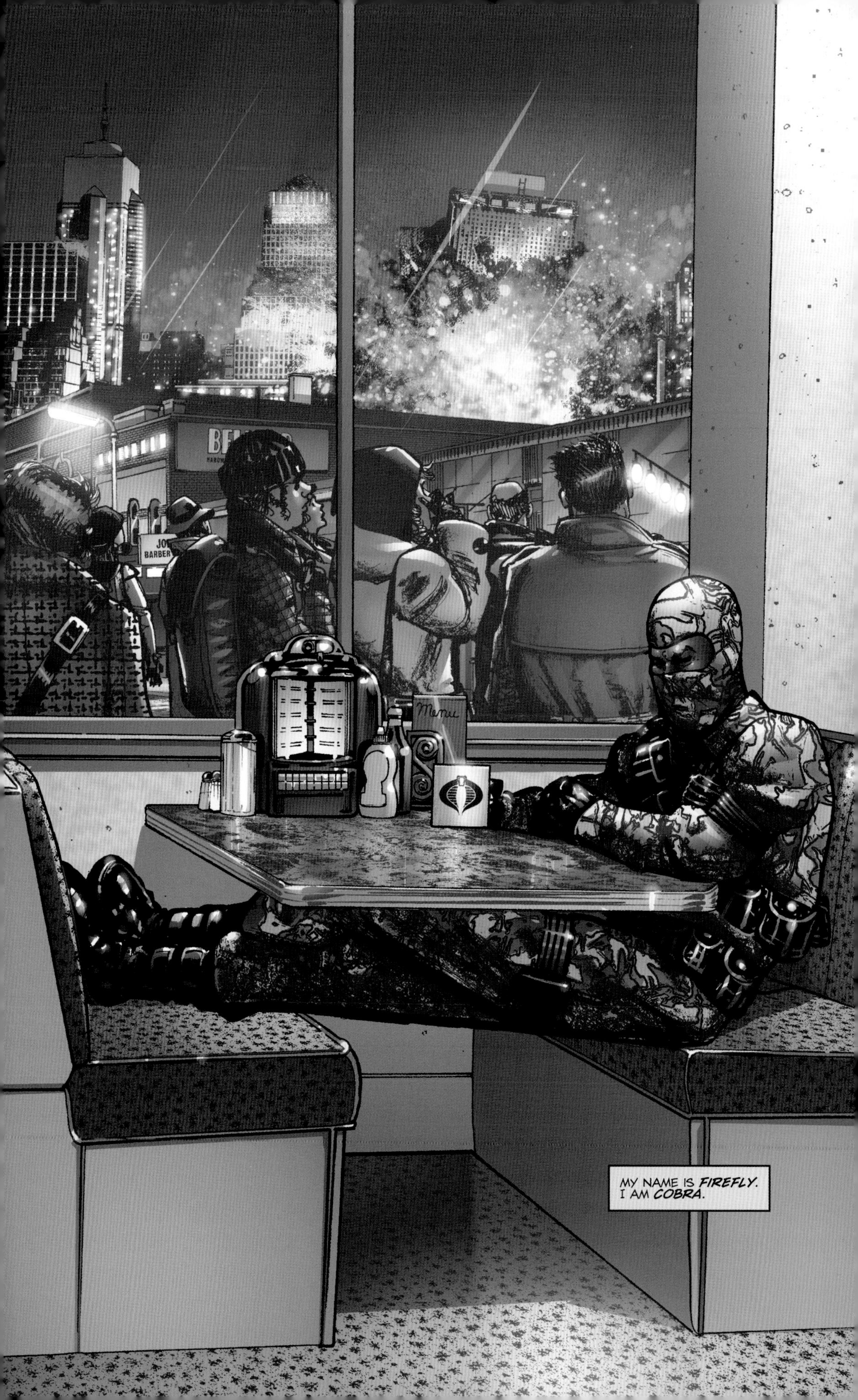
Menu
MY NAME IS *FIREFLY*. I AM *COBRA*.

TRIPWIRE

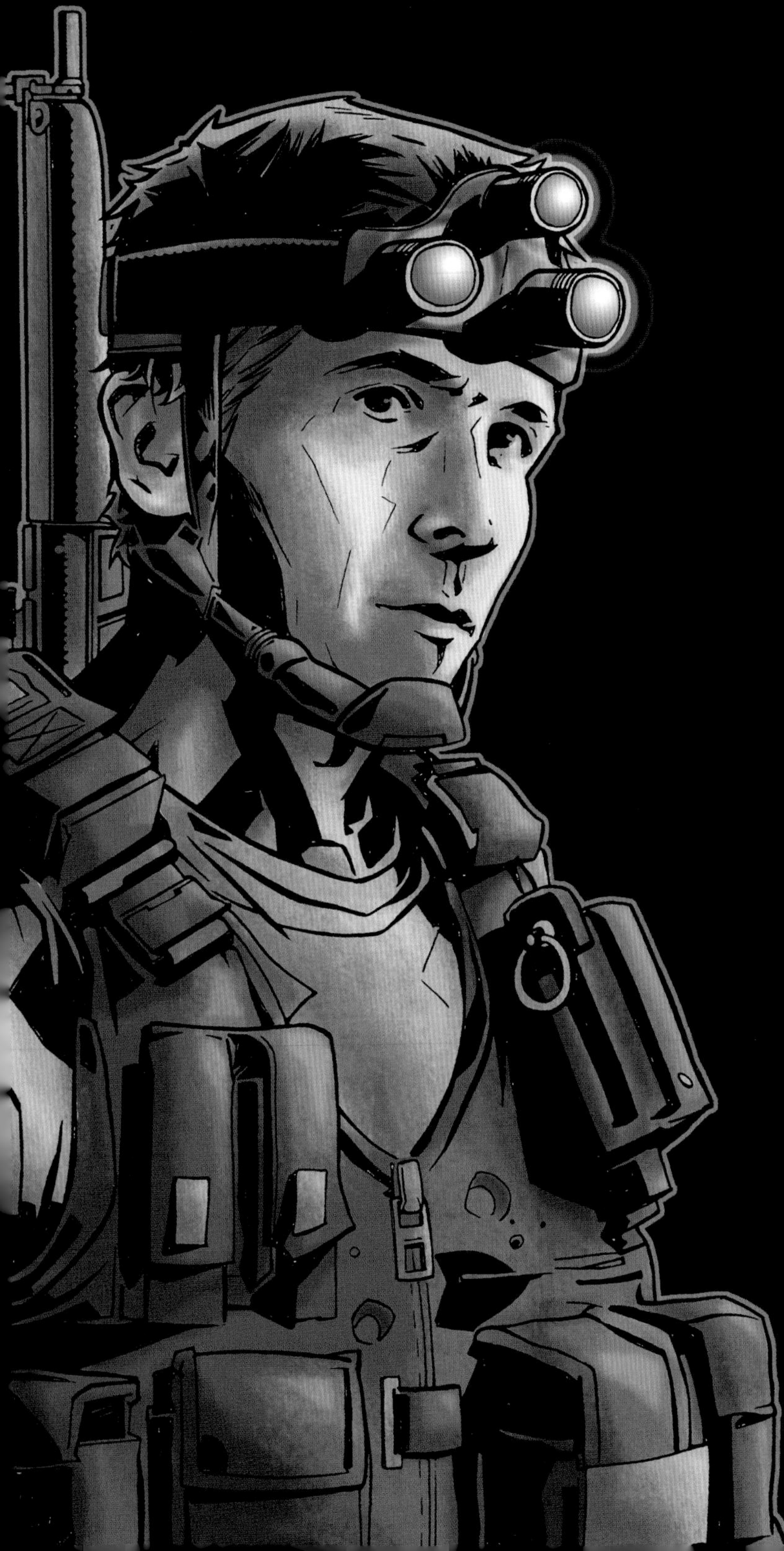

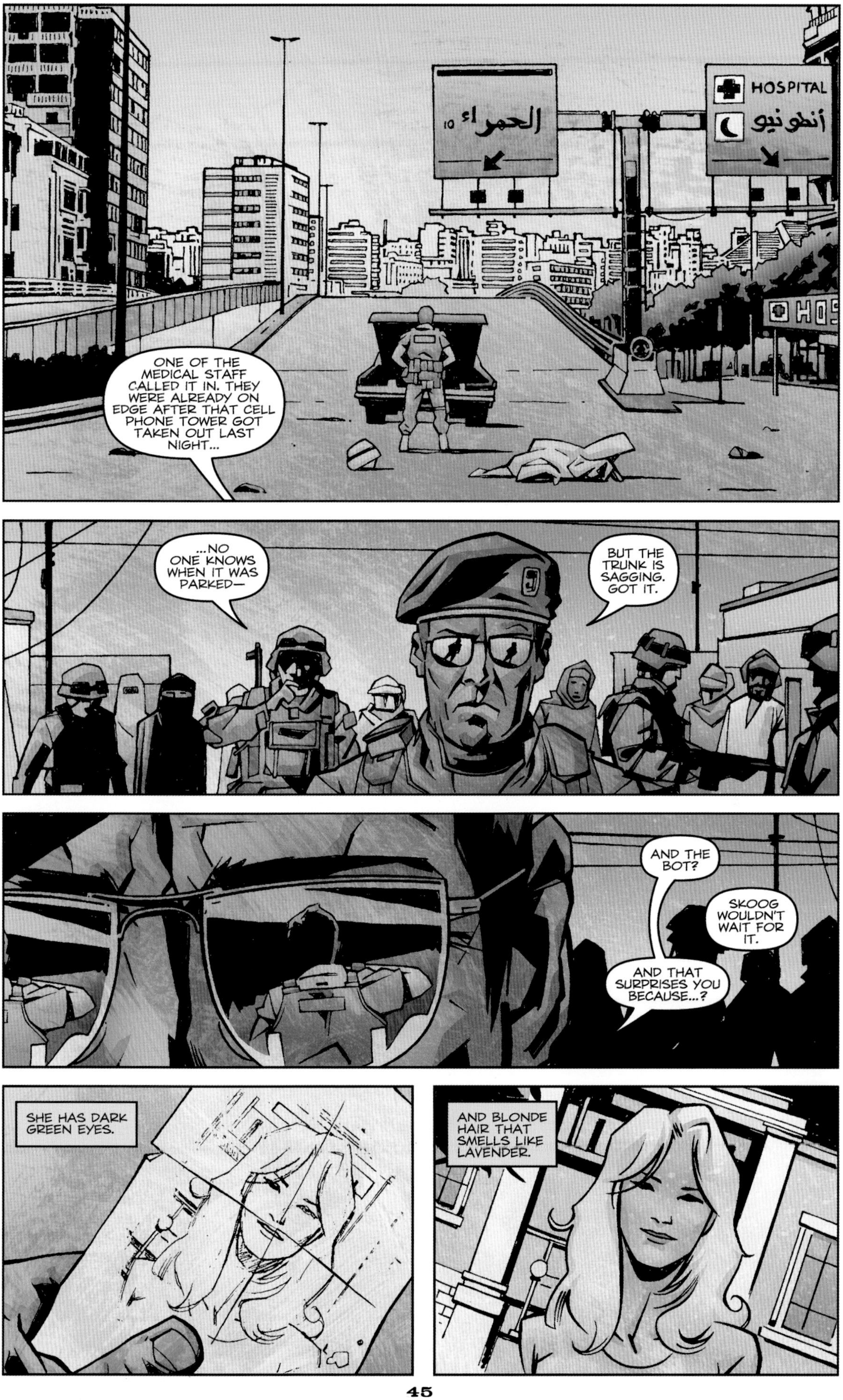
الحمراء
HOSPITAL
أنطونيو
ONE OF THE MEDICAL STAFF CALLED IT IN. THEY WERE ALREADY ON EDGE AFTER THAT CELL PHONE TOWER GOT TAKEN OUT LAST NIGHT...
...NO ONE KNOWS WHEN IT WAS PARKED—
BUT THE TRUNK IS SAGGING. GOT IT.
AND THE BOT?
SKOOG WOULDN'T WAIT FOR IT.
AND THAT SURPRISES YOU BECAUSE...?
SHE HAS DARK GREEN EYES.
AND BLONDE HAIR THAT SMELLS LIKE LAVENDER.

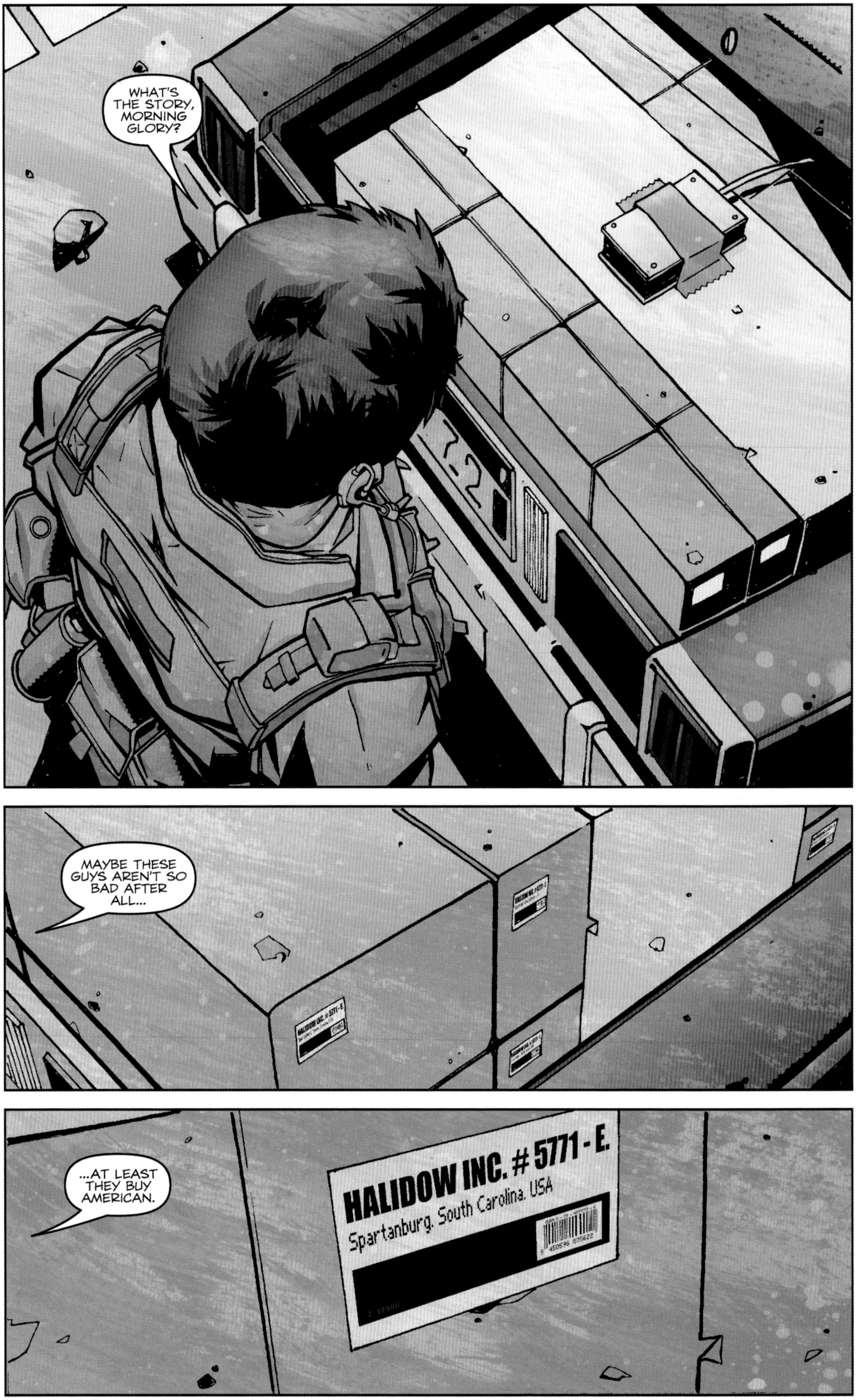
WHAT'S THE STORY, MORNING GLORY?
MAYBE THESE GUYS AREN'T SO BAD AFTER ALL...
...AT LEAST THEY BUY AMERICAN.
HALIDOW INC. # 5771 - E.
Spartanburg, South Carolina, USA

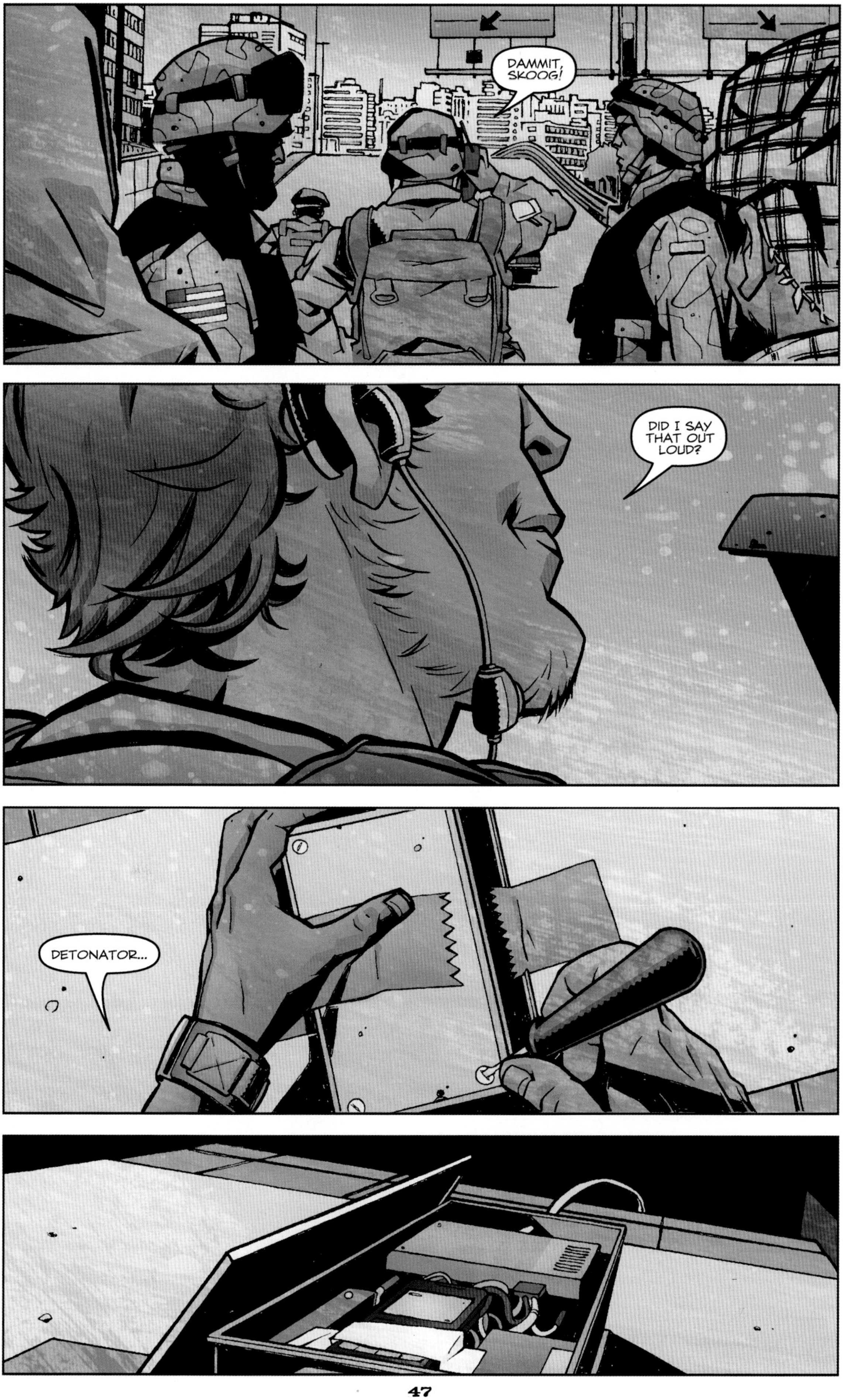
DAMMIT, SKOOG!
DID I SAY THAT OUT LOUD?
DETONATOR...

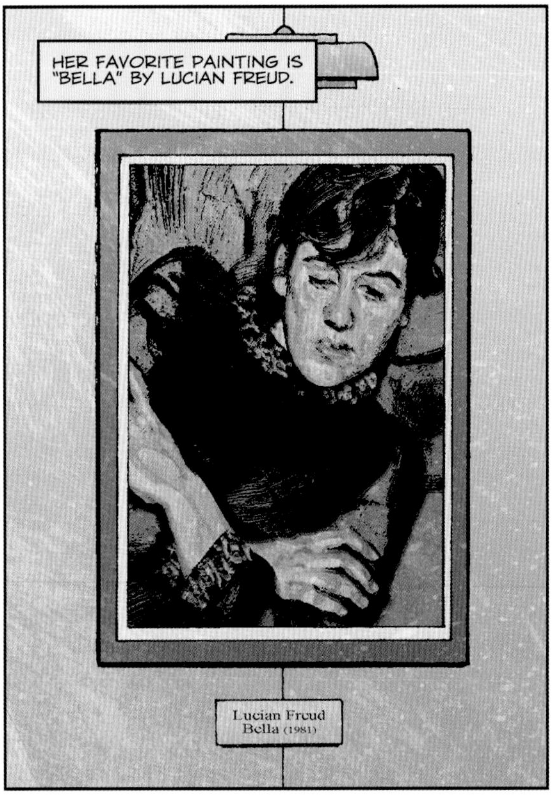
HER FAVORITE PAINTING IS "BELLA" BY LUCIAN FREUD.
Lucian Freud
Bella (1981)

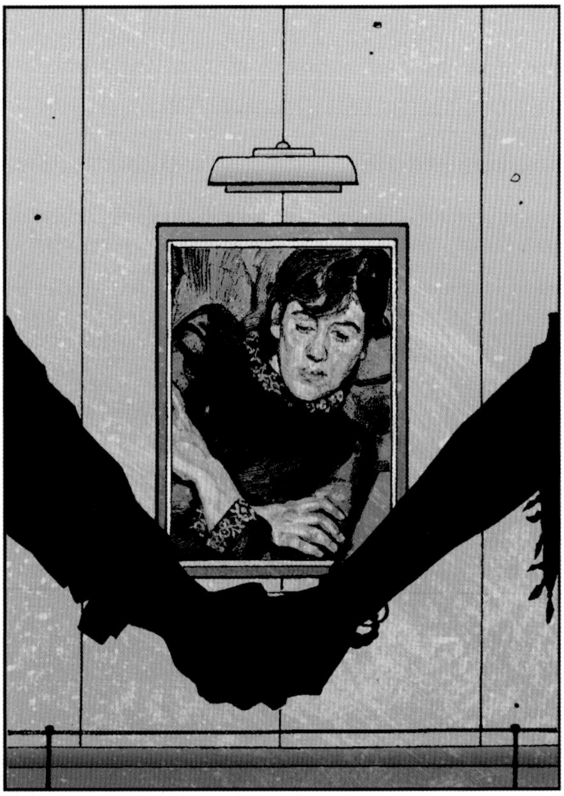

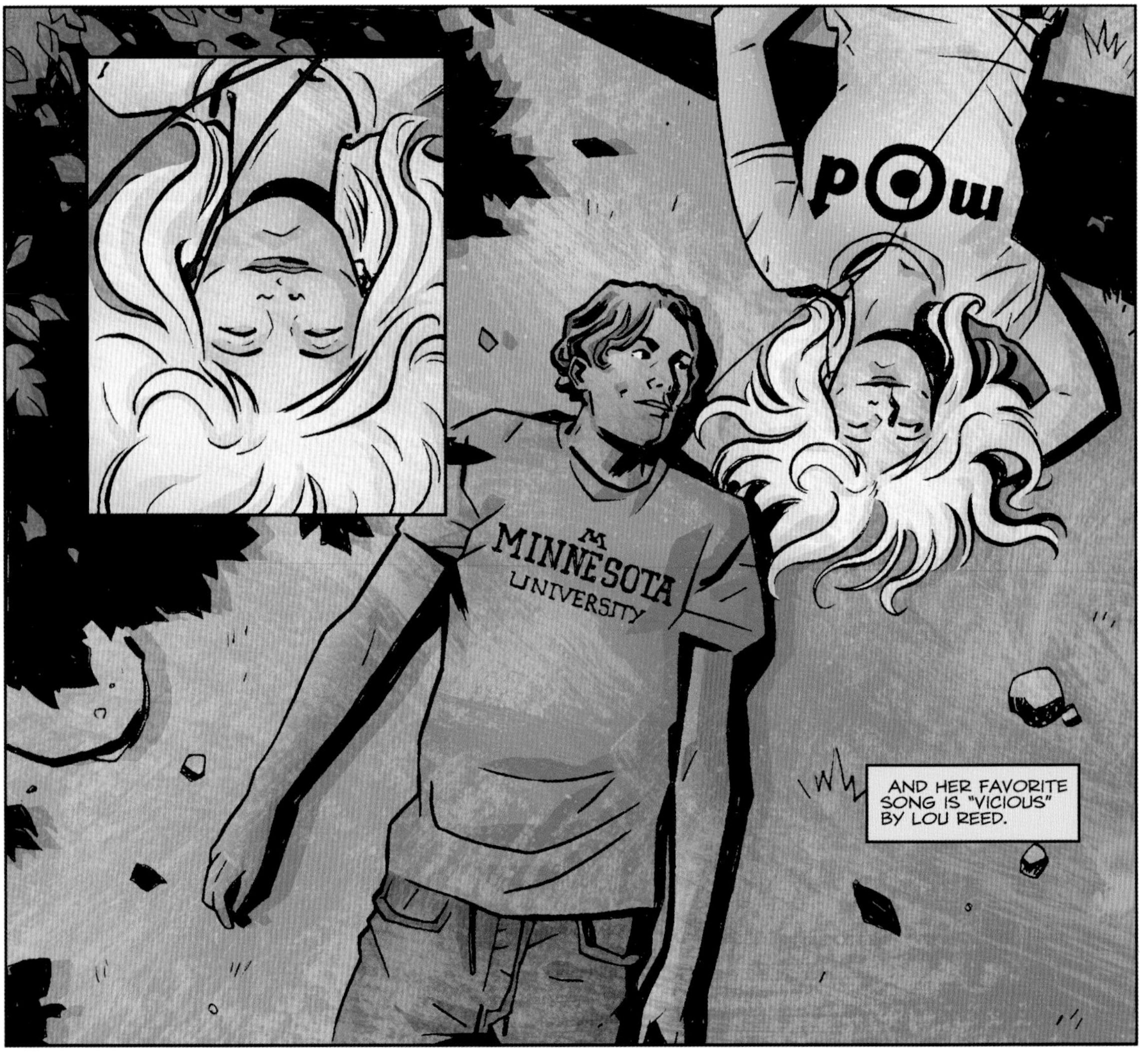
POW
MINNESOTA
UNIVERSITY
AND HER FAVORITE SONG IS "VICIOUS" BY LOU REED.

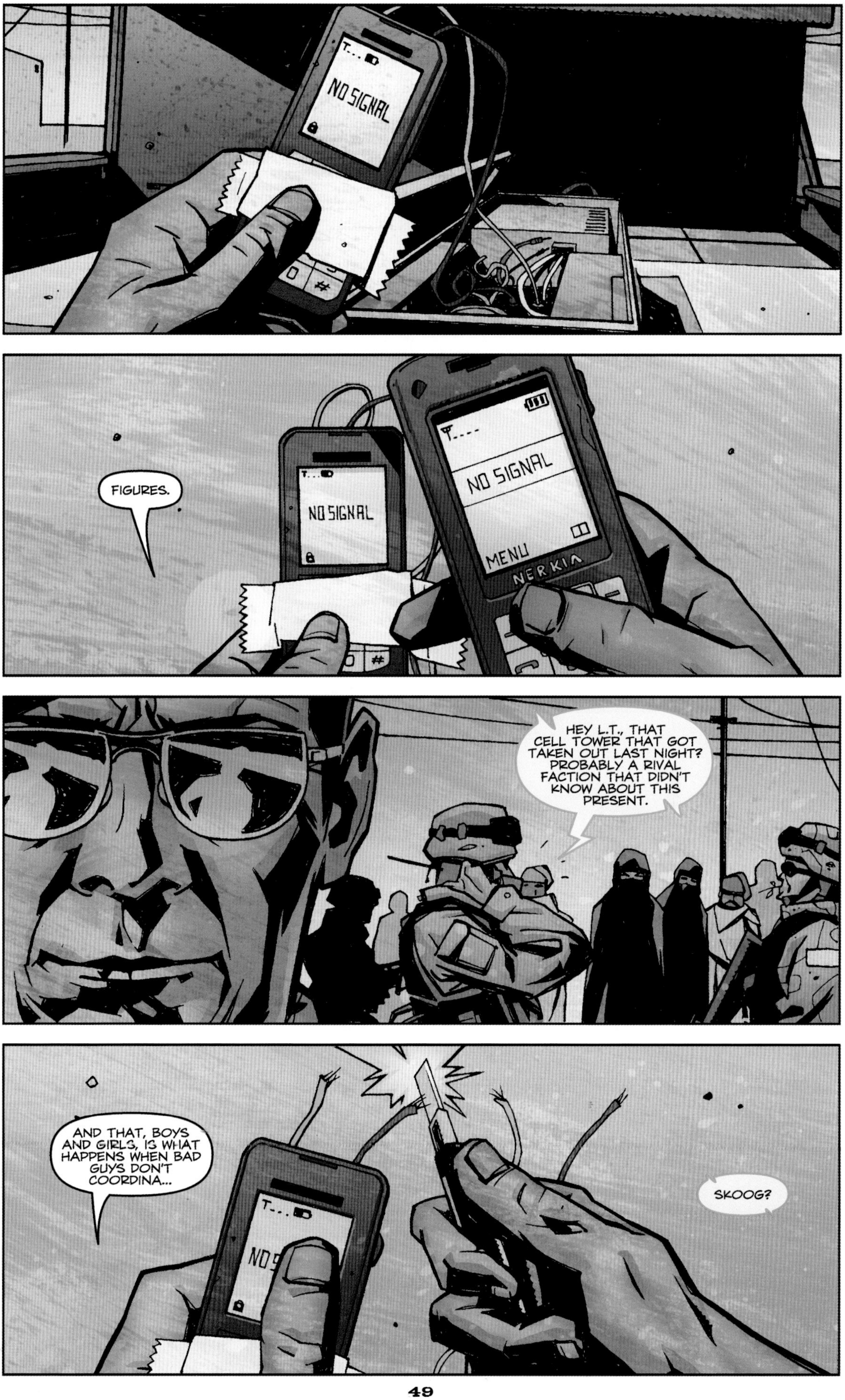
NO SIGNAL
FIGURES.
NO SIGNAL
NO SIGNAL
MENU
NERKIA
HEY L.T., THAT CELL TOWER THAT GOT TAKEN OUT LAST NIGHT? PROBABLY A RIVAL FACTION THAT DIDN'T KNOW ABOUT THIS PRESENT.
AND THAT, BOYS AND GIRLS, IS WHAT HAPPENS WHEN BAD GUYS DON'T COORDINA...
SKOOG?

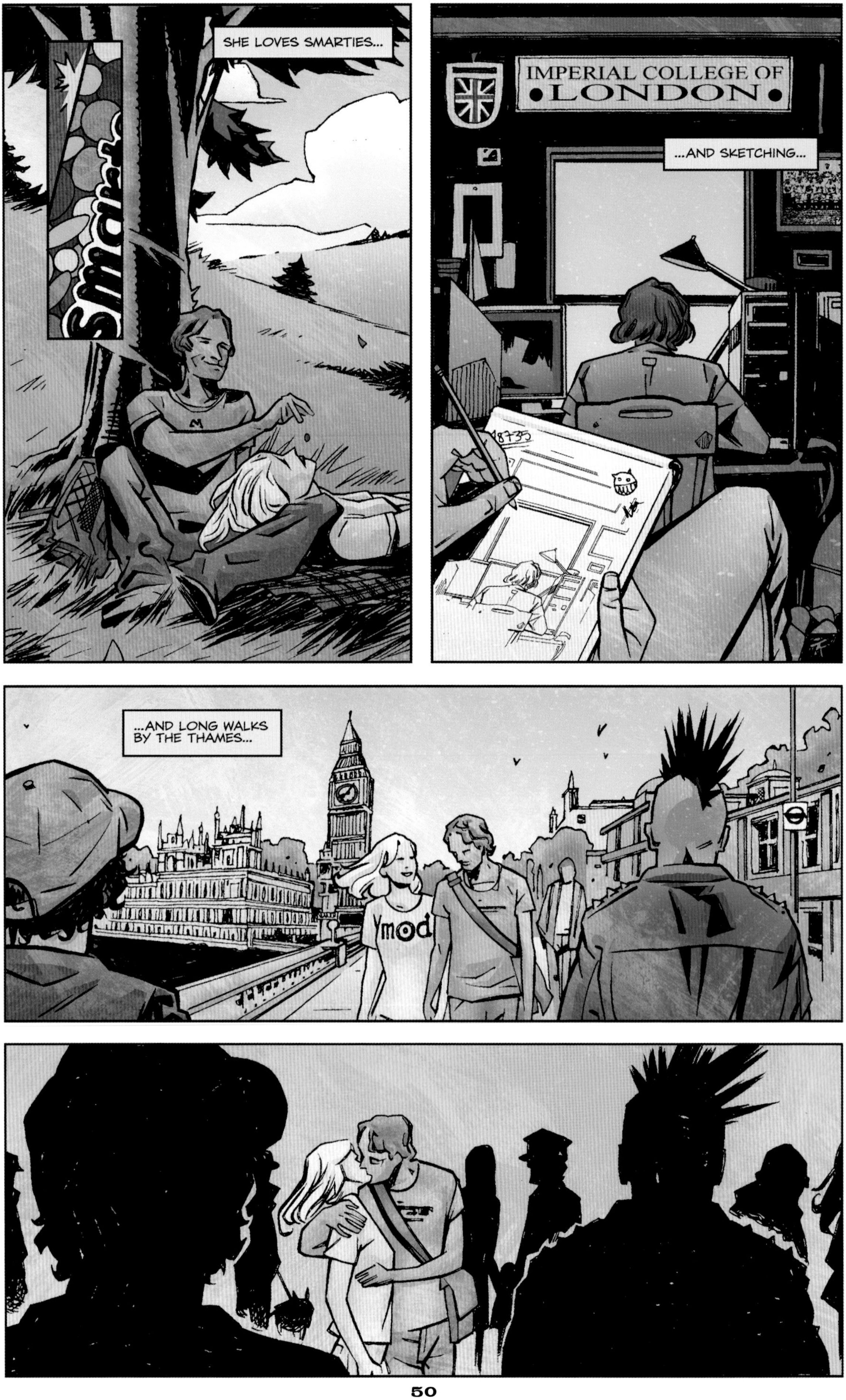
SHE LOVES SMARTIES...
IMPERIAL COLLEGE OF
LONDON
...AND SKETCHING...
...AND LONG WALKS
BY THE THAMES...
mod

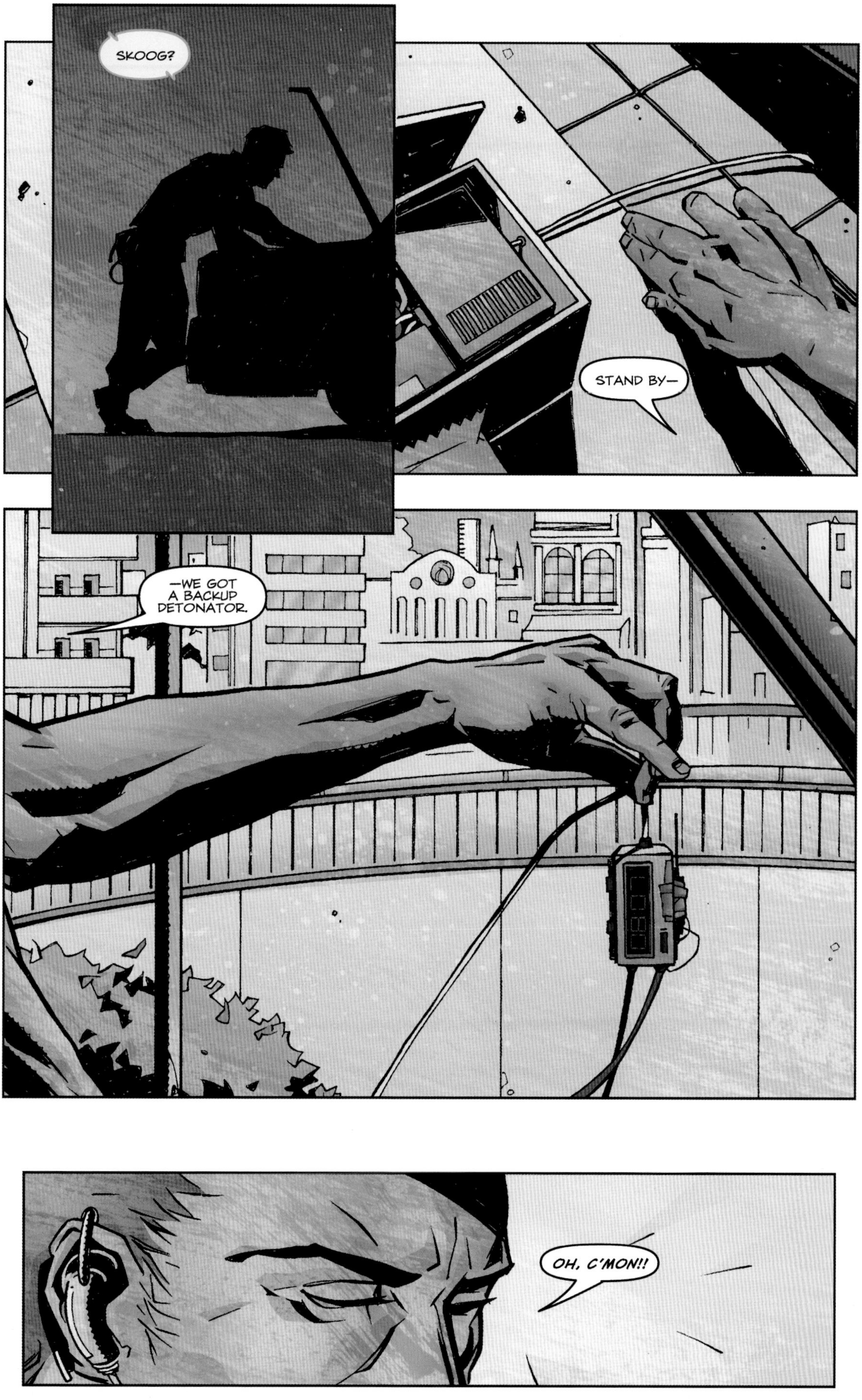
SKOOG?
STAND BY—
—WE GOT A BACKUP DETONATOR.
OH, C'MON!!

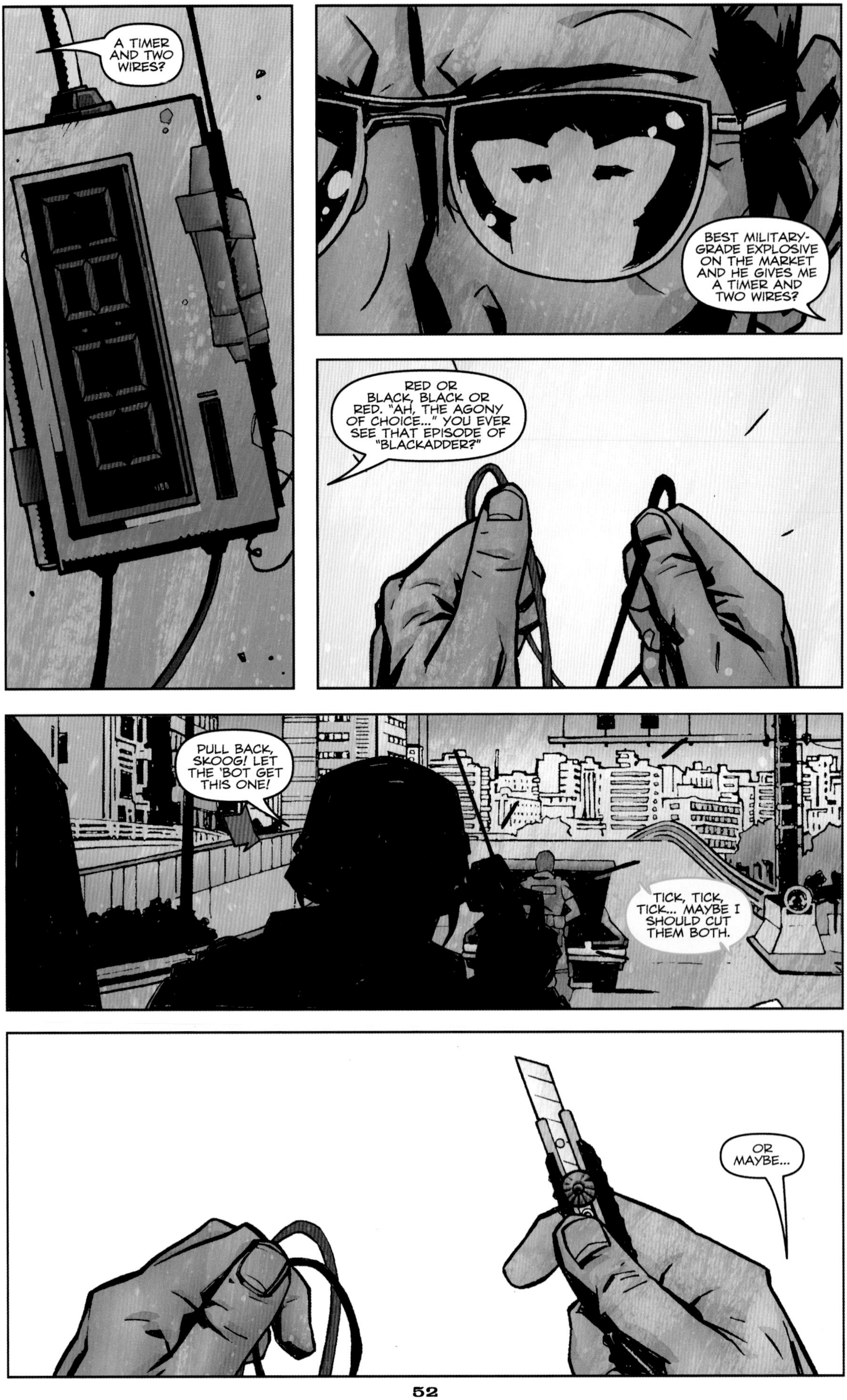
A TIMER AND TWO WIRES?
BEST MILITARY-GRADE EXPLOSIVE ON THE MARKET AND HE GIVES ME A TIMER AND TWO WIRES?
RED OR BLACK, BLACK OR RED. "AH, THE AGONY OF CHOICE..." YOU EVER SEE THAT EPISODE OF "BLACKADDER?"
PULL BACK, SKOOG! LET THE 'BOT GET THIS ONE!
TICK, TICK, TICK... MAYBE I SHOULD CUT THEM BOTH.
OR MAYBE...

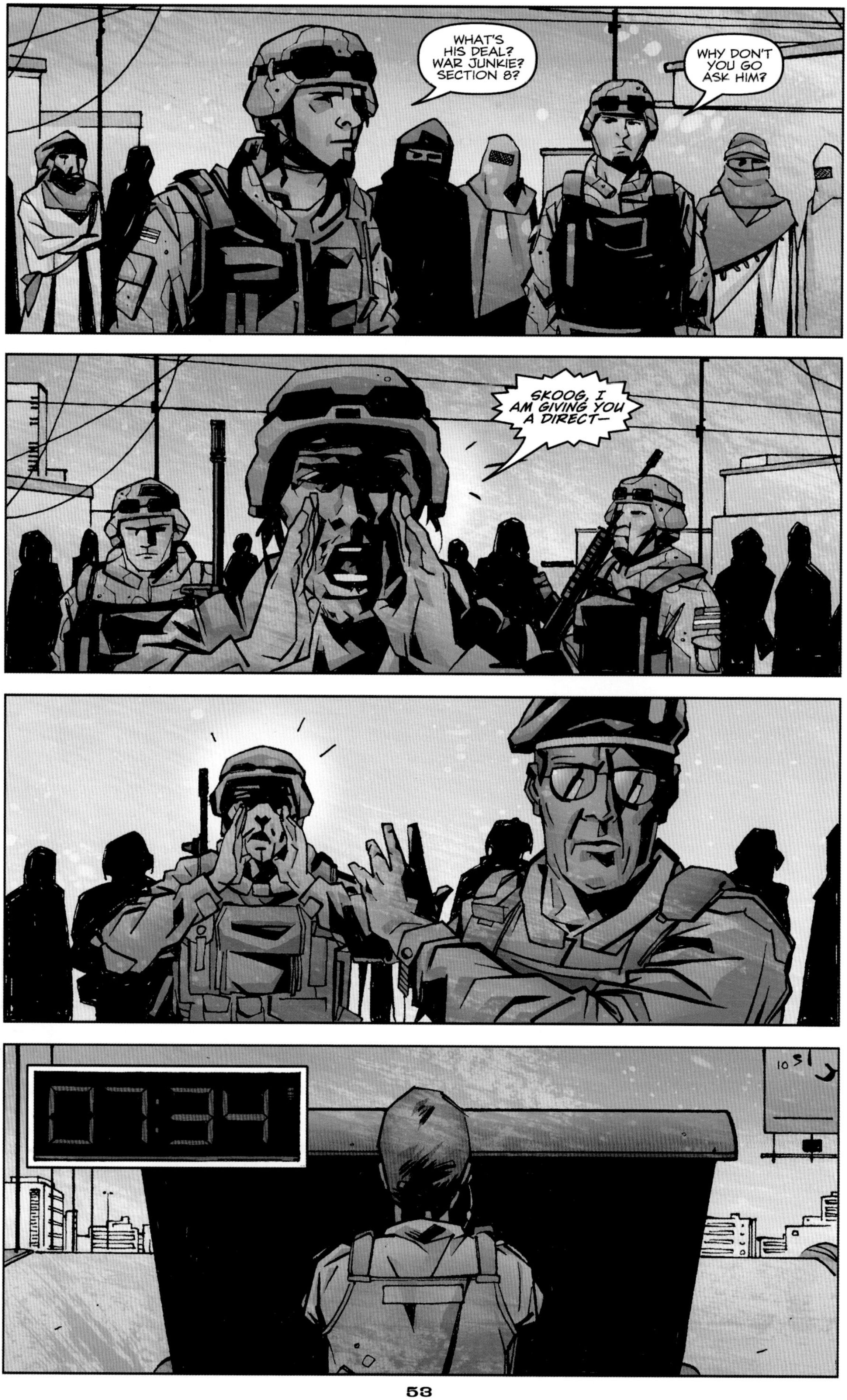
WHAT'S HIS DEAL? WAR JUNKIE? SECTION 8?
WHY DON'T YOU GO ASK HIM?
SKOOG, I AM GIVING YOU A DIRECT—
07:34

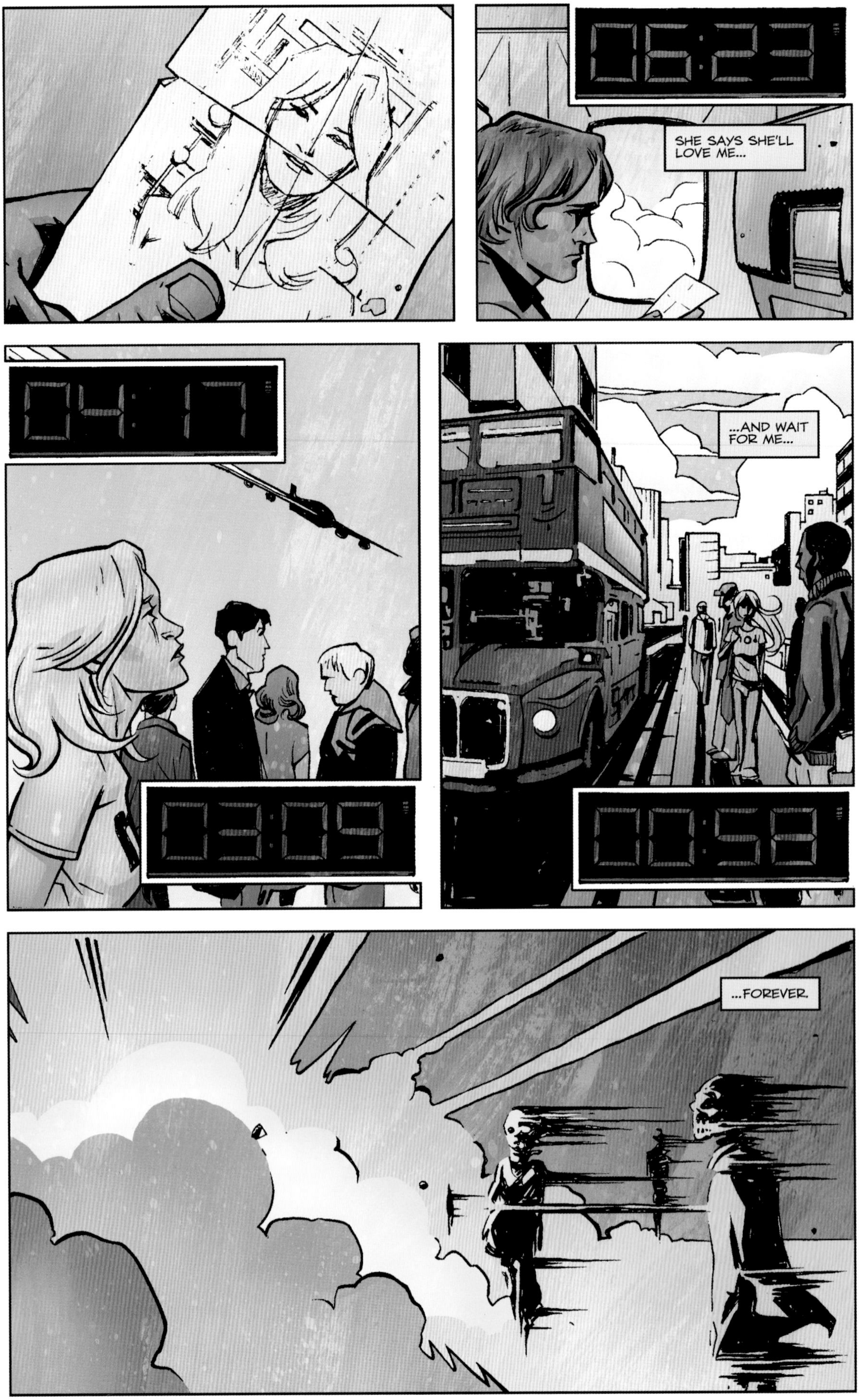
05:23
SHE SAYS SHE'LL LOVE ME...
04:17
03:09
...AND WAIT FOR ME...
00:59
...FOREVER.

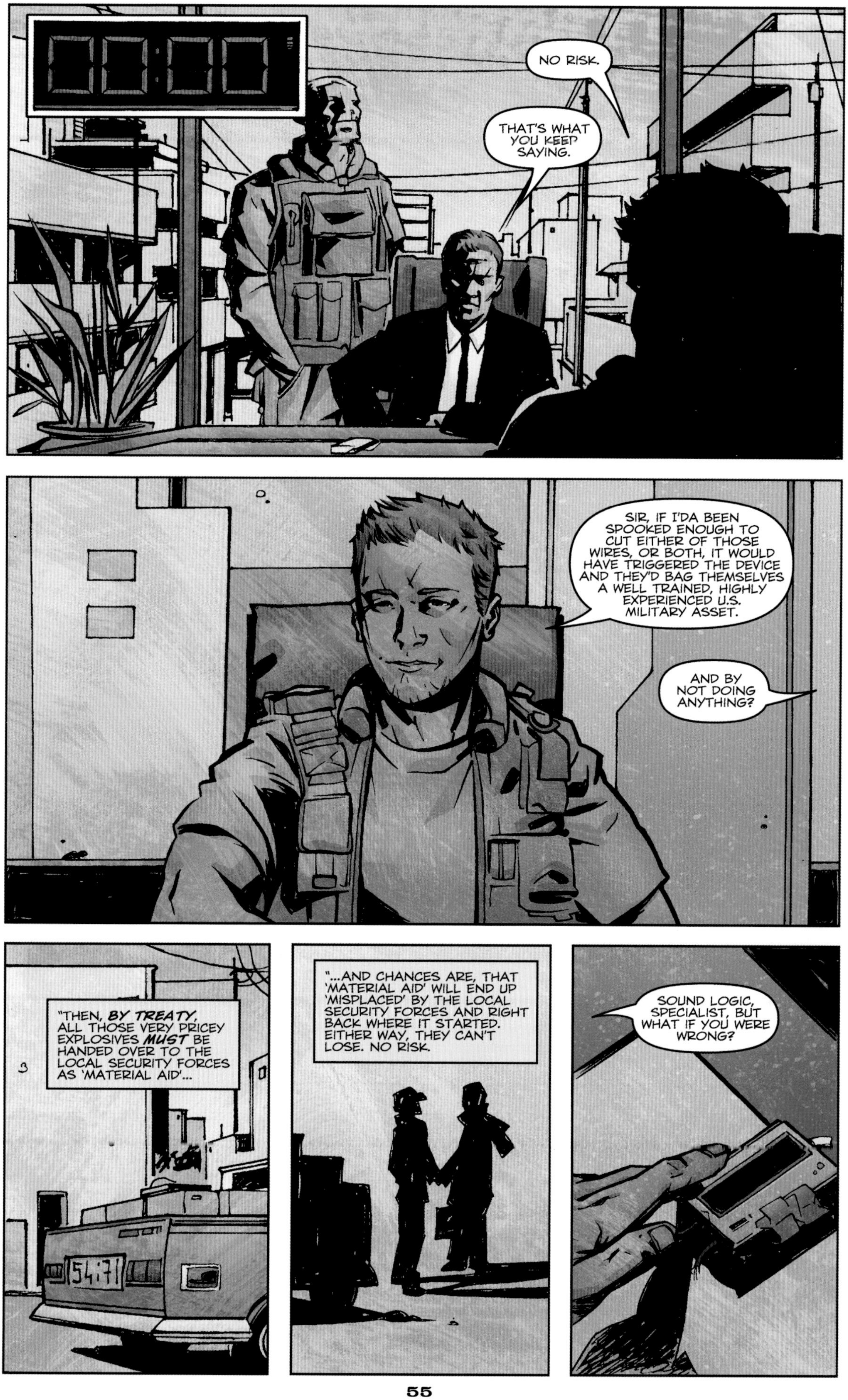
NO RISK.
THAT'S WHAT YOU KEEP SAYING.
SIR, IF I'DA BEEN SPOOKED ENOUGH TO CUT EITHER OF THOSE WIRES, OR BOTH, IT WOULD HAVE TRIGGERED THE DEVICE AND THEY'D BAG THEMSELVES A WELL TRAINED, HIGHLY EXPERIENCED U.S. MILITARY ASSET.
AND BY NOT DOING ANYTHING?
"THEN, *BY TREATY*, ALL THOSE VERY PRICEY EXPLOSIVES *MUST* BE HANDED OVER TO THE LOCAL SECURITY FORCES AS 'MATERIAL AID'...
54:71
"...AND CHANCES ARE, THAT 'MATERIAL AID' WILL END UP 'MISPLACED' BY THE LOCAL SECURITY FORCES AND RIGHT BACK WHERE IT STARTED. EITHER WAY, THEY CAN'T LOSE. NO RISK.
SOUND LOGIC, SPECIALIST, BUT WHAT IF YOU WERE WRONG?

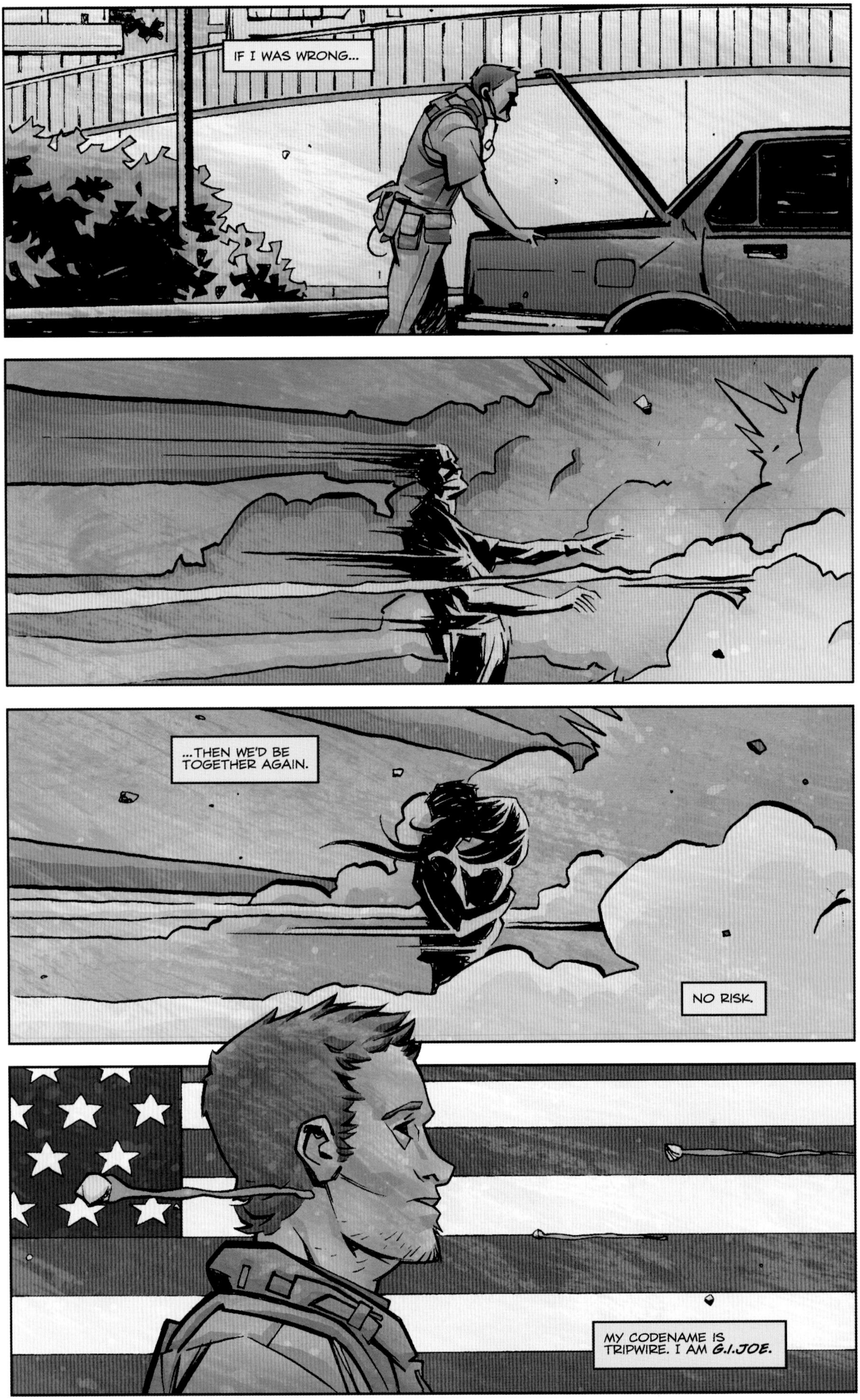

IF I WAS WRONG...
...THEN WE'D BE TOGETHER AGAIN.
NO RISK.
MY CODENAME IS TRIPWIRE. I AM *G.I.JOE.*

DEEP SIX

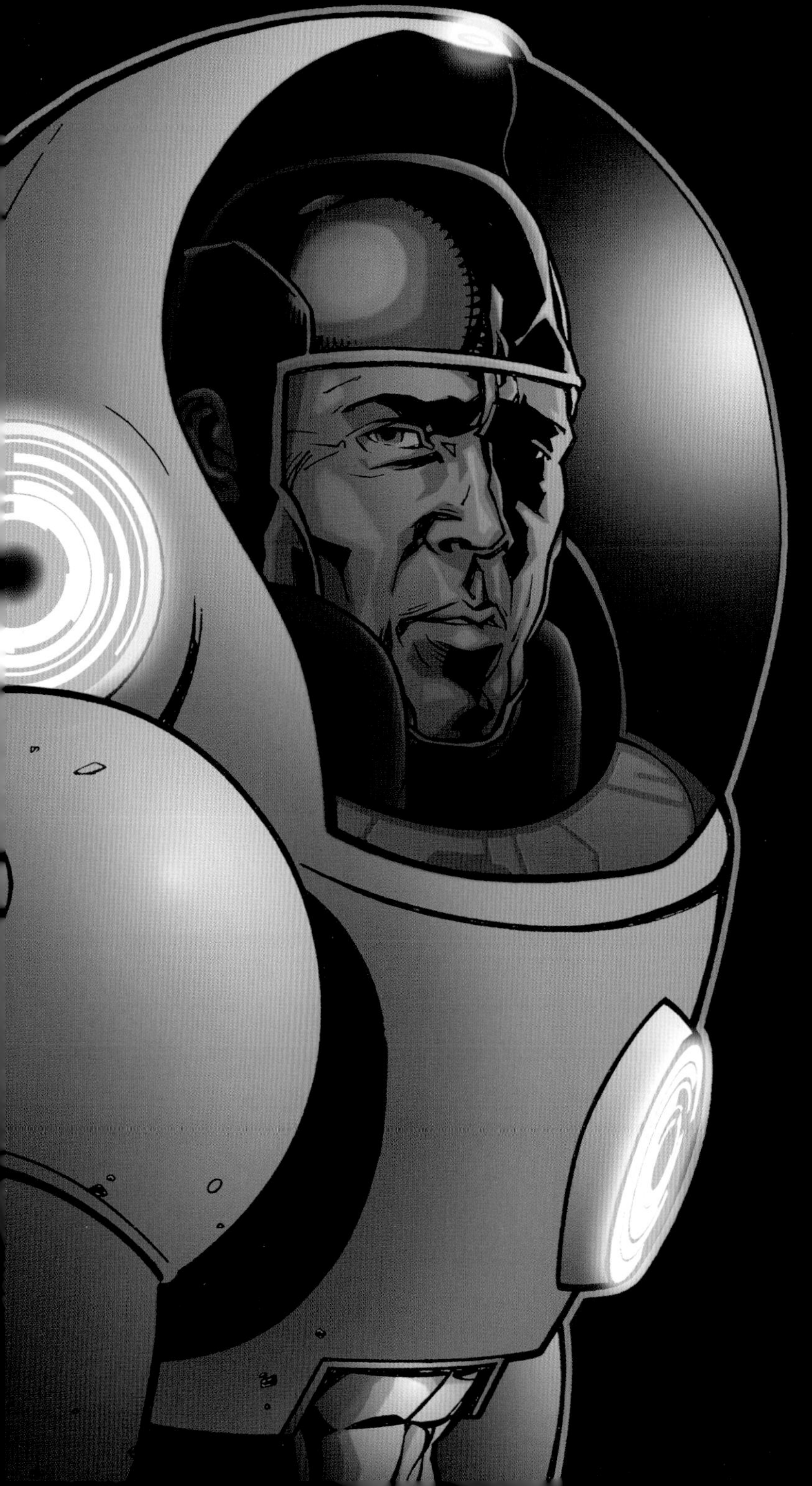

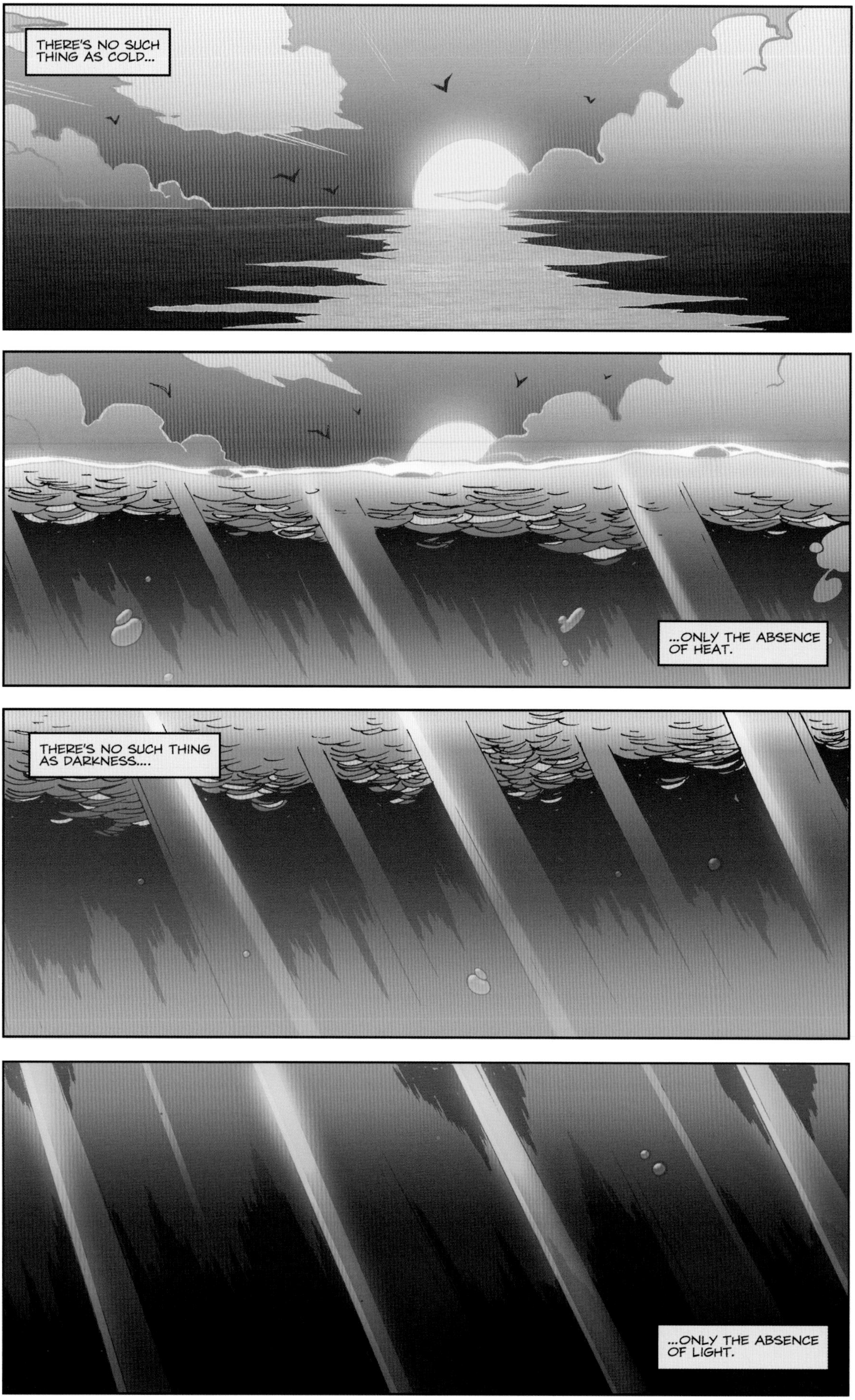
THERE'S NO SUCH THING AS COLD...
...ONLY THE ABSENCE OF HEAT.
THERE'S NO SUCH THING AS DARKNESS....
...ONLY THE ABSENCE OF LIGHT.

HYDROGEN AND OXYGEN.

SODIUM AND CHLORINE.

SALTWATER...

...AND TIME.

TIME.

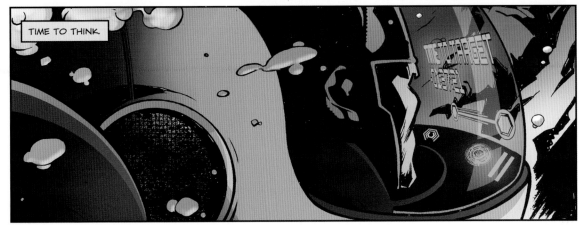

TIME TO THINK.

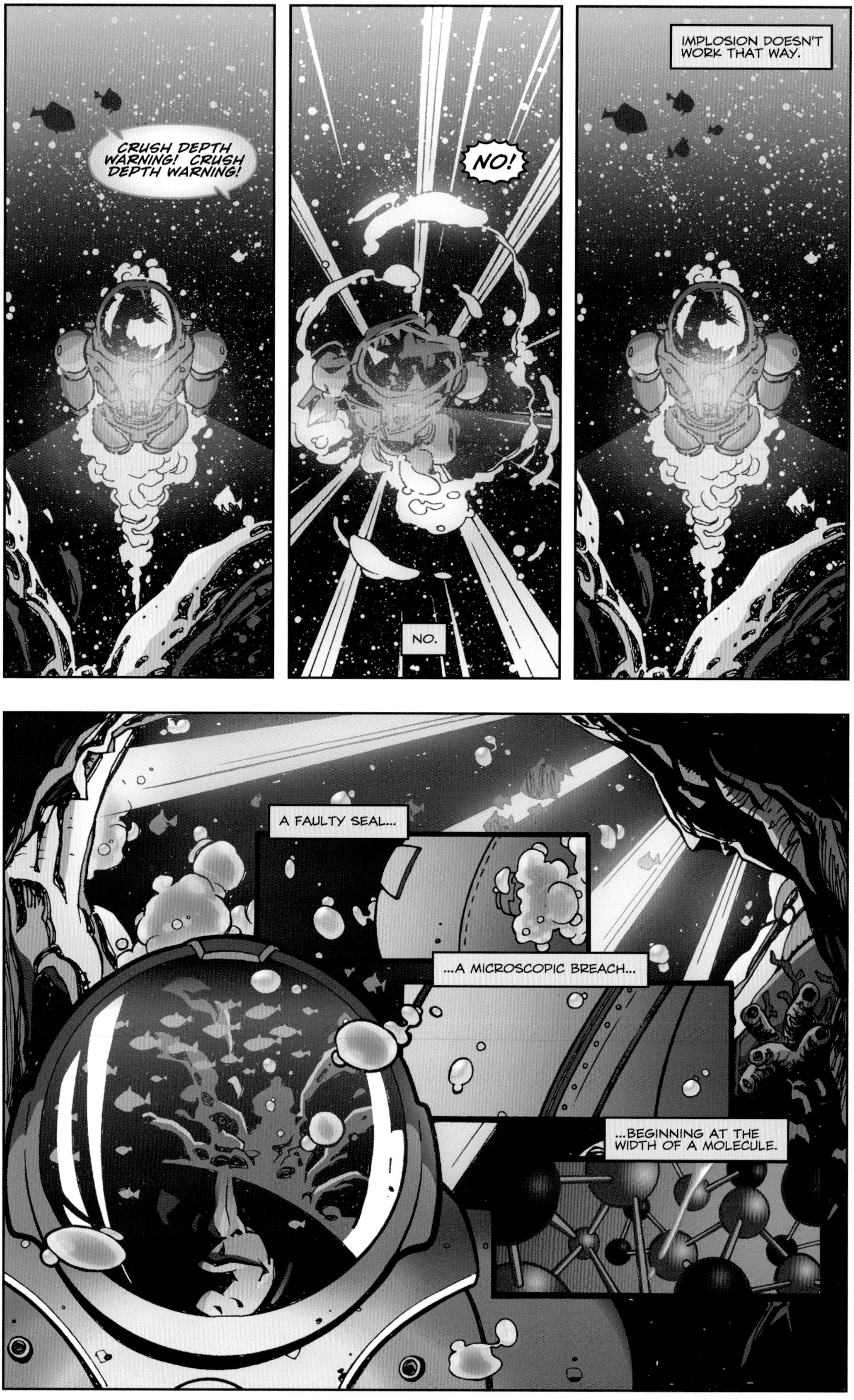
CRUSH DEPTH WARNING! CRUSH DEPTH WARNING!
NO!
NO.
IMPLOSION DOESN'T WORK THAT WAY.
A FAULTY SEAL...
...A MICROSCOPIC BREACH...
...BEGINNING AT THE WIDTH OF A MOLECULE.

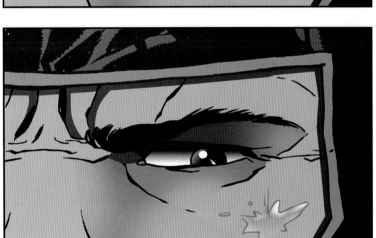

OVER 1,000 POUNDS PER SQUARE INCH.

AT LEAST THAT'D BE QUICK.

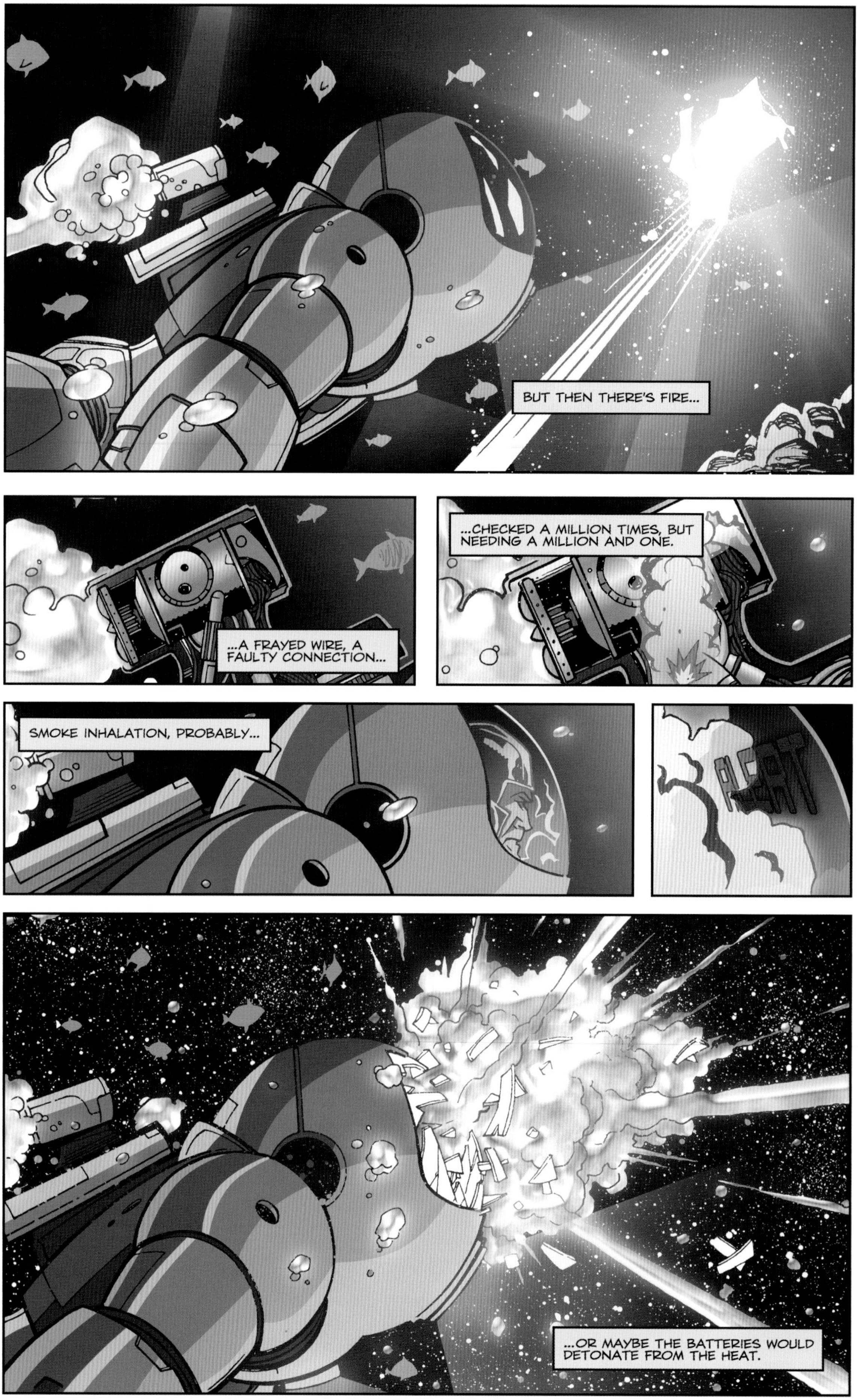
BUT THEN THERE'S FIRE...
...A FRAYED WIRE, A FAULTY CONNECTION...
...CHECKED A MILLION TIMES, BUT NEEDING A MILLION AND ONE.
SMOKE INHALATION, PROBABLY...
...OR MAYBE THE BATTERIES WOULD DETONATE FROM THE HEAT.

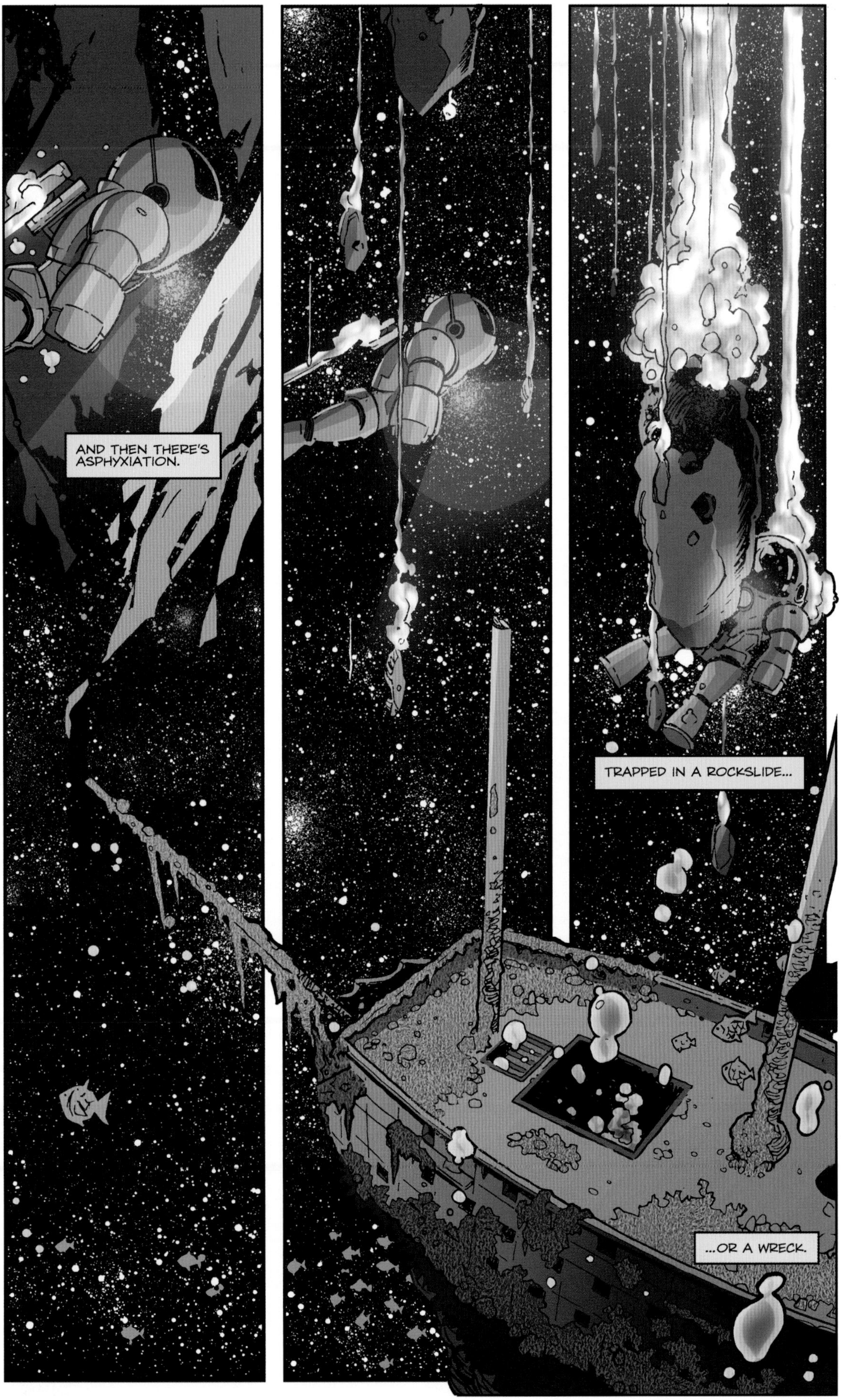
AND THEN THERE'S ASPHYXIATION.
TRAPPED IN A ROCKSLIDE...
...OR A WRECK.

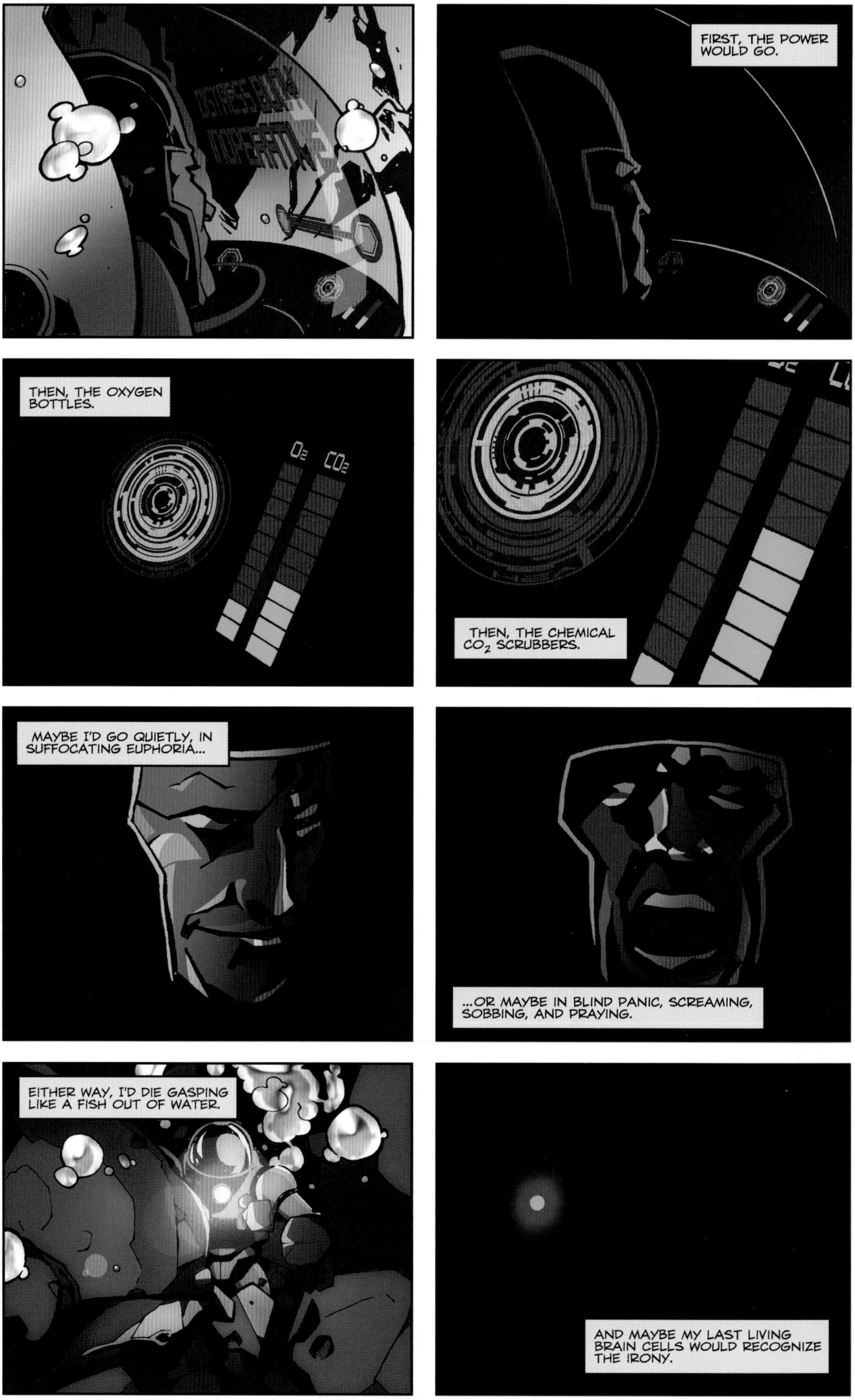
FIRST, THE POWER WOULD GO.
THEN, THE OXYGEN BOTTLES.
O_2
CO_2
THEN, THE CHEMICAL CO_2 SCRUBBERS.
MAYBE I'D GO QUIETLY, IN SUFFOCATING EUPHORIA...
...OR MAYBE IN BLIND PANIC, SCREAMING, SOBBING, AND PRAYING.
EITHER WAY, I'D DIE GASPING LIKE A FISH OUT OF WATER.
AND MAYBE MY LAST LIVING BRAIN CELLS WOULD RECOGNIZE THE IRONY.

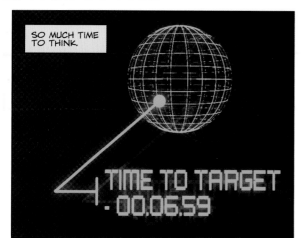

SO MUCH TIME TO THINK.

TIME TO TARGET - 00.06.59

SO MANY WAYS TO DIE.

FIRING SOLUTION - 99%

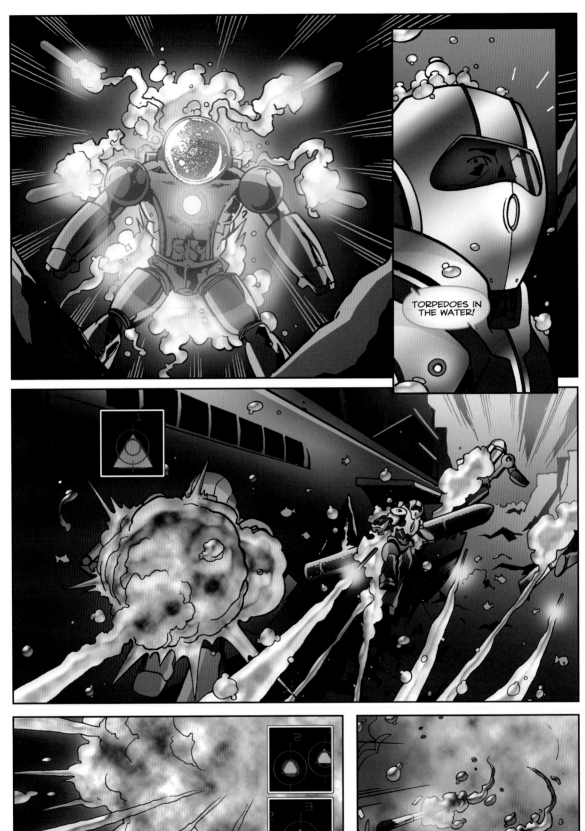

TORPEDOES IN
THE WATER!

TARGETS
DESTROYED.

HOSTILE
TORPEDOES
INBOUND.

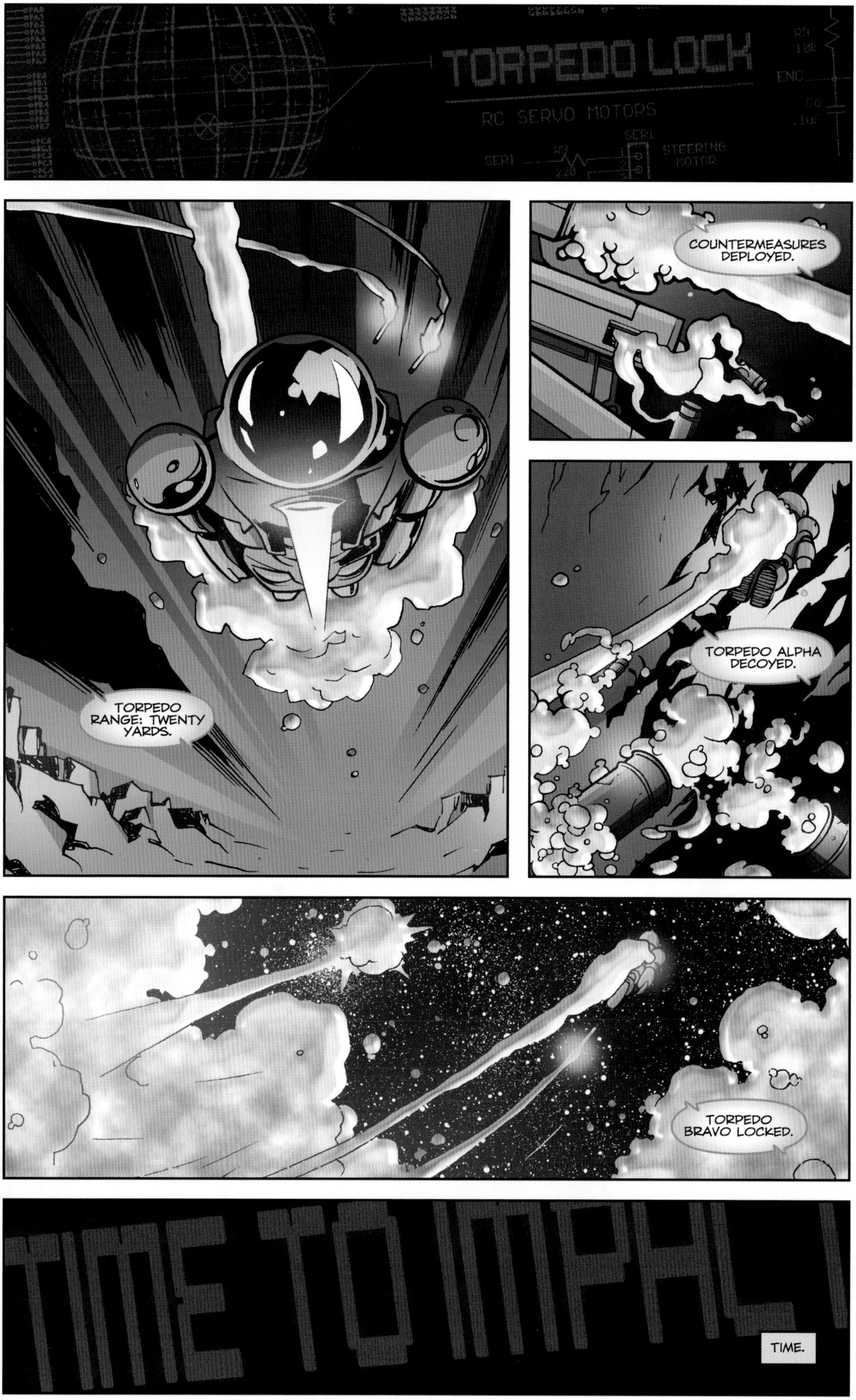
TORPEDO LOCK
RC SERVO MOTORS
STEERING MOTOR
TORPEDO RANGE: TWENTY YARDS.
COUNTERMEASURES DEPLOYED.
TORPEDO ALPHA DECOYED.
TORPEDO BRAVO LOCKED.
TIME TO
TIME.

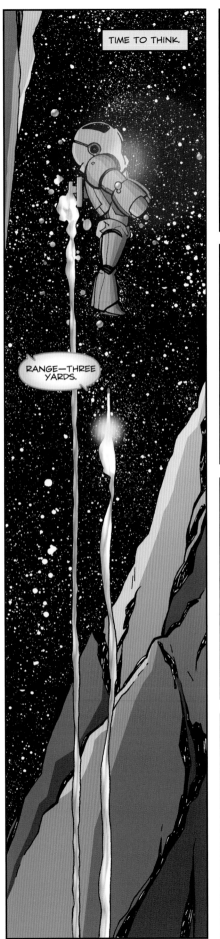

TIME TO THINK.

RANGE—THREE YARDS.

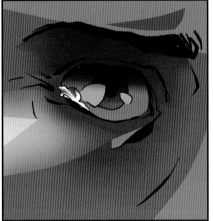

TWO YARDS.

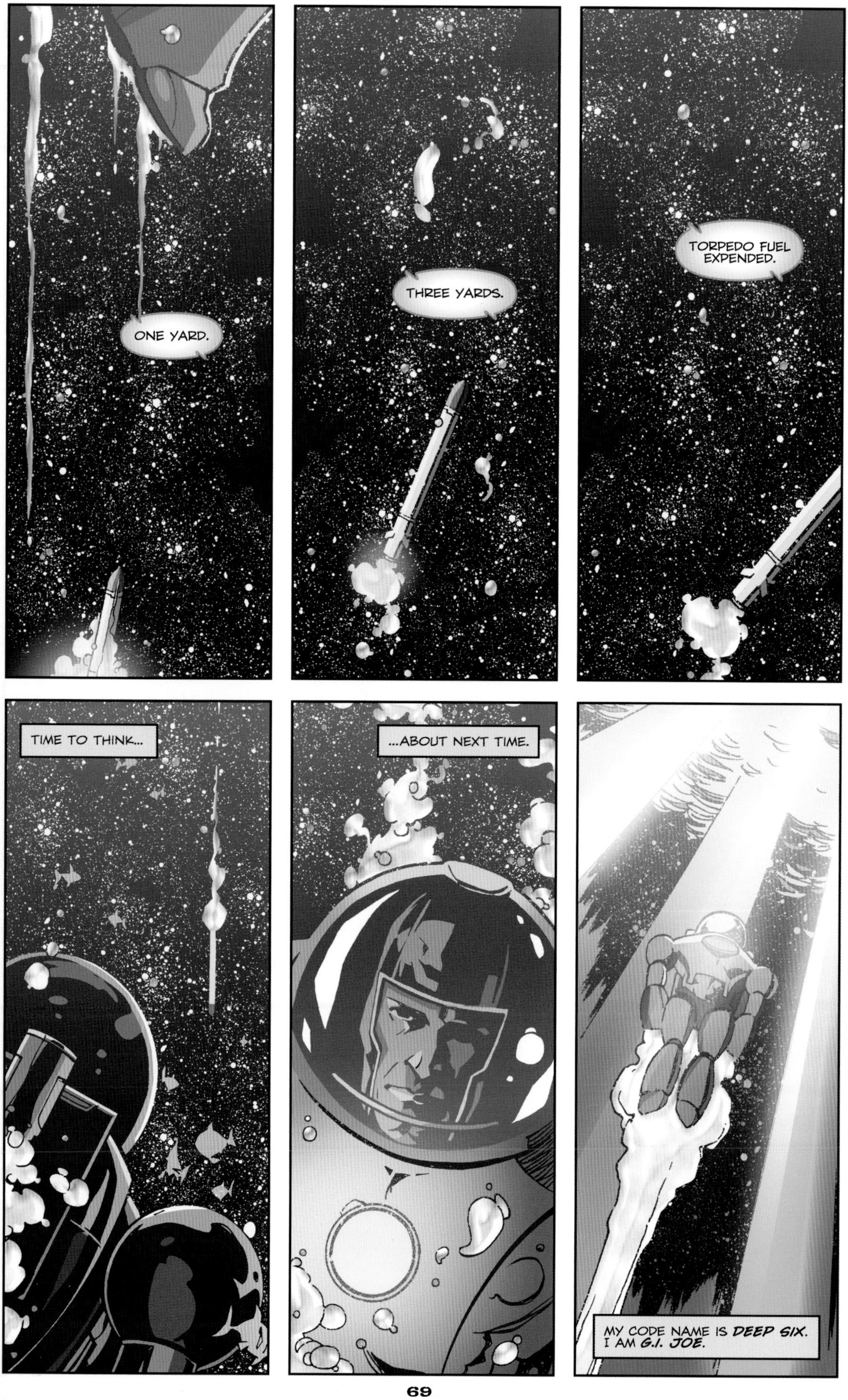
ONE YARD.
THREE YARDS.
TORPEDO FUEL EXPENDED.
TIME TO THINK...
...ABOUT NEXT TIME.
MY CODE NAME IS *DEEP SIX*.
I AM *G.I. JOE*.

INTERROGATOR

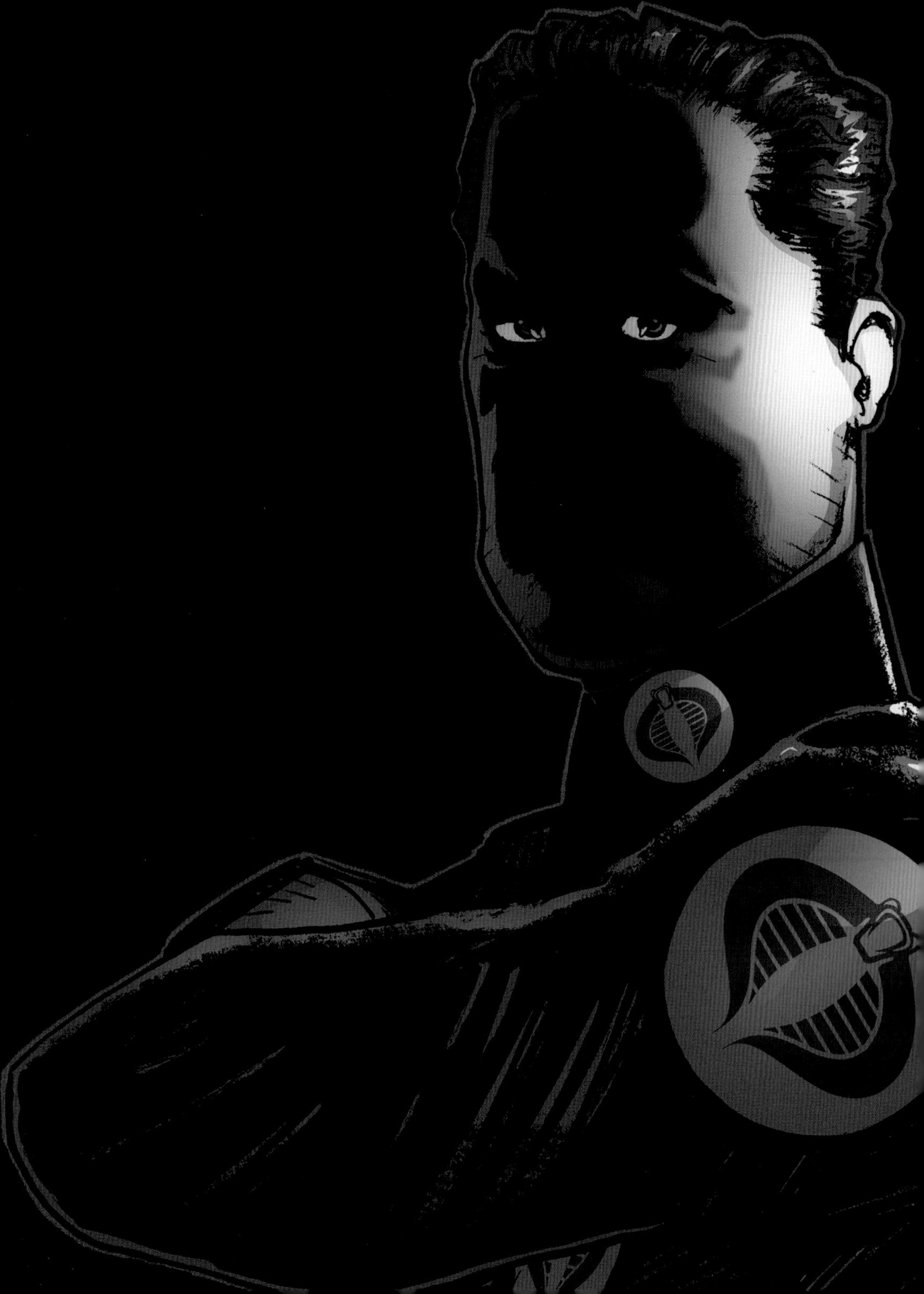

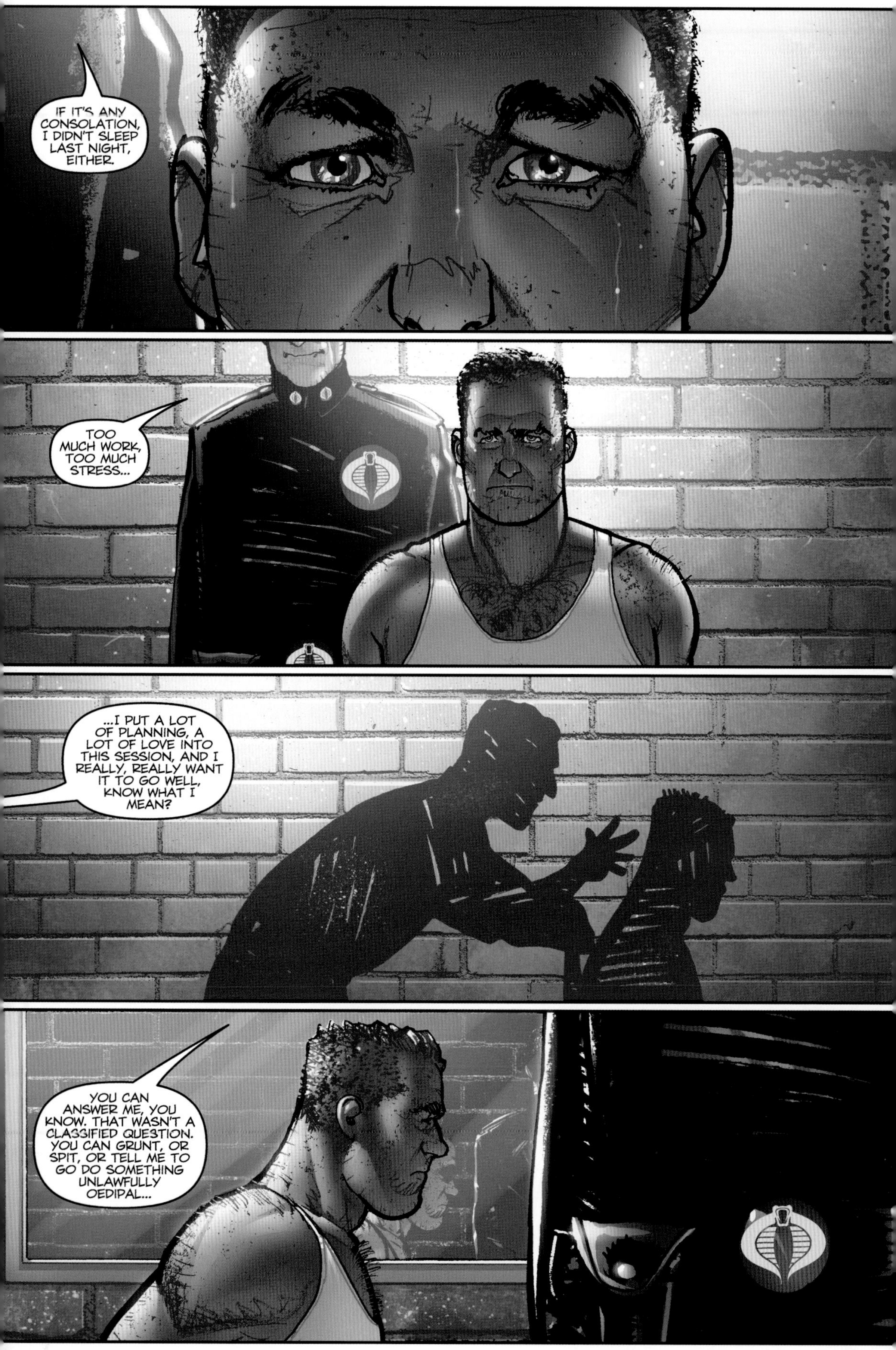
IF IT'S ANY CONSOLATION, I DIDN'T SLEEP LAST NIGHT, EITHER.
TOO MUCH WORK, TOO MUCH STRESS...
...I PUT A LOT OF PLANNING, A LOT OF LOVE INTO THIS SESSION, AND I REALLY, REALLY WANT IT TO GO WELL, KNOW WHAT I MEAN?
YOU CAN ANSWER ME, YOU KNOW. THAT WASN'T A CLASSIFIED QUESTION. YOU CAN GRUNT, OR SPIT, OR TELL ME TO GO DO SOMETHING UNLAWFULLY OEDIPAL...

...OR YOU COULD ASK ME SOMETHING, ANYTHING. WHERE AM I FROM? WHO DO I WORK FOR? WHY DO I HAVE THIS PRETENTIOUS NEED TO BRING UP SOPHOCLES?
SERIOUSLY, I'D LIKE THIS TO BE A GENUINE CONVERSATION. IT'S JUST... NICER.
NO? NOTHING? TOUGH ROOM.
DO YOU KNOW WHAT THIS IS... AND NO, DON'T BE CUTE AND SAY IT'S A RHETORICAL QUESTION.
WELL, TECHNICALLY, IT'S YOUR OWN SIDEARM, CLEANED, OILED, AND NOW WITH ONE LIVE ROUND IN THE CHAMBER. AND THAT ROUND IS WHY I CALL THIS A "CHOICE."
WON'T WORK...
PARDON?

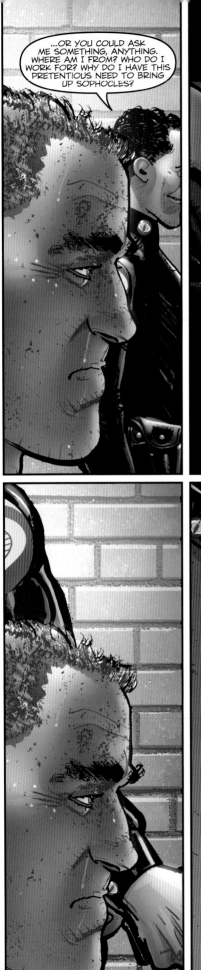

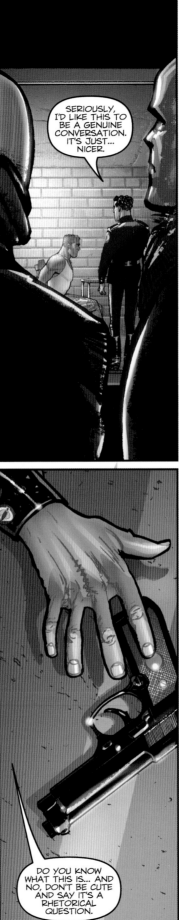

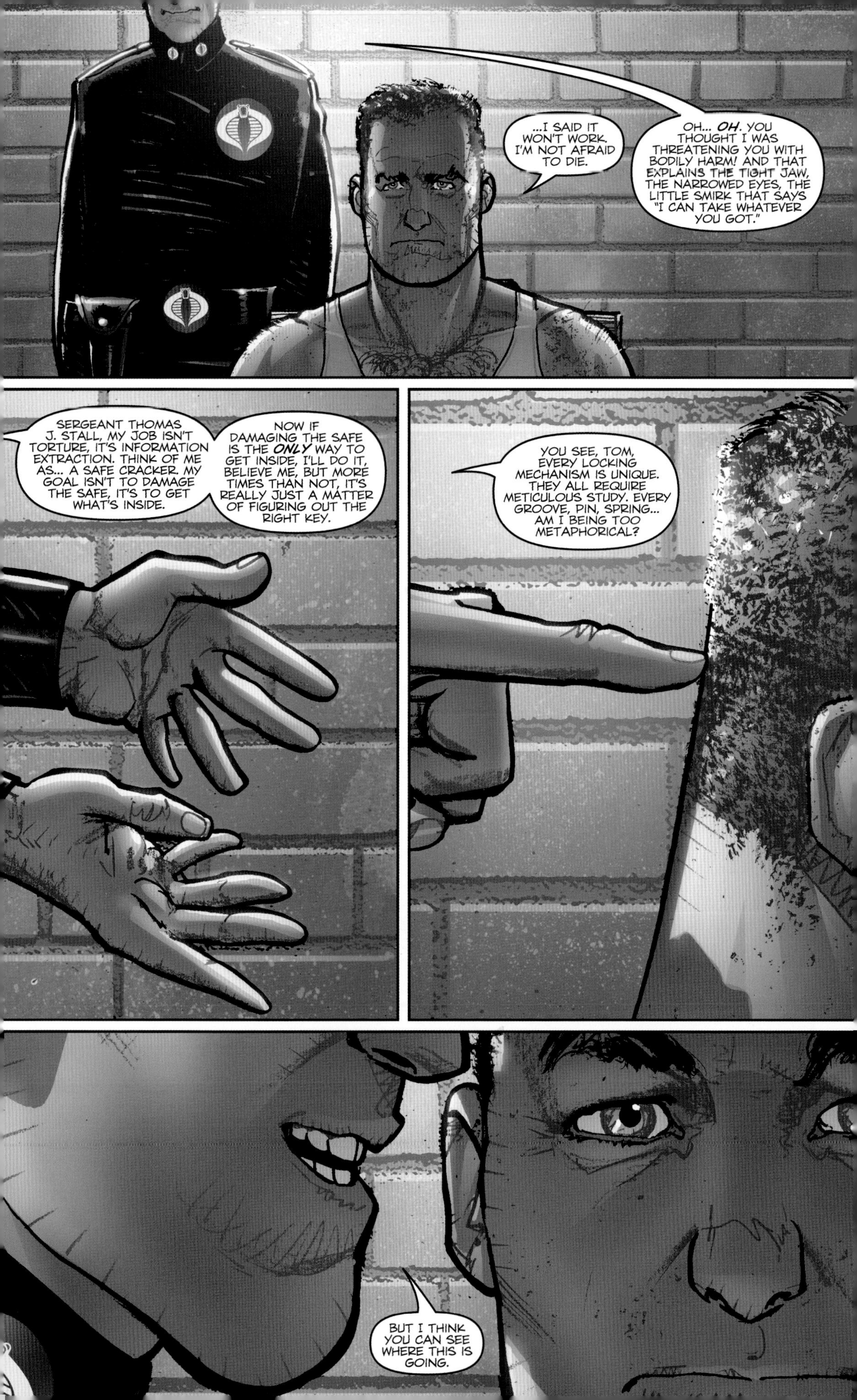
...I SAID IT WON'T WORK. I'M NOT AFRAID TO DIE.
OH... ***OH***. YOU THOUGHT I WAS THREATENING YOU WITH BODILY HARM! AND THAT EXPLAINS THE TIGHT JAW, THE NARROWED EYES, THE LITTLE SMIRK THAT SAYS "I CAN TAKE WHATEVER YOU GOT."
SERGEANT THOMAS J. STALL, MY JOB ISN'T TORTURE, IT'S INFORMATION EXTRACTION. THINK OF ME AS... A SAFE CRACKER. MY GOAL ISN'T TO DAMAGE THE SAFE, IT'S TO GET WHAT'S INSIDE.
NOW IF DAMAGING THE SAFE IS THE ***ONLY*** WAY TO GET INSIDE, I'LL DO IT, BELIEVE ME, BUT MORE TIMES THAN NOT, IT'S REALLY JUST A MATTER OF FIGURING OUT THE RIGHT KEY.
YOU SEE, TOM, EVERY LOCKING MECHANISM IS UNIQUE. THEY ALL REQUIRE METICULOUS STUDY. EVERY GROOVE, PIN, SPRING... AM I BEING TOO METAPHORICAL?
BUT I THINK YOU CAN SEE WHERE THIS IS GOING.

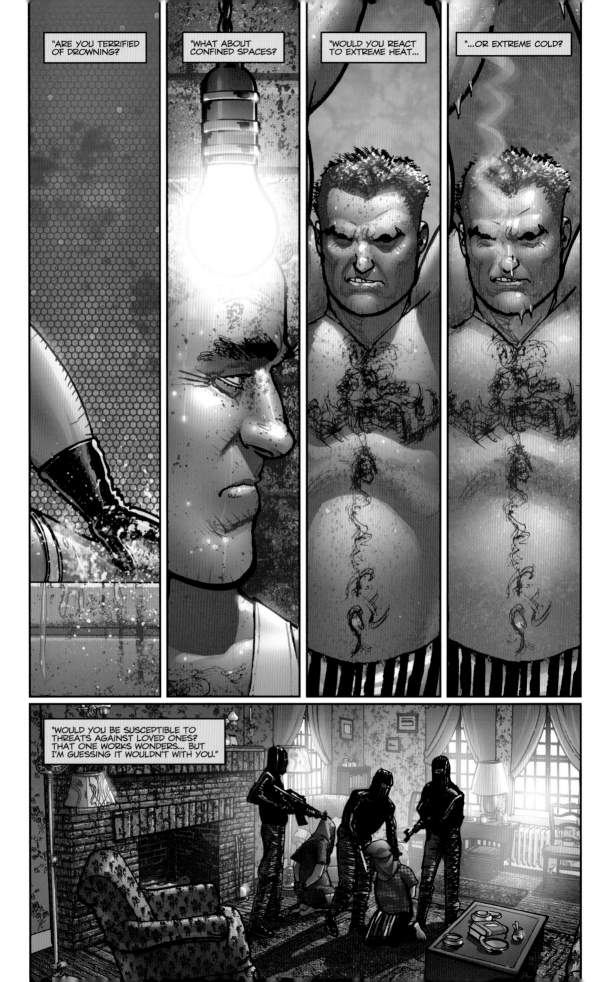

"ARE YOU TERRIFIED OF DROWNING?

"WHAT ABOUT CONFINED SPACES?

"WOULD YOU REACT TO EXTREME HEAT...

"...OR EXTREME COLD?

"WOULD YOU BE SUSCEPTIBLE TO THREATS AGAINST LOVED ONES? THAT ONE WORKS WONDERS... BUT I'M GUESSING IT WOULDN'T WITH YOU."

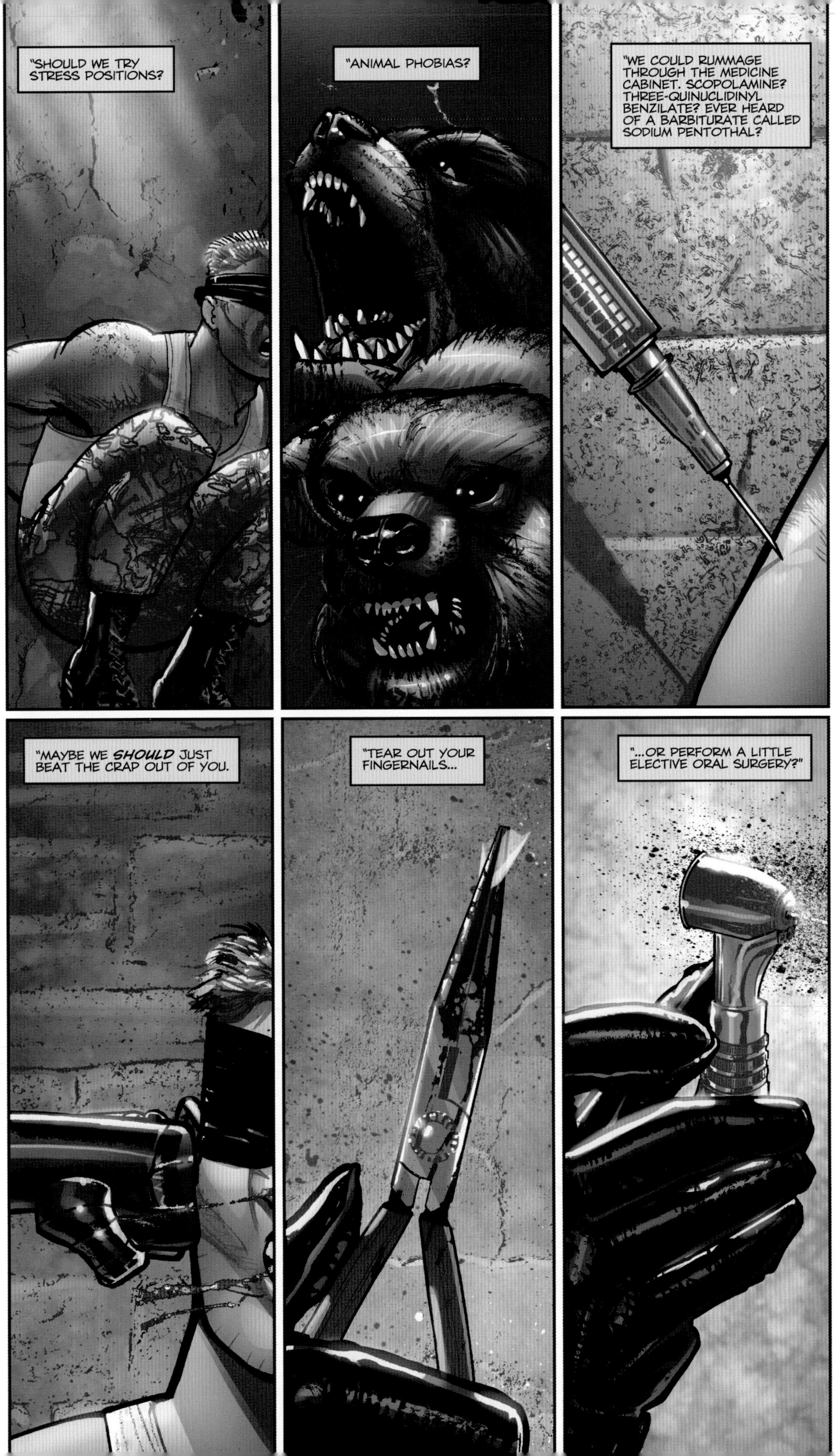
"SHOULD WE TRY STRESS POSITIONS?
"ANIMAL PHOBIAS?
"WE COULD RUMMAGE THROUGH THE MEDICINE CABINET. SCOPOLAMINE? THREE-QUINUCLIDINYL BENZILATE? EVER HEARD OF A BARBITURATE CALLED SODIUM PENTOTHAL?
"MAYBE WE *SHOULD* JUST BEAT THE CRAP OUT OF YOU.
"TEAR OUT YOUR FINGERNAILS...
"...OR PERFORM A LITTLE ELECTIVE ORAL SURGERY?"

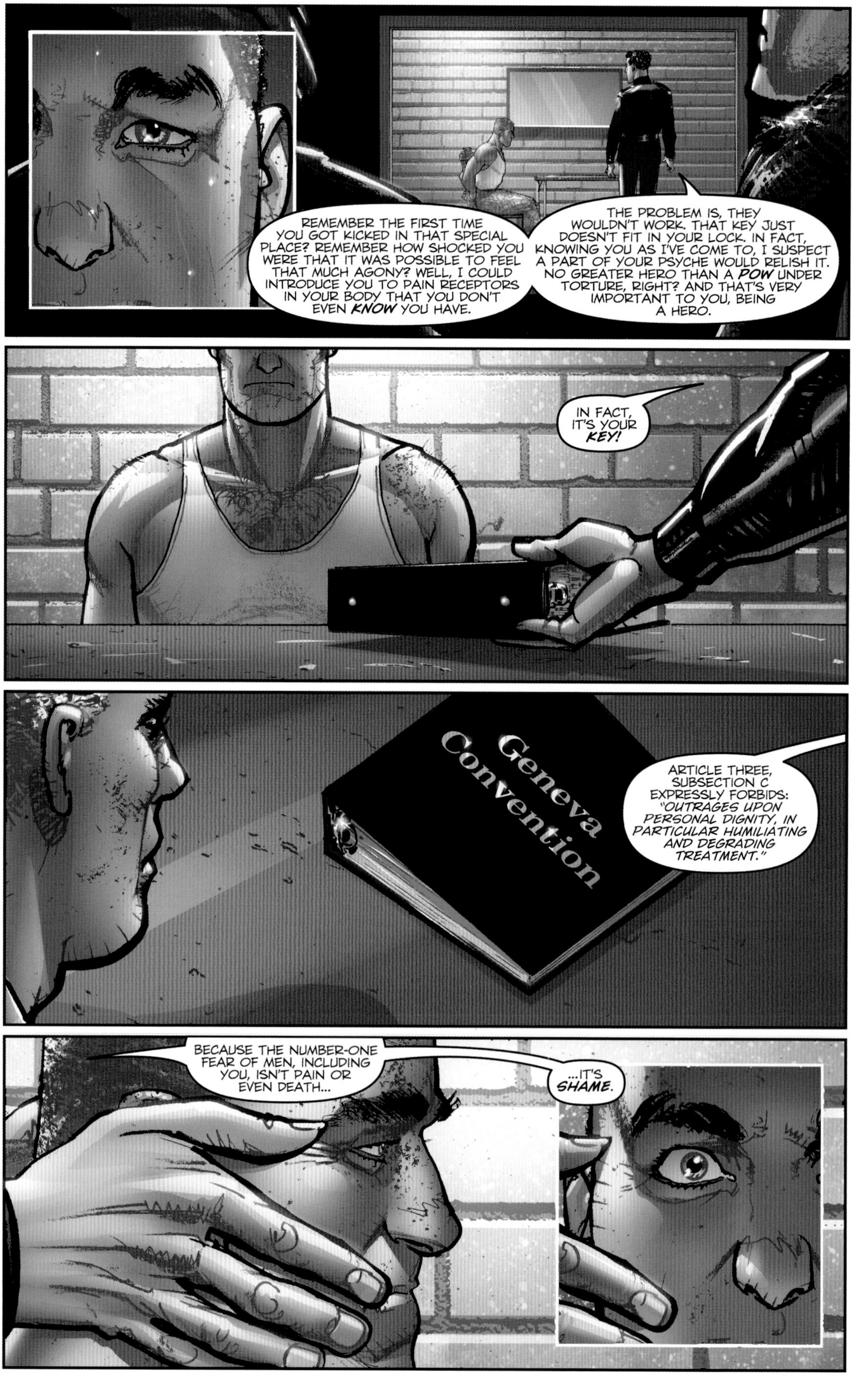
REMEMBER THE FIRST TIME YOU GOT KICKED IN THAT SPECIAL PLACE? REMEMBER HOW SHOCKED YOU WERE THAT IT WAS POSSIBLE TO FEEL THAT MUCH AGONY? WELL, I COULD INTRODUCE YOU TO PAIN RECEPTORS IN YOUR BODY THAT YOU DON'T EVEN *KNOW* YOU HAVE.
THE PROBLEM IS, THEY WOULDN'T WORK. THAT KEY JUST DOESN'T FIT IN YOUR LOCK. IN FACT, KNOWING YOU AS I'VE COME TO, I SUSPECT A PART OF YOUR PSYCHE WOULD RELISH IT. NO GREATER HERO THAN A *POW* UNDER TORTURE, RIGHT? AND THAT'S VERY IMPORTANT TO YOU, BEING A HERO.
IN FACT, IT'S YOUR *KEY!*
Geneva Convention
ARTICLE THREE, SUBSECTION C EXPRESSLY FORBIDS: *"OUTRAGES UPON PERSONAL DIGNITY, IN PARTICULAR HUMILIATING AND DEGRADING TREATMENT."*
BECAUSE THE NUMBER-ONE FEAR OF MEN, INCLUDING YOU, ISN'T PAIN OR EVEN DEATH...
...IT'S *SHAME*.

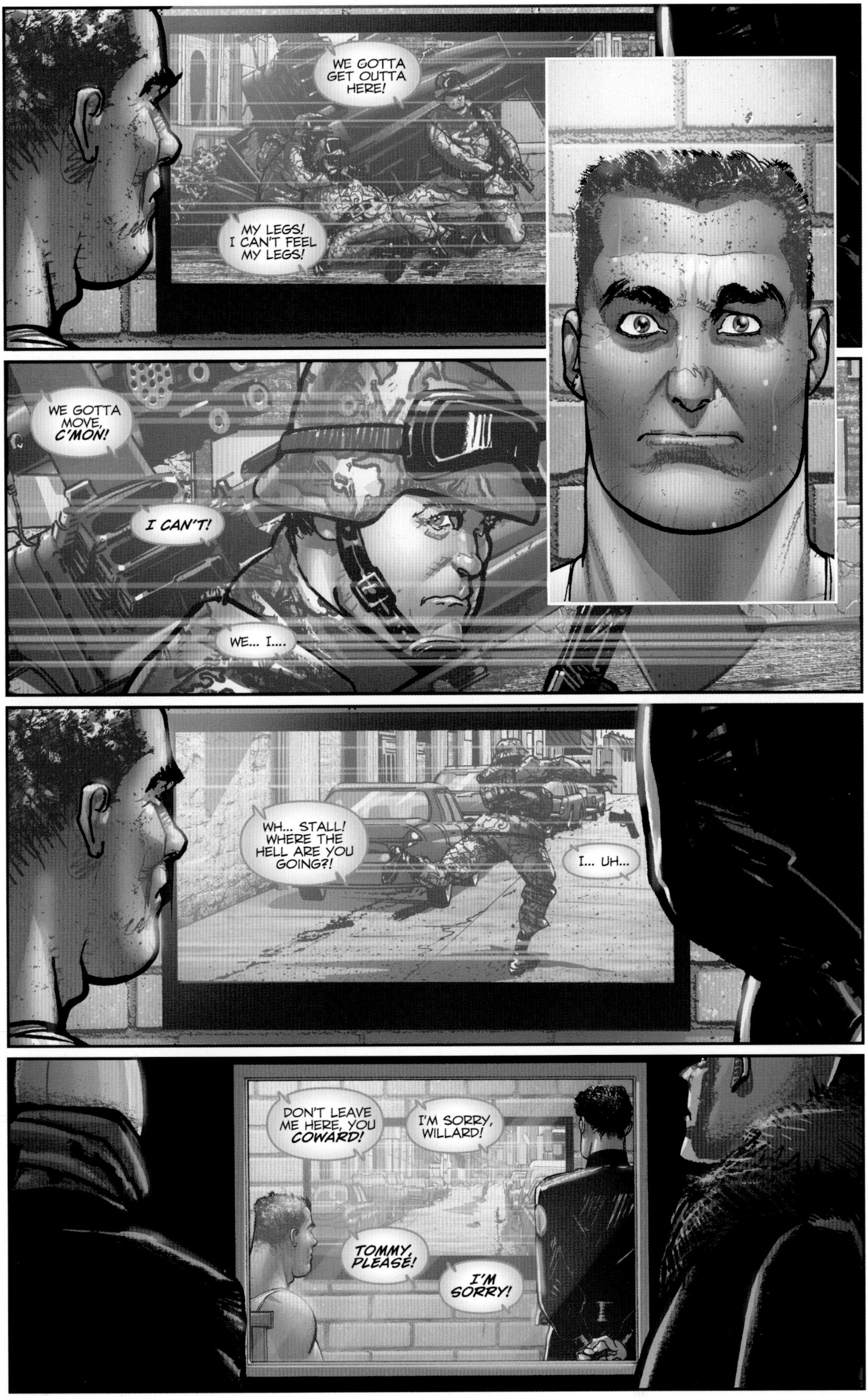

WE GOTTA GET OUTTA HERE!
MY LEGS! I CAN'T FEEL MY LEGS!
WE GOTTA MOVE, C'MON!
I CAN'T!
WE... I....
WH... STALL! WHERE THE HELL ARE YOU GOING?!
I... UH...
DON'T LEAVE ME HERE, YOU COWARD!
I'M SORRY, WILLARD!
TOMMY, PLEASE!
I'M SORRY!

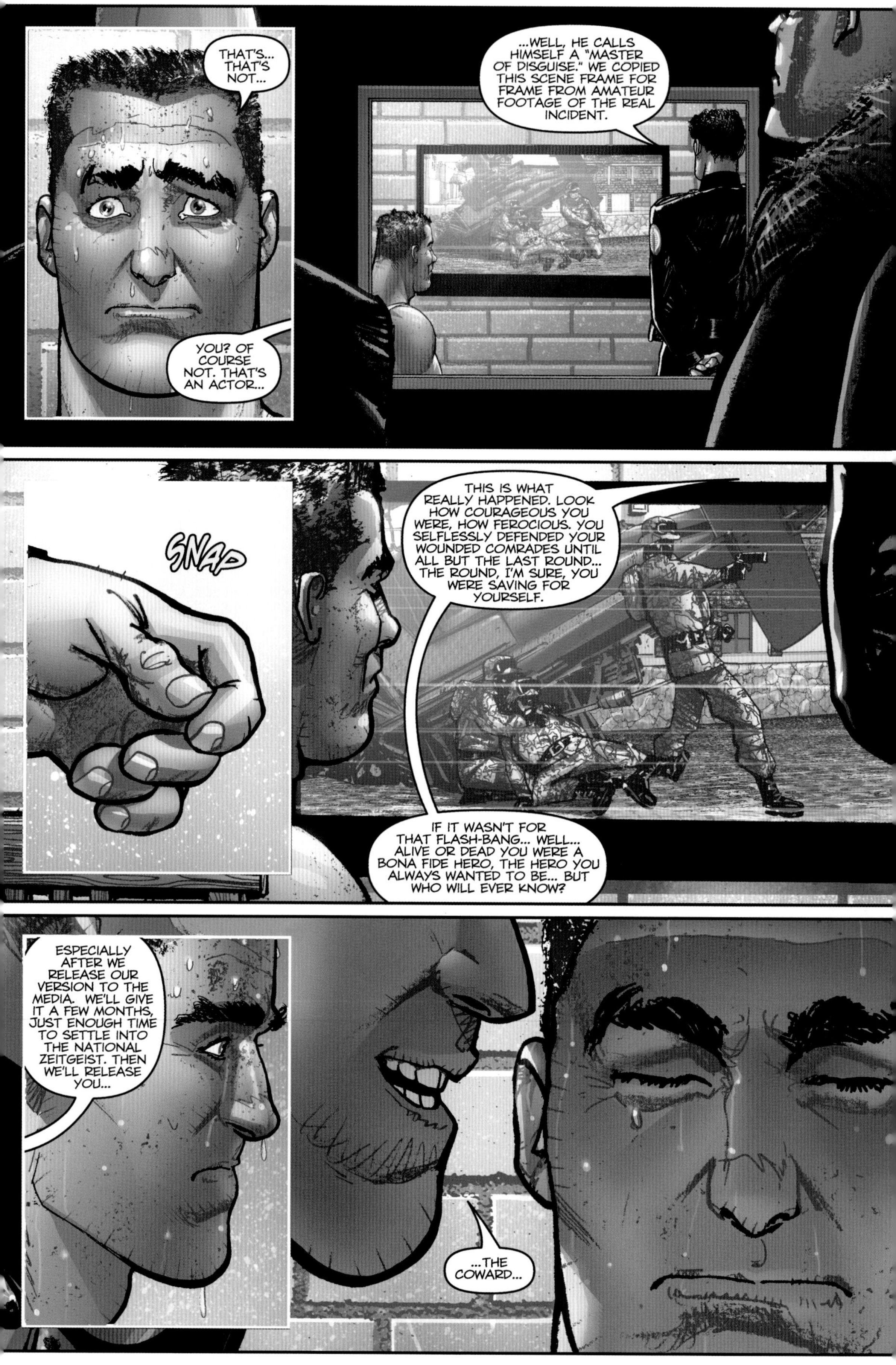
THAT'S... THAT'S NOT...
...WELL, HE CALLS HIMSELF A "MASTER OF DISGUISE." WE COPIED THIS SCENE FRAME FOR FRAME FROM AMATEUR FOOTAGE OF THE REAL INCIDENT.
YOU? OF COURSE NOT. THAT'S AN ACTOR...
SNAP
THIS IS WHAT REALLY HAPPENED. LOOK HOW COURAGEOUS YOU WERE, HOW FEROCIOUS. YOU SELFLESSLY DEFENDED YOUR WOUNDED COMRADES UNTIL ALL BUT THE LAST ROUND... THE ROUND, I'M SURE, YOU WERE SAVING FOR YOURSELF.
IF IT WASN'T FOR THAT FLASH-BANG... WELL... ALIVE OR DEAD YOU WERE A BONA FIDE HERO, THE HERO YOU ALWAYS WANTED TO BE... BUT WHO WILL EVER KNOW?
ESPECIALLY AFTER WE RELEASE OUR VERSION TO THE MEDIA. WE'LL GIVE IT A FEW MONTHS, JUST ENOUGH TIME TO SETTLE INTO THE NATIONAL ZEITGEIST. THEN WE'LL RELEASE YOU...
...THE COWARD...

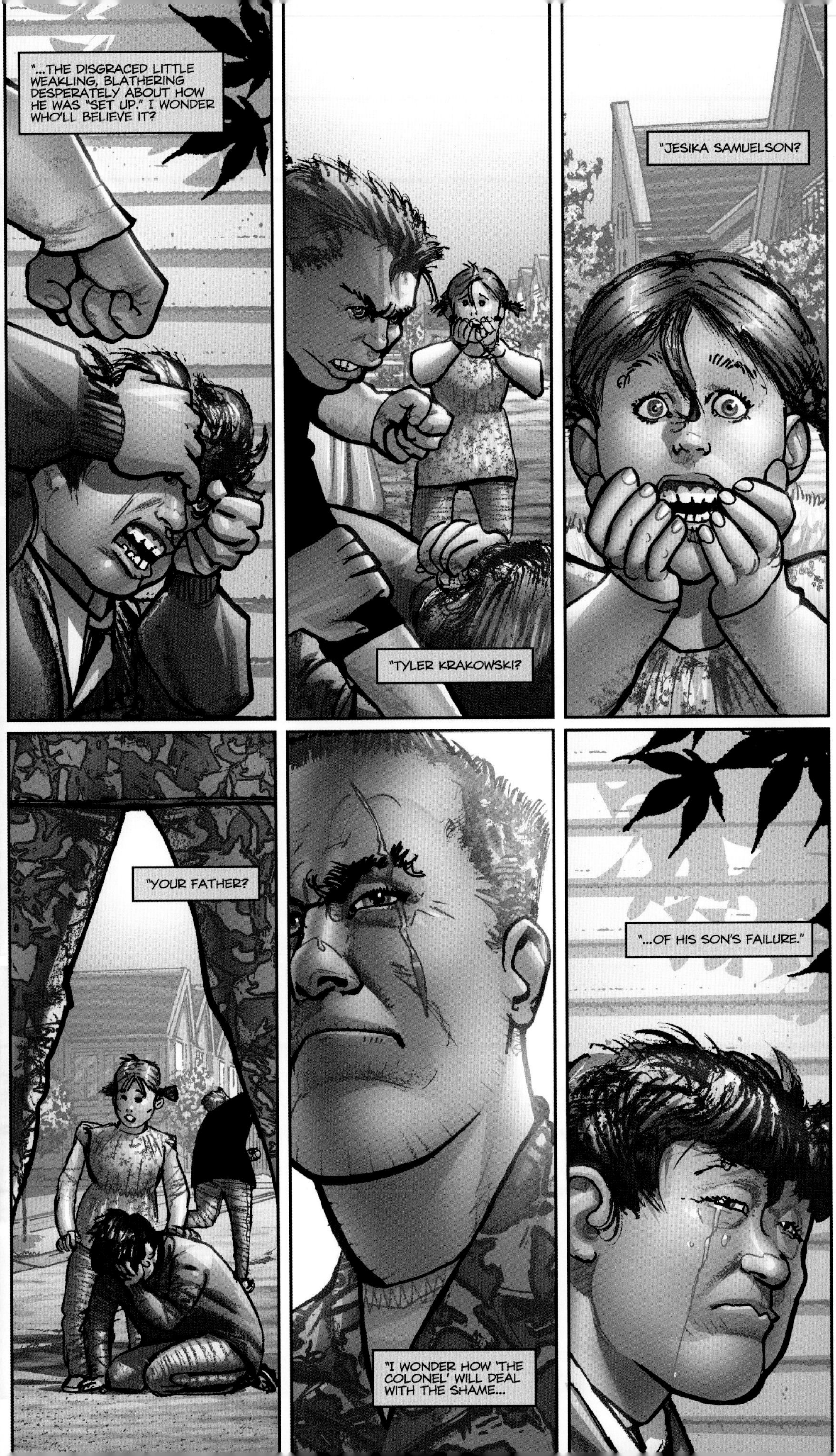
"...THE DISGRACED LITTLE WEAKLING, BLATHERING DESPERATELY ABOUT HOW HE WAS "SET UP." I WONDER WHO'LL BELIEVE IT?
"TYLER KRAKOWSKI?
"JESIKA SAMUELSON?
"YOUR FATHER?
"I WONDER HOW 'THE COLONEL' WILL DEAL WITH THE SHAME...
"...OF HIS SON'S FAILURE."

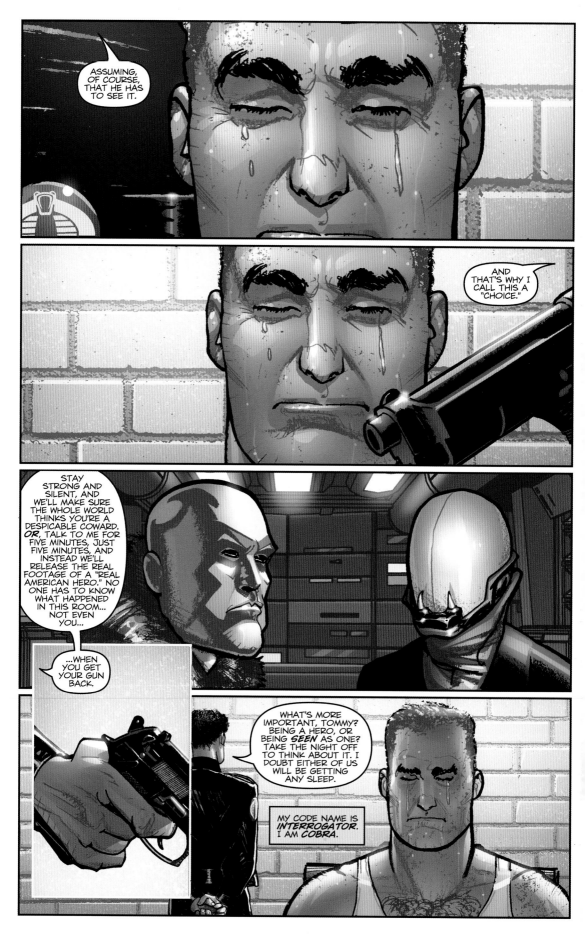

ASSUMING, OF COURSE, THAT HE HAS TO SEE IT.

AND THAT'S WHY I CALL THIS A "CHOICE."

STAY STRONG AND SILENT, AND WE'LL MAKE SURE THE WHOLE WORLD THINKS YOU'RE A DESPICABLE COWARD. *OR*, TALK TO ME FOR FIVE MINUTES, JUST FIVE MINUTES, AND INSTEAD WE'LL RELEASE THE REAL FOOTAGE OF A "REAL AMERICAN HERO." NO ONE HAS TO KNOW WHAT HAPPENED IN THIS ROOM... NOT EVEN YOU...

...WHEN YOU GET YOUR GUN BACK.

WHAT'S MORE IMPORTANT, TOMMY? BEING A HERO, OR BEING *SEEN* AS ONE? TAKE THE NIGHT OFF TO THINK ABOUT IT. I DOUBT EITHER OF US WILL BE GETTING ANY SLEEP.

MY CODE NAME IS *INTERROGATOR*. I AM *COBRA*.

DR. MINDBENDER

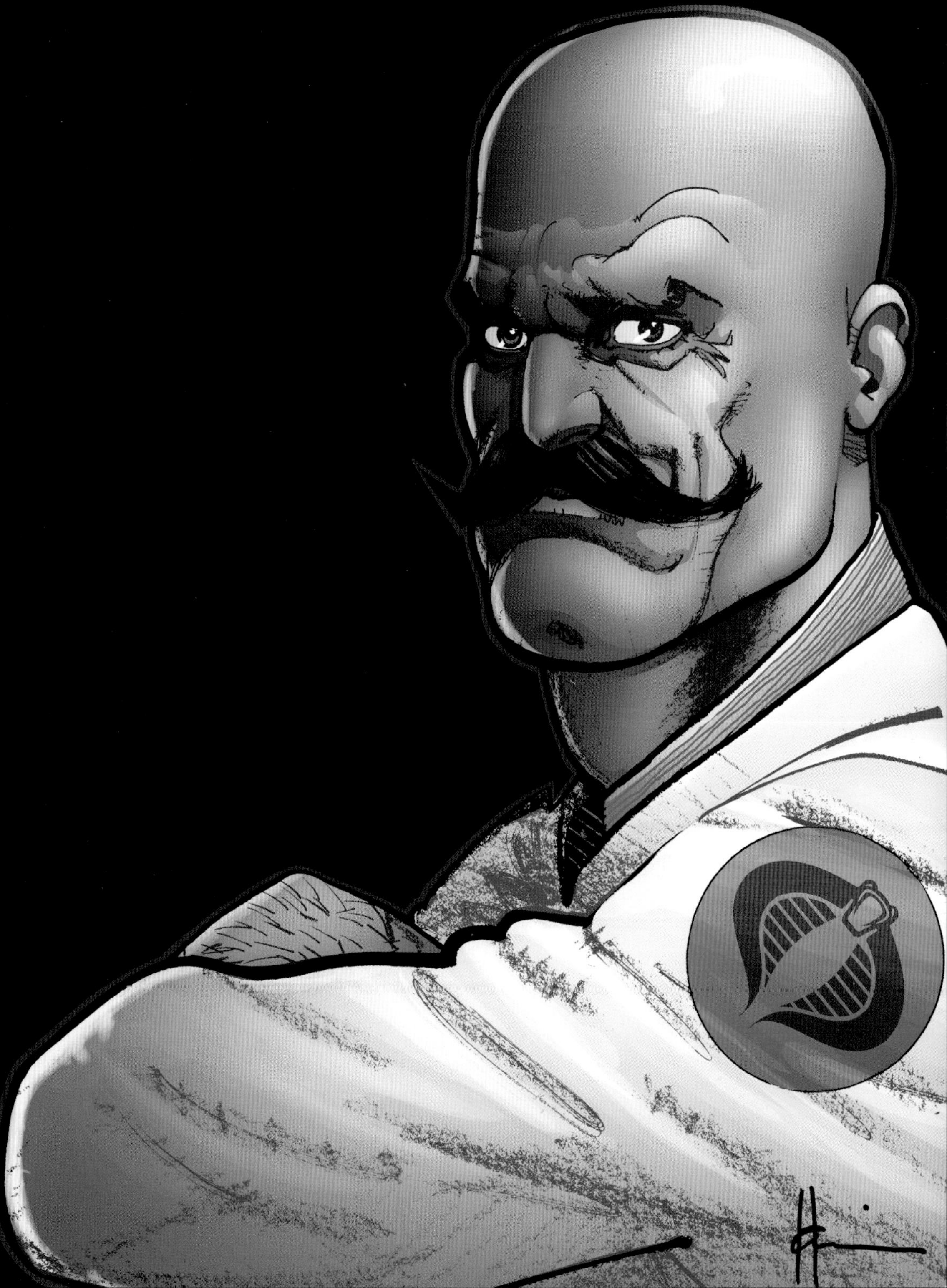

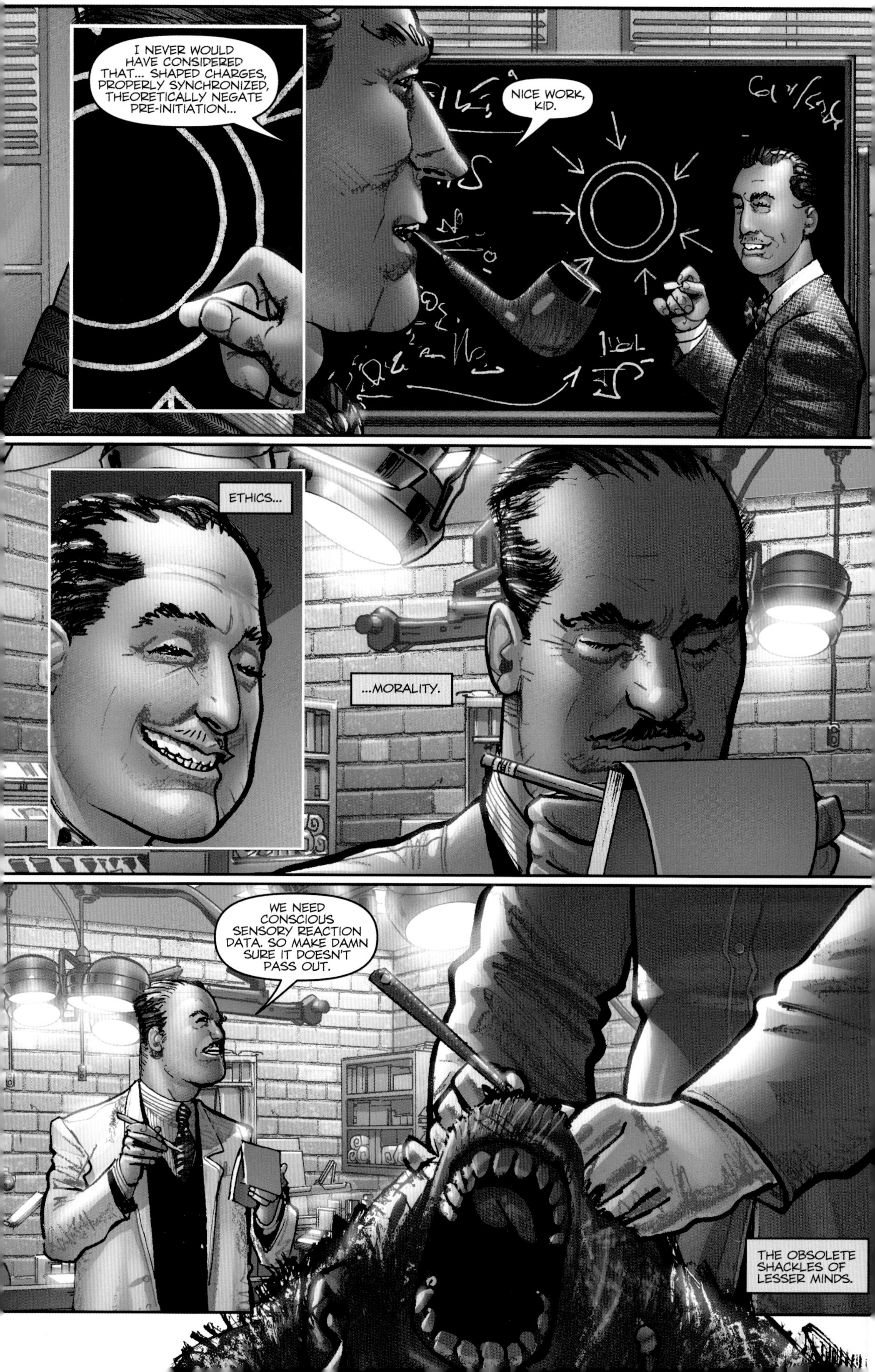
I NEVER WOULD HAVE CONSIDERED THAT... SHAPED CHARGES, PROPERLY SYNCHRONIZED, THEORETICALLY NEGATE PRE-INITIATION...
NICE WORK, KID.
ETHICS...
...MORALITY.
WE NEED CONSCIOUS SENSORY REACTION DATA. SO MAKE DAMN SURE IT DOESN'T PASS OUT.
THE OBSOLETE SHACKLES OF LESSER MINDS.

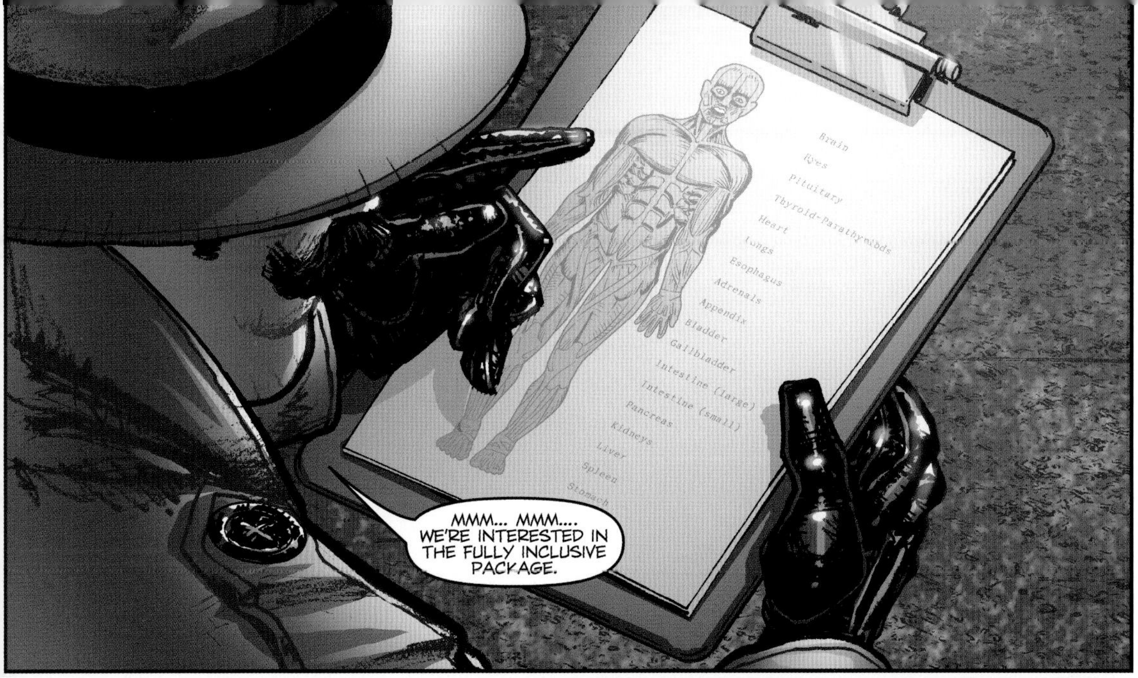
Brain
Eyes
Pituitary
Thyroid-Parathyroids
Heart
Lungs
Esophagus
Adrenals
Appendix
Bladder
Gallbladder
Intestine (large)
Intestine (small)
Pancreas
Kidneys
Liver
Spleen
Stomach
MMM... MMM.... WE'RE INTERESTED IN THE FULLY INCLUSIVE PACKAGE.

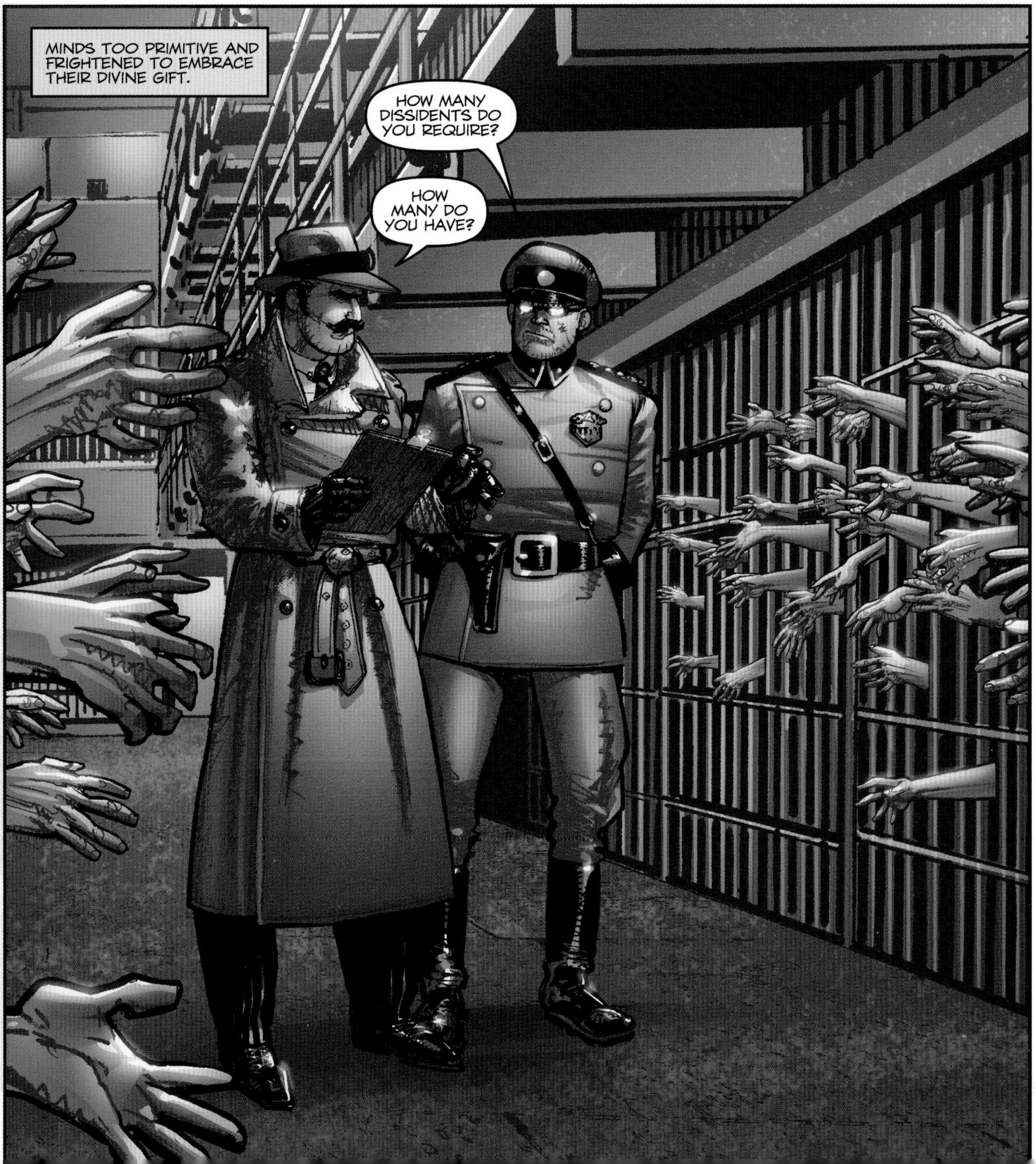
MINDS TOO PRIMITIVE AND FRIGHTENED TO EMBRACE THEIR DIVINE GIFT.
HOW MANY DISSIDENTS DO YOU REQUIRE?
HOW MANY DO YOU HAVE?

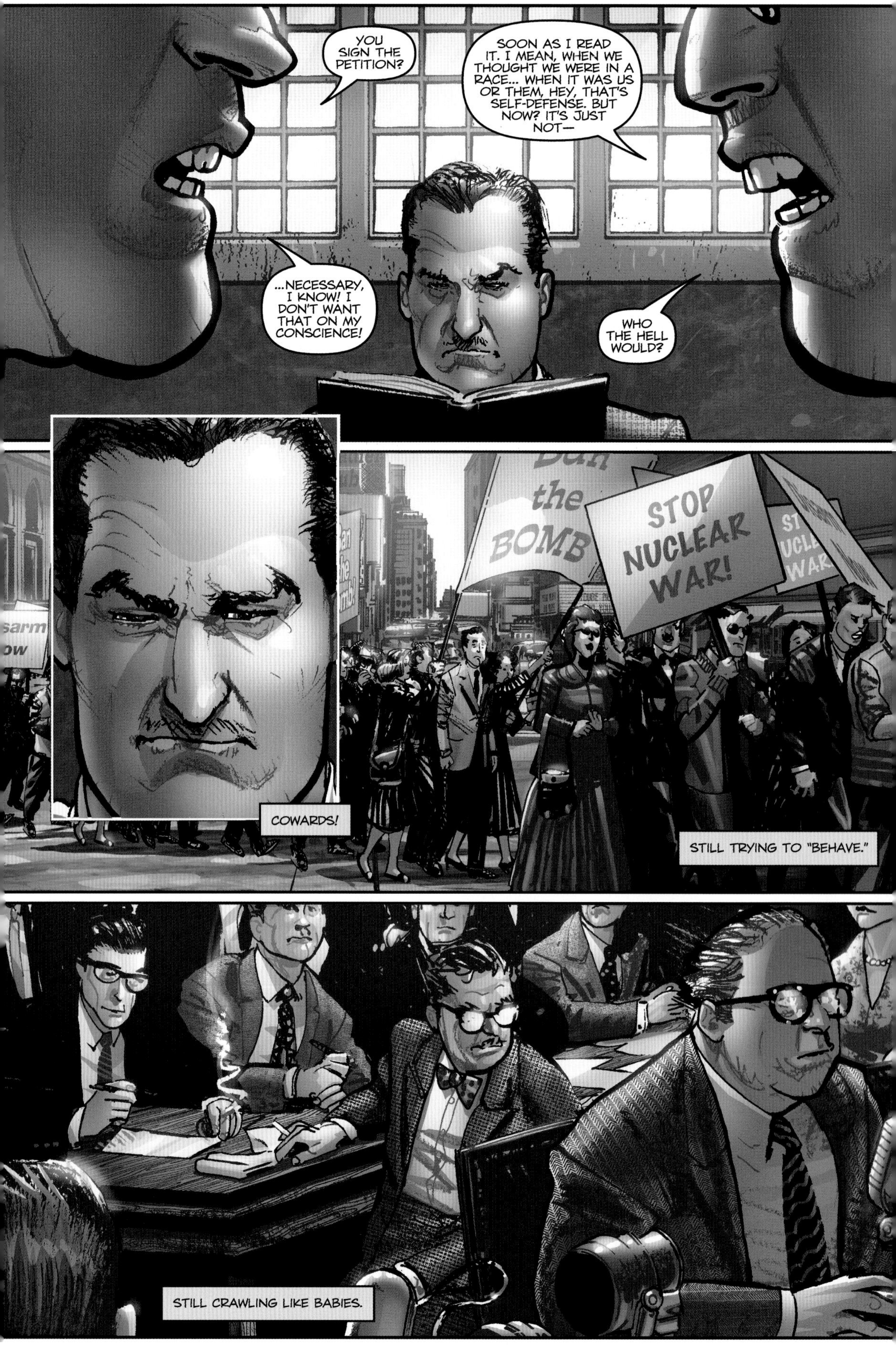
YOU SIGN THE PETITION?
SOON AS I READ IT. I MEAN, WHEN WE THOUGHT WE WERE IN A RACE... WHEN IT WAS US OR THEM, HEY, THAT'S SELF-DEFENSE. BUT NOW? IT'S JUST NOT—
...NECESSARY, I KNOW! I DON'T WANT THAT ON MY CONSCIENCE!
WHO THE HELL WOULD?
Ban the BOMB
STOP NUCLEAR WAR!
COWARDS!
STILL TRYING TO "BEHAVE."
STILL CRAWLING LIKE BABIES.

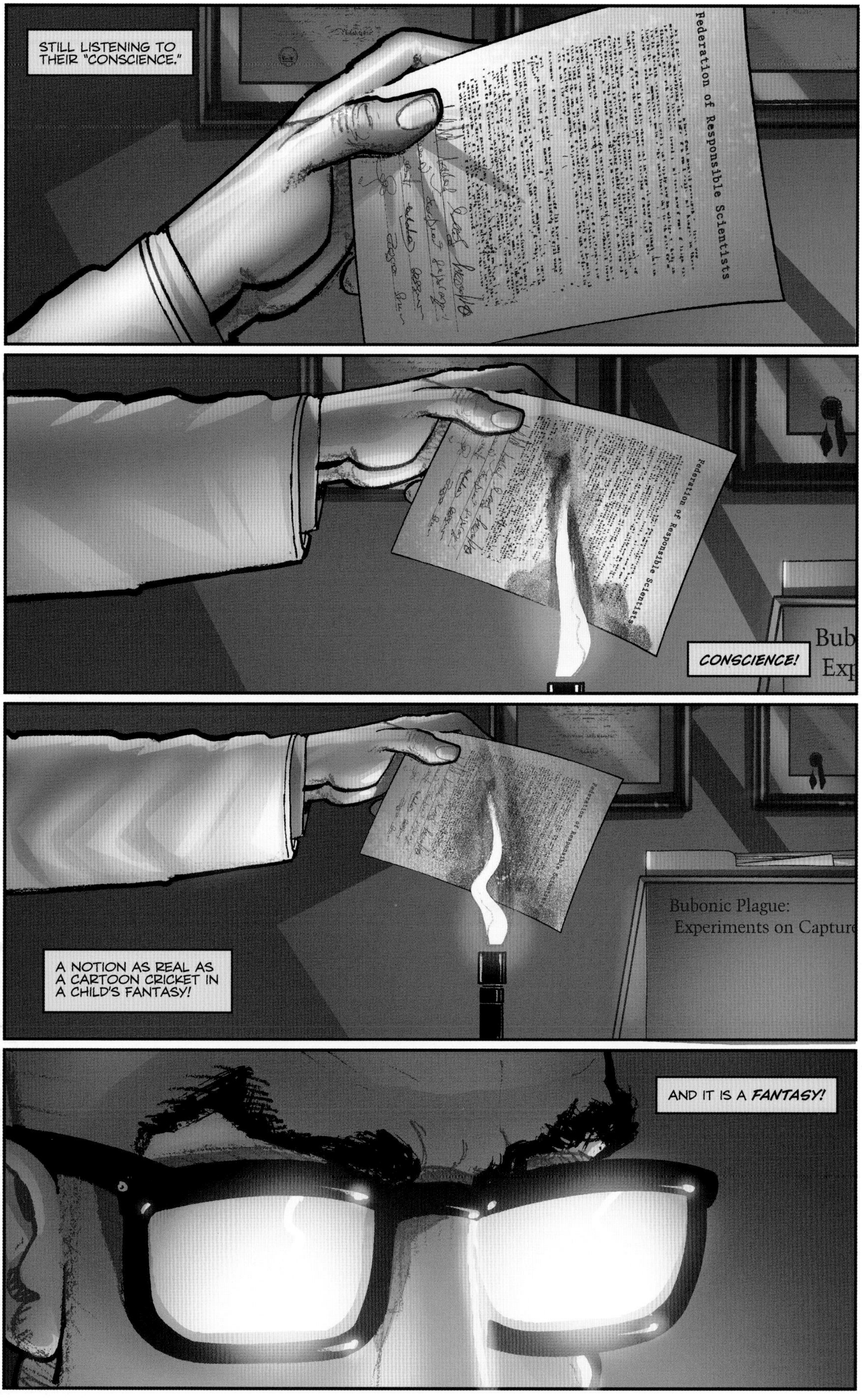
STILL LISTENING TO THEIR "CONSCIENCE."
Federation of Responsible Scientists
Federation of Responsible Scientists
CONSCIENCE!
Bubonic Plague:
Experiments on Captur
A NOTION AS REAL AS A CARTOON CRICKET IN A CHILD'S FANTASY!
AND IT IS A *FANTASY!*

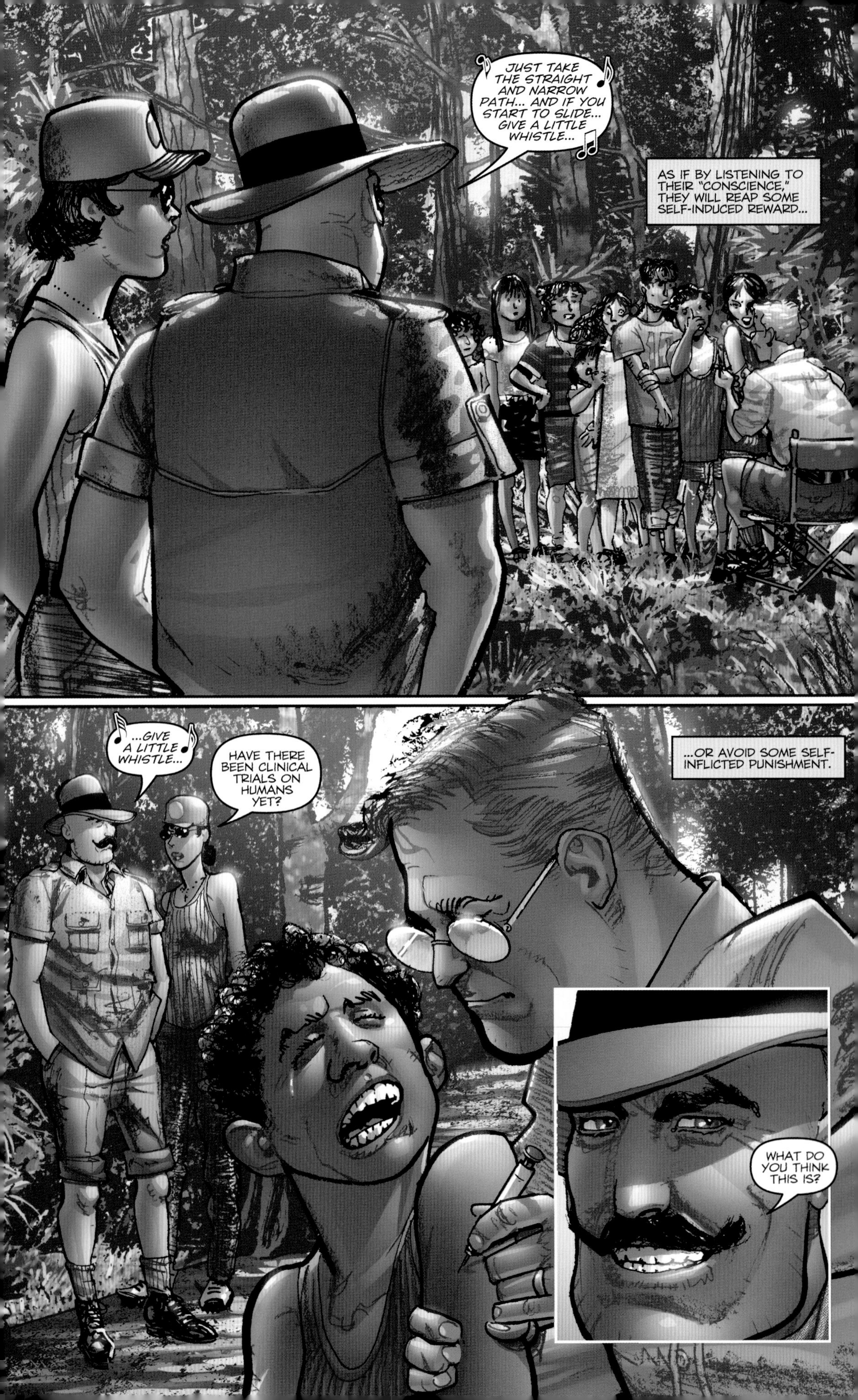
JUST TAKE THE STRAIGHT AND NARROW PATH... AND IF YOU START TO SLIDE... GIVE A LITTLE WHISTLE...
AS IF BY LISTENING TO THEIR "CONSCIENCE," THEY WILL REAP SOME SELF-INDUCED REWARD...
...GIVE A LITTLE WHISTLE...
HAVE THERE BEEN CLINICAL TRIALS ON HUMANS YET?
...OR AVOID SOME SELF-INFLICTED PUNISHMENT.
WHAT DO YOU THINK THIS IS?

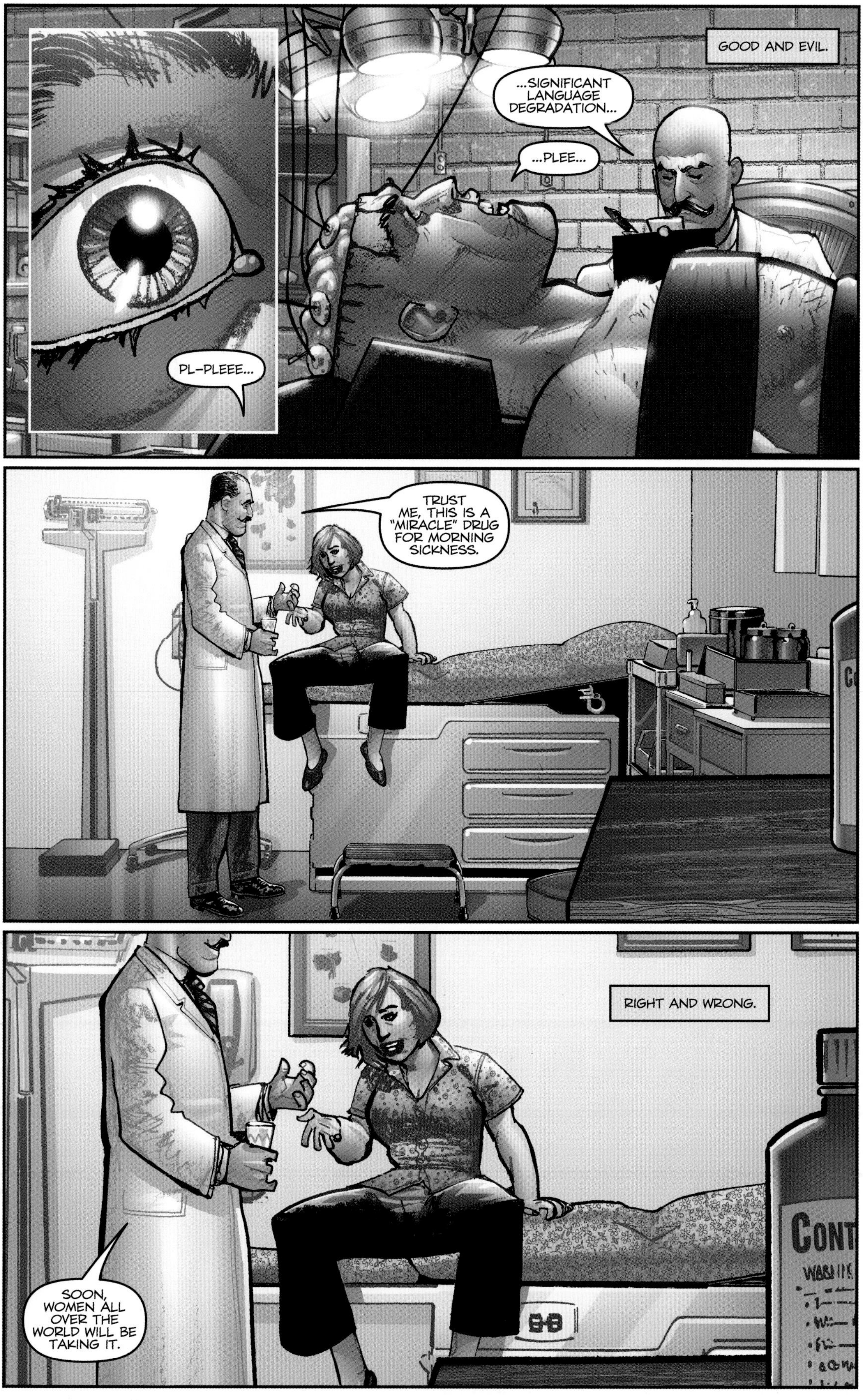
GOOD AND EVIL.
...SIGNIFICANT LANGUAGE DEGRADATION...
...PLEE...
PL-PLEEE...
TRUST ME, THIS IS A "MIRACLE" DRUG FOR MORNING SICKNESS.
RIGHT AND WRONG.
SOON, WOMEN ALL OVER THE WORLD WILL BE TAKING IT.

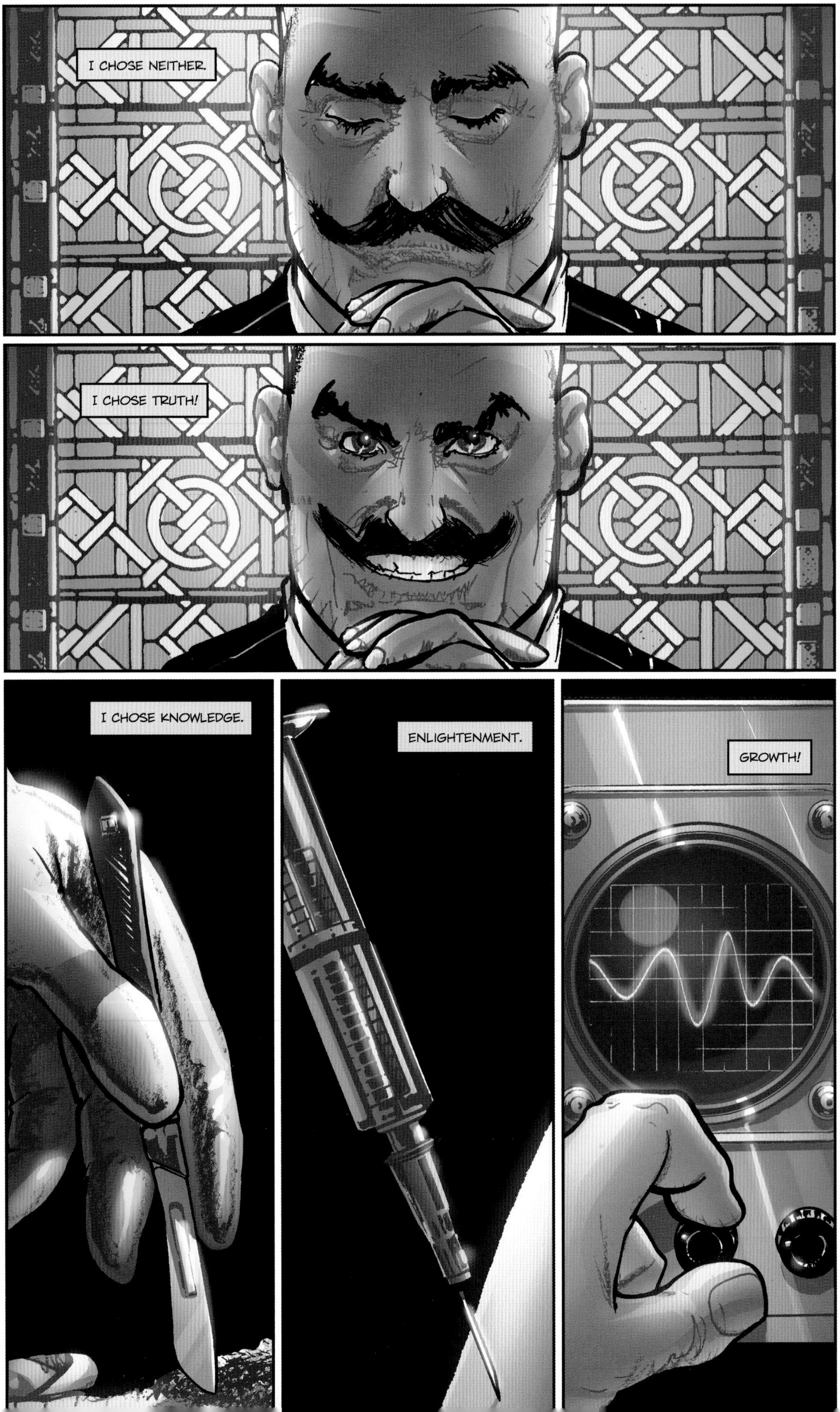
I CHOSE NEITHER.
I CHOSE TRUTH!
I CHOSE KNOWLEDGE.
ENLIGHTENMENT.
GROWTH!

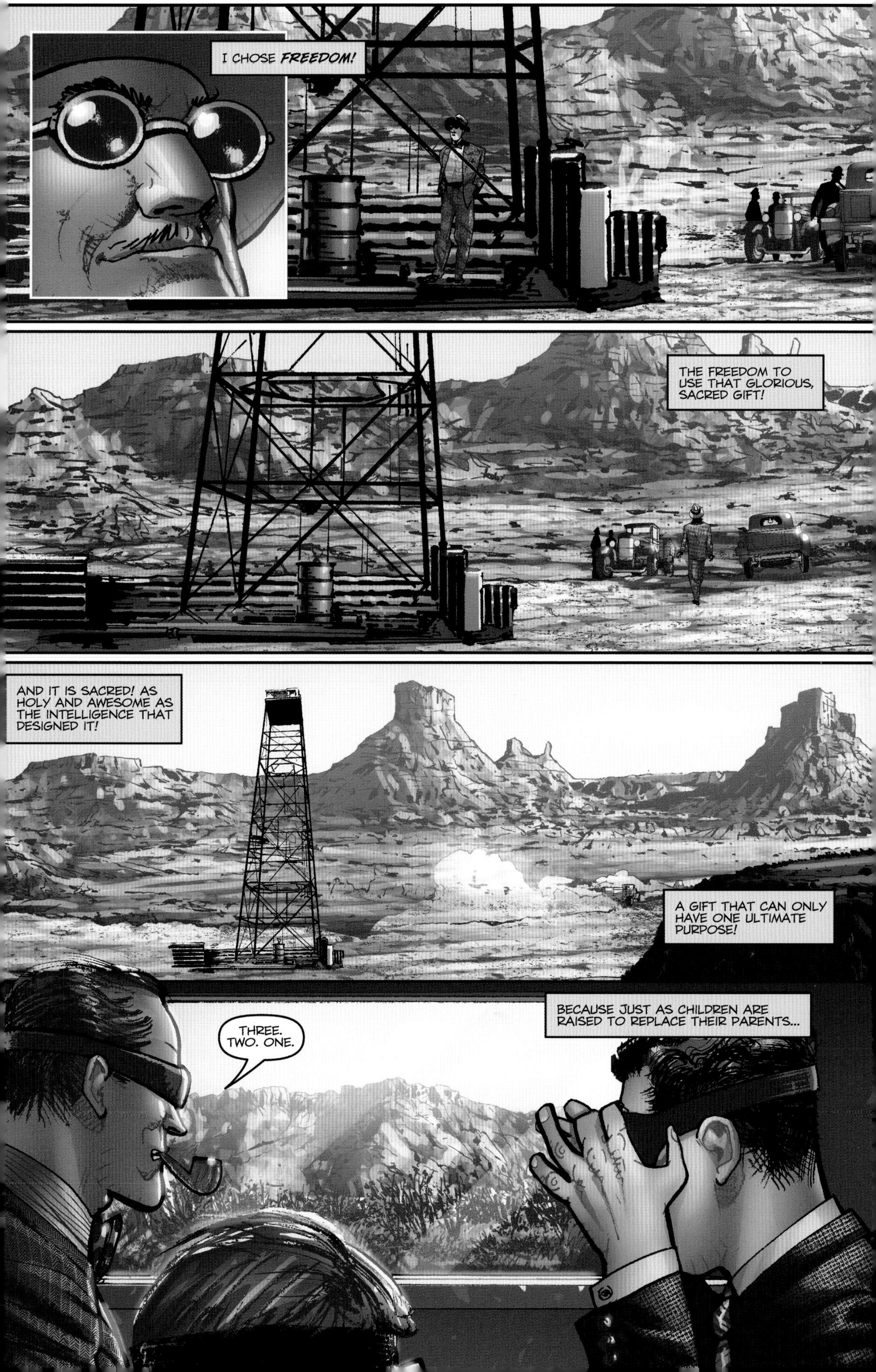
I CHOSE FREEDOM!
THE FREEDOM TO USE THAT GLORIOUS, SACRED GIFT!
AND IT IS SACRED! AS HOLY AND AWESOME AS THE INTELLIGENCE THAT DESIGNED IT!
A GIFT THAT CAN ONLY HAVE ONE ULTIMATE PURPOSE!
BECAUSE JUST AS CHILDREN ARE RAISED TO REPLACE THEIR PARENTS...
THREE. TWO. ONE.

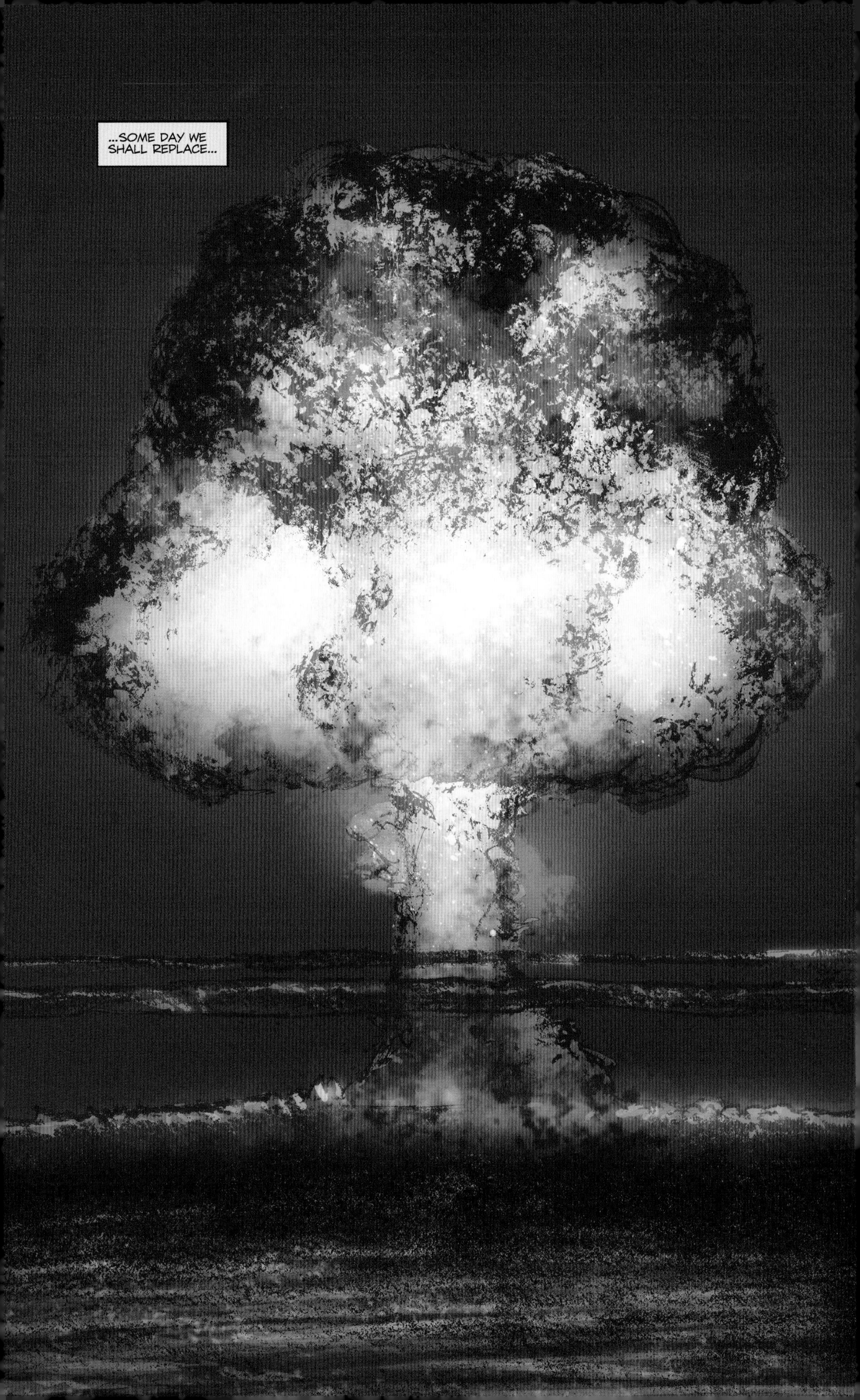
...SOME DAY WE SHALL REPLACE...

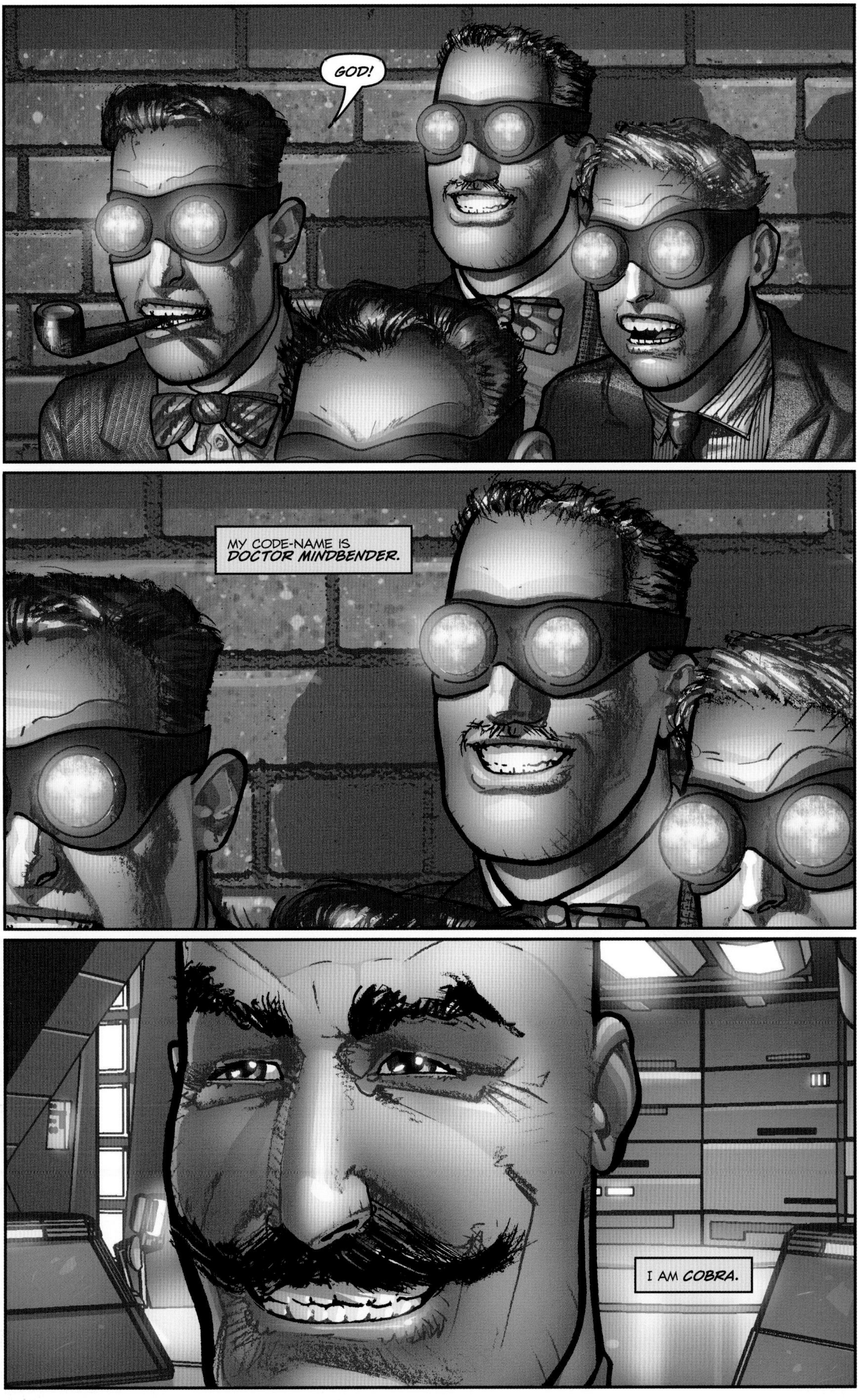
GOD!
MY CODE-NAME IS DOCTOR MINDBENDER.
I AM COBRA.

DOC

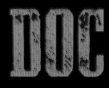

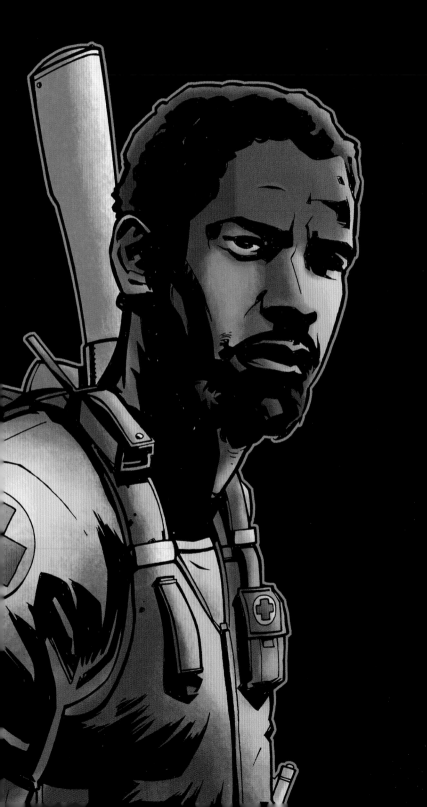

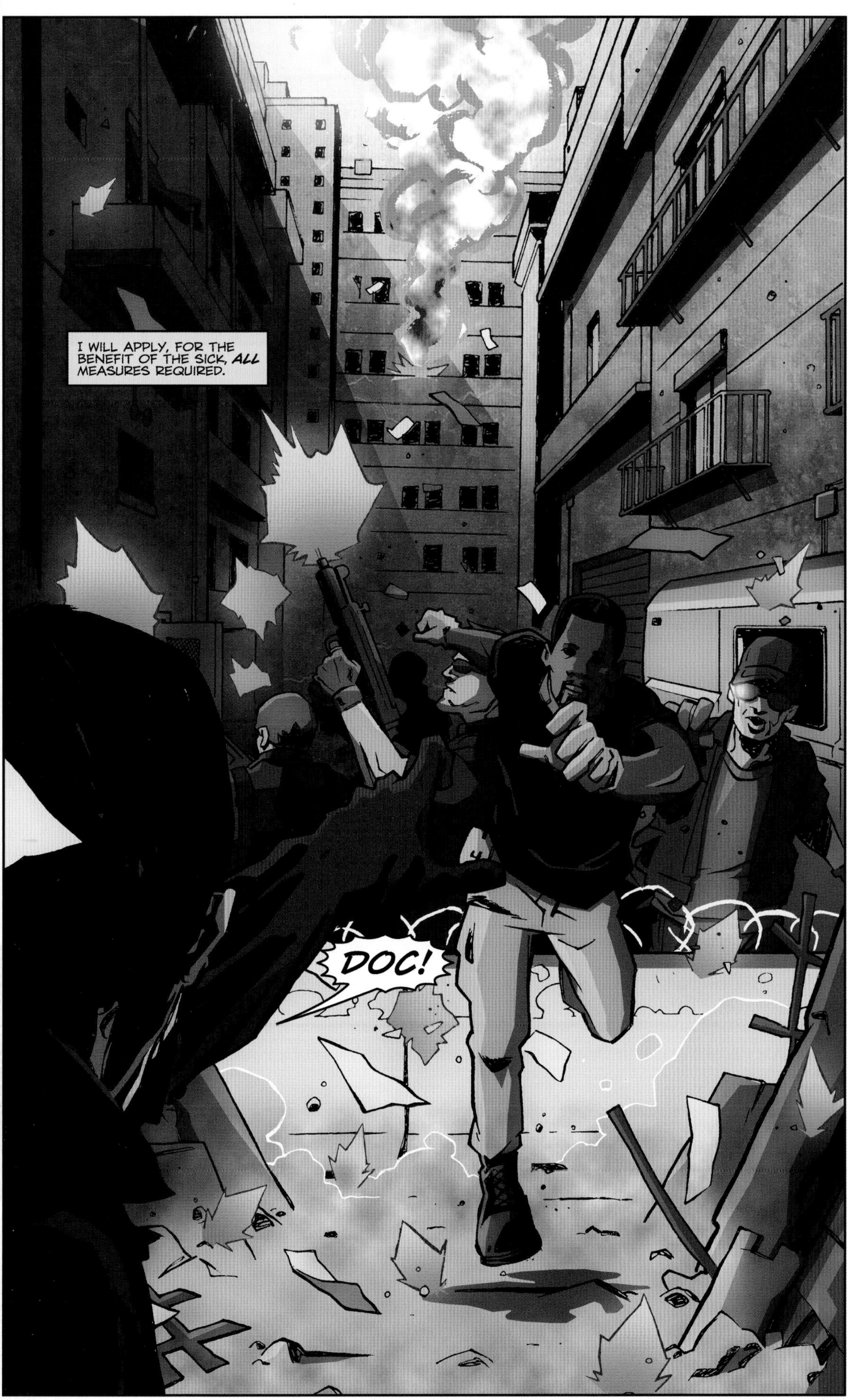
I WILL APPLY, FOR THE BENEFIT OF THE SICK, ALL MEASURES REQUIRED.
DOC!

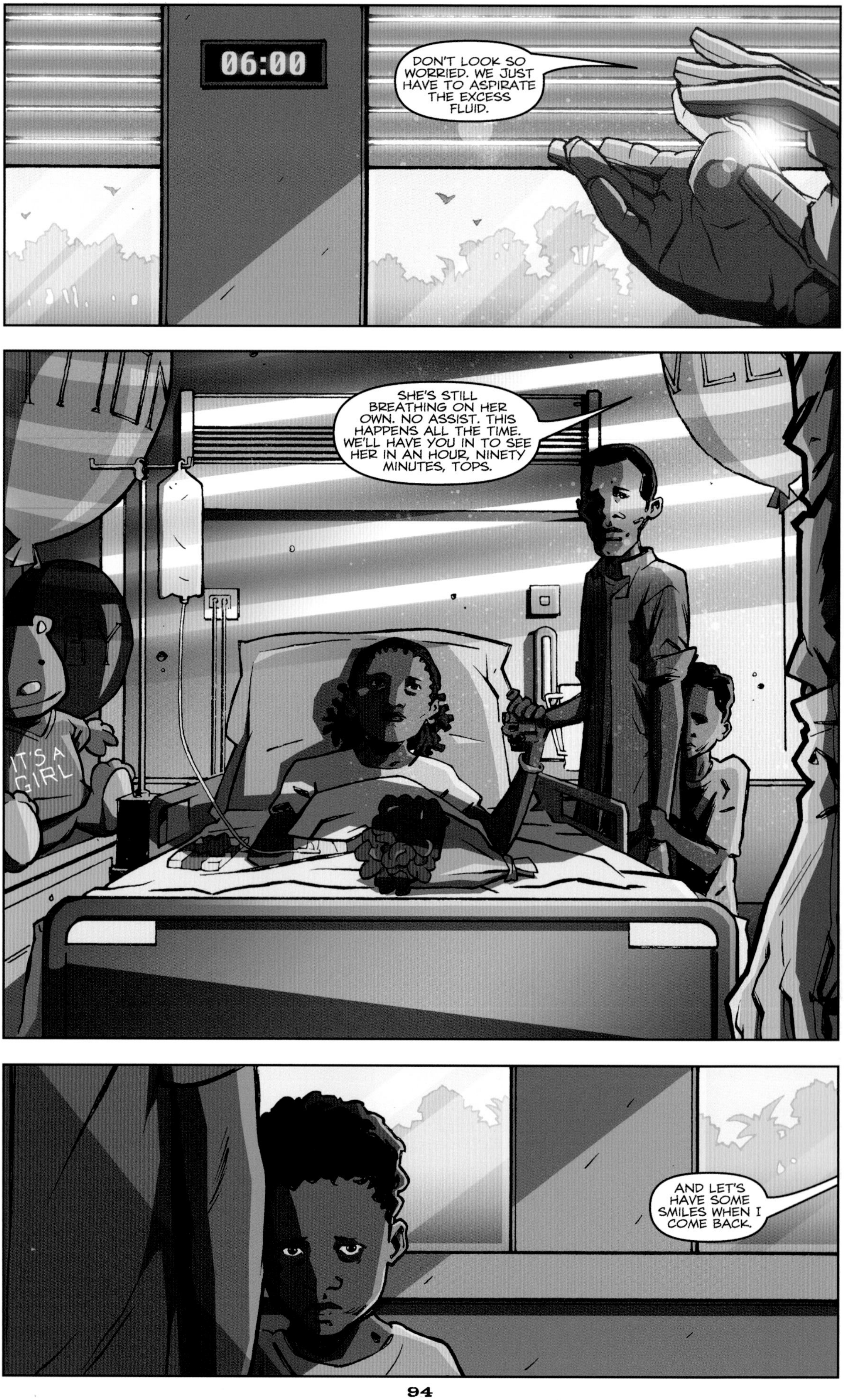
06:00
DON'T LOOK SO WORRIED. WE JUST HAVE TO ASPIRATE THE EXCESS FLUID.
SHE'S STILL BREATHING ON HER OWN. NO ASSIST. THIS HAPPENS ALL THE TIME. WE'LL HAVE YOU IN TO SEE HER IN AN HOUR, NINETY MINUTES, TOPS.
IT'S A GIRL
AND LET'S HAVE SOME SMILES WHEN I COME BACK.

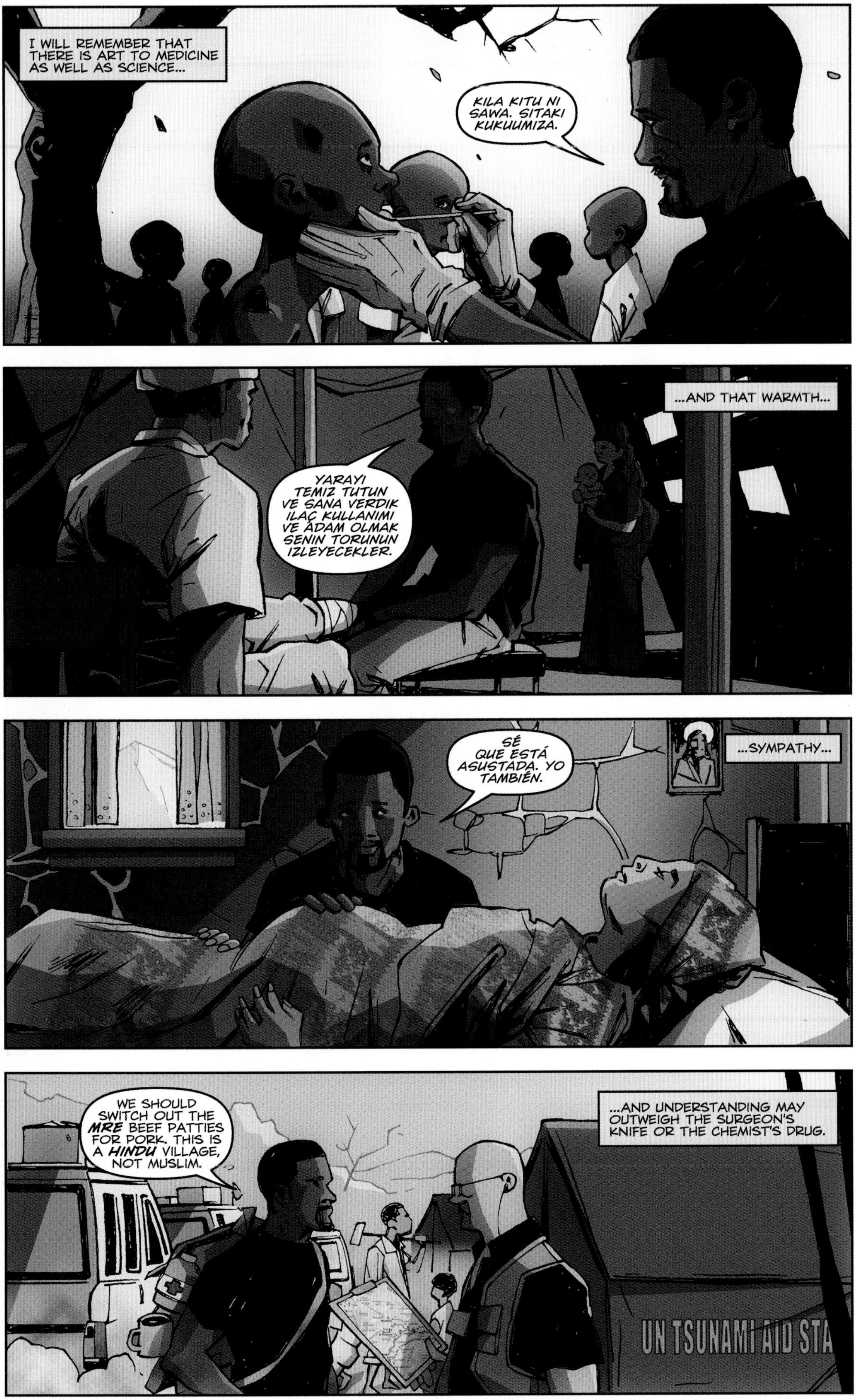
I WILL REMEMBER THAT THERE IS ART TO MEDICINE AS WELL AS SCIENCE...
KILA KITU NI SAWA. SITAKI KUKUUMIZA.
...AND THAT WARMTH...
YARAYI TEMIZ TUTUN VE SANA VERDIK ILAÇ KULLANIMI VE ÄDAM OLMAK SENIN TORUNUN IZLEYECEKLER.
...SYMPATHY...
SÉ QUE ESTÁ ASUSTADA. YO TAMBIÉN.
WE SHOULD SWITCH OUT THE MRE BEEF PATTIES FOR PORK. THIS IS A HINDU VILLAGE, NOT MUSLIM.
...AND UNDERSTANDING MAY OUTWEIGH THE SURGEON'S KNIFE OR THE CHEMIST'S DRUG.
UN TSUNAMI AID STA

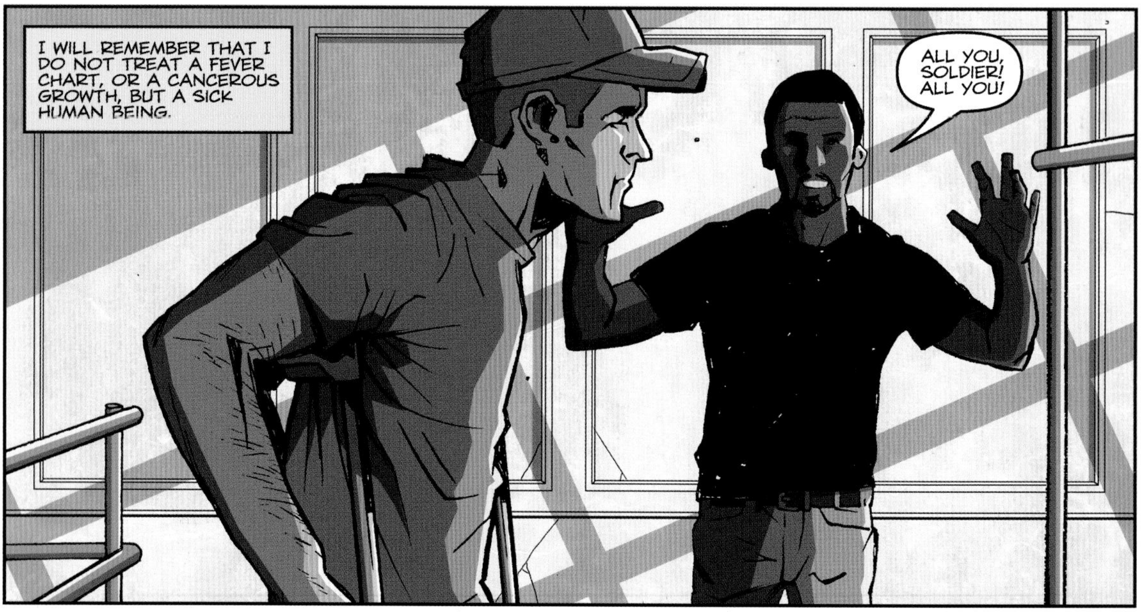
I WILL REMEMBER THAT I DO NOT TREAT A FEVER CHART, OR A CANCEROUS GROWTH, BUT A SICK HUMAN BEING.
ALL YOU, SOLDIER! ALL YOU!

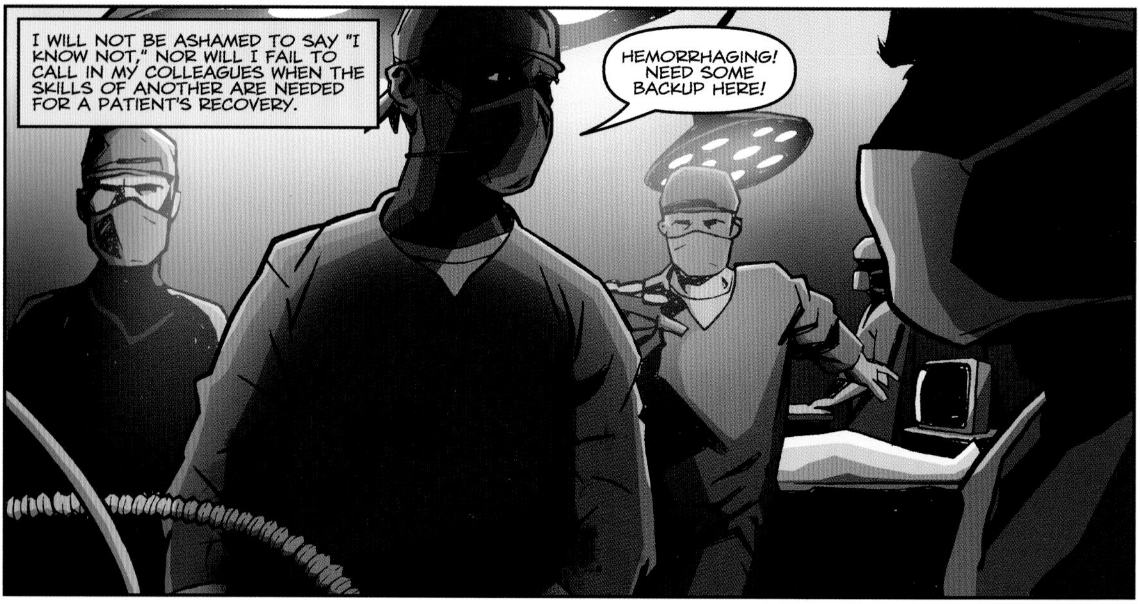
I WILL NOT BE ASHAMED TO SAY "I KNOW NOT," NOR WILL I FAIL TO CALL IN MY COLLEAGUES WHEN THE SKILLS OF ANOTHER ARE NEEDED FOR A PATIENT'S RECOVERY.
HEMORRHAGING! NEED SOME BACKUP HERE!

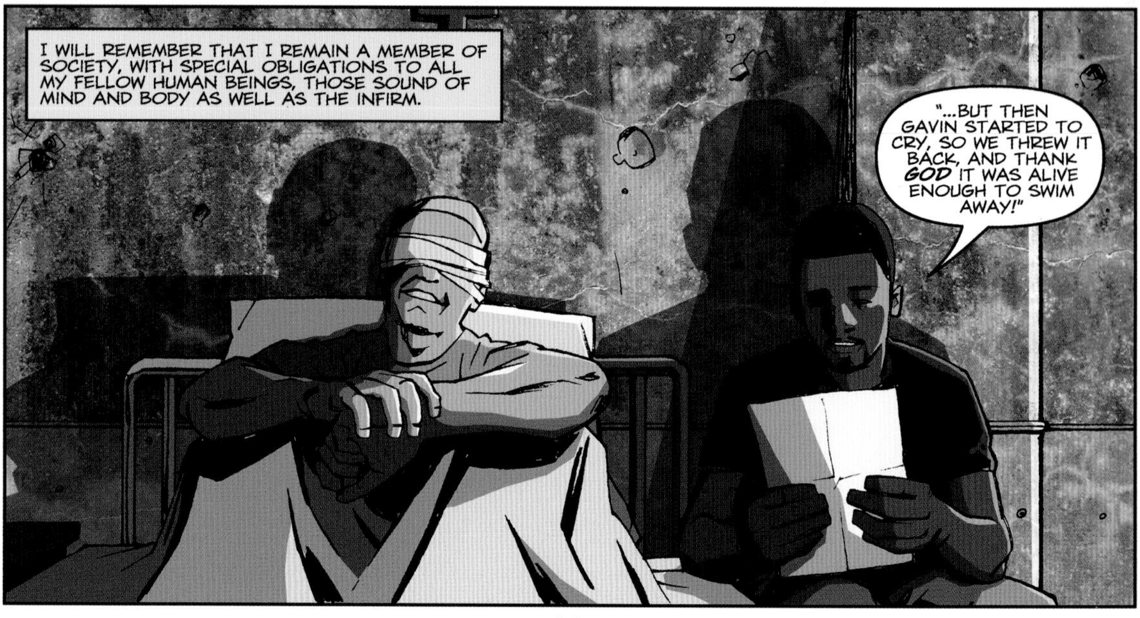
I WILL REMEMBER THAT I REMAIN A MEMBER OF SOCIETY, WITH SPECIAL OBLIGATIONS TO ALL MY FELLOW HUMAN BEINGS, THOSE SOUND OF MIND AND BODY AS WELL AS THE INFIRM.
"...BUT THEN GAVIN STARTED TO CRY, SO WE THREW IT BACK, AND THANK GOD IT WAS ALIVE ENOUGH TO SWIM AWAY!"

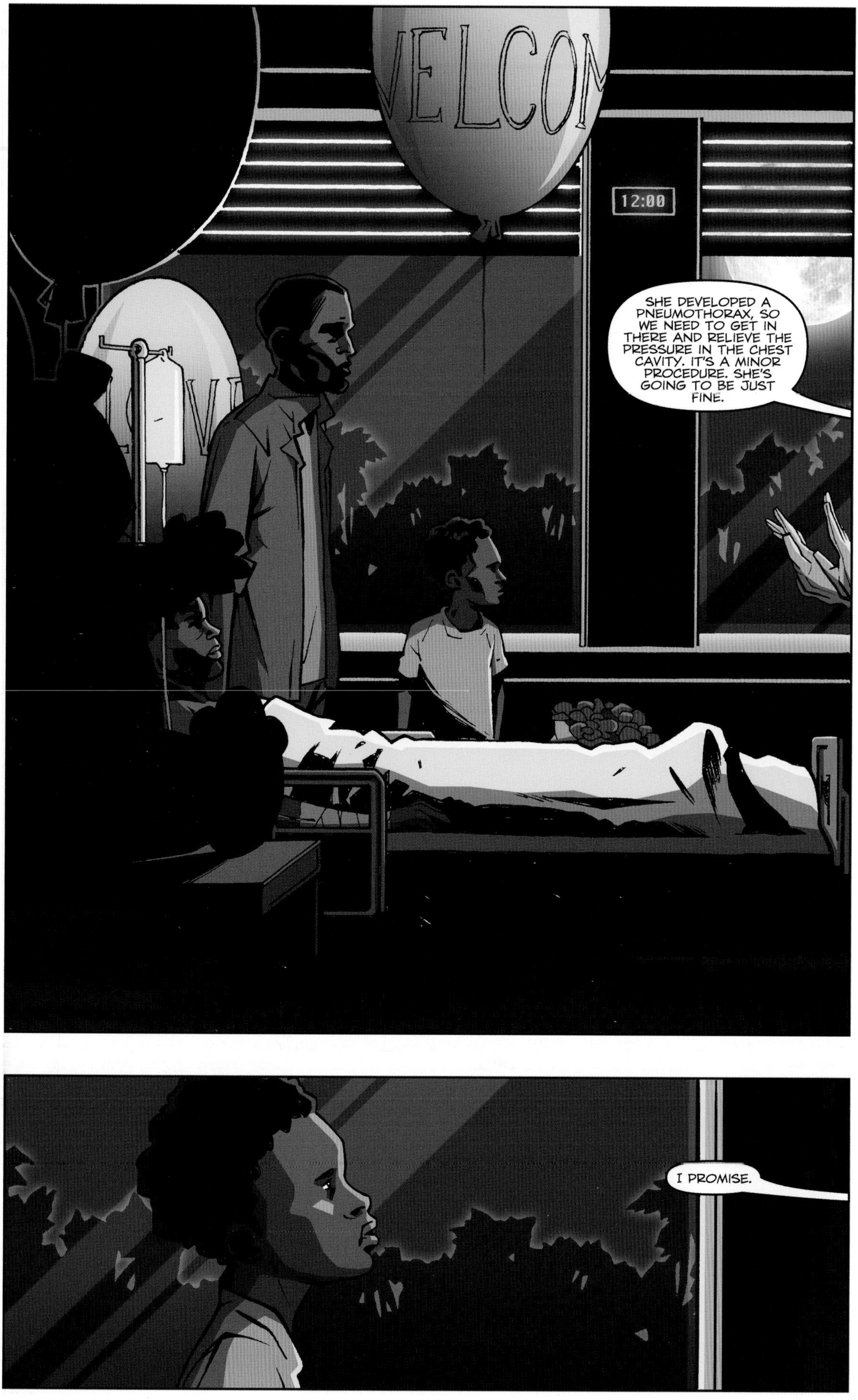
VELCOM
12:00
SHE DEVELOPED A PNEUMOTHORAX, SO WE NEED TO GET IN THERE AND RELIEVE THE PRESSURE IN THE CHEST CAVITY. IT'S A MINOR PROCEDURE. SHE'S GOING TO BE JUST FINE.
I PROMISE.

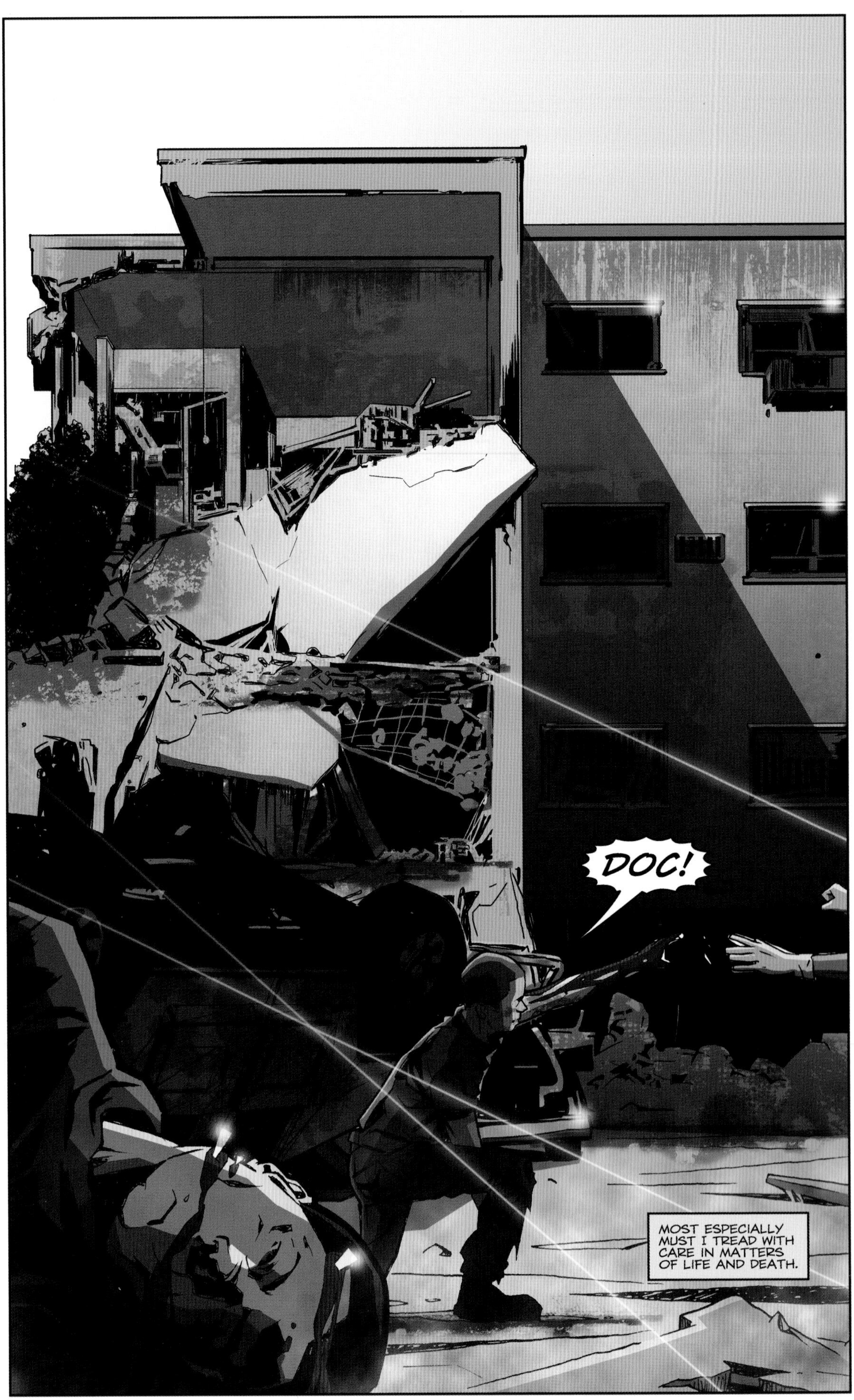
DOC!
MOST ESPECIALLY MUST I TREAD WITH CARE IN MATTERS OF LIFE AND DEATH.

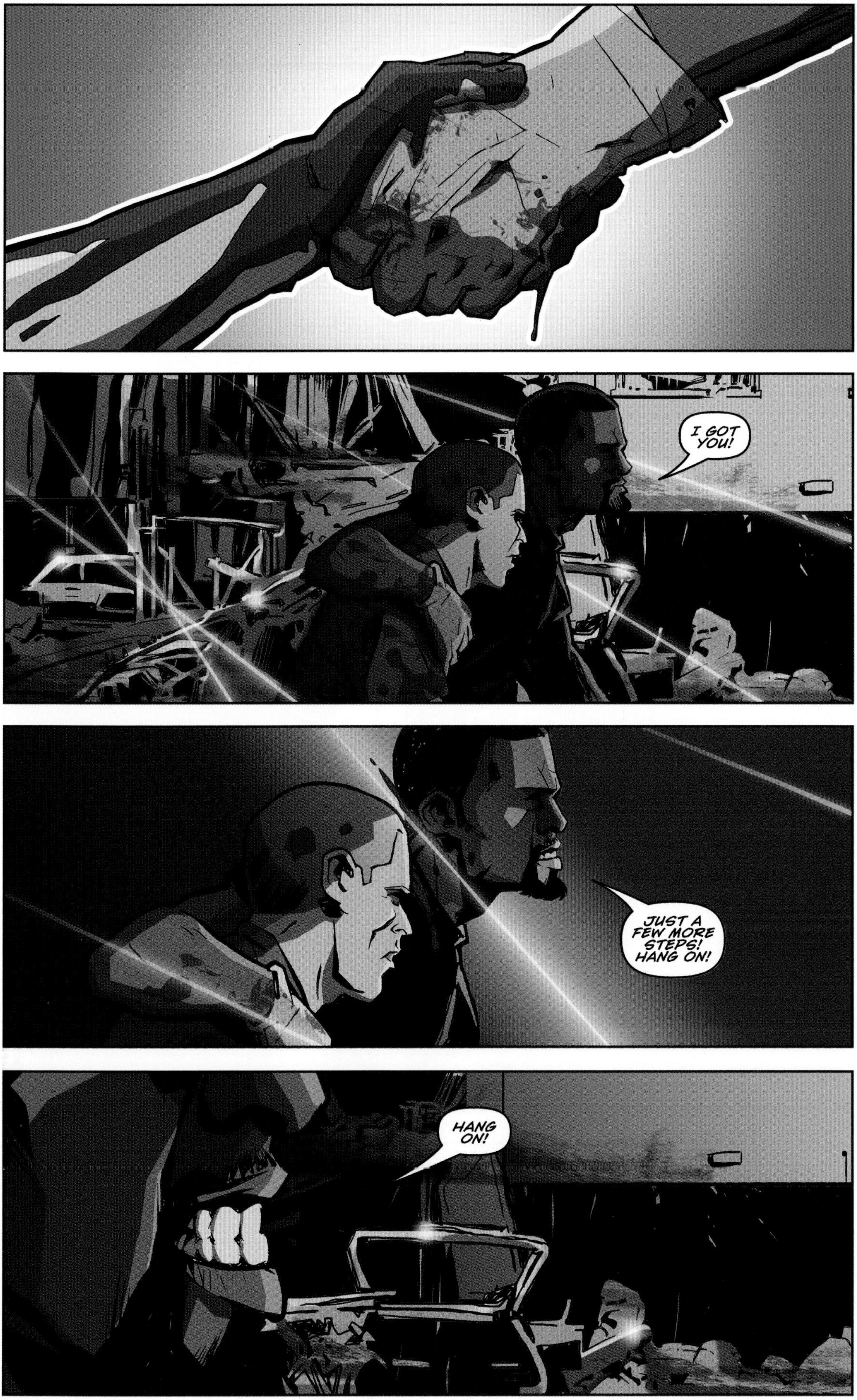
I GOT YOU!
JUST A FEW MORE STEPS! HANG ON!
HANG ON!

IF IT IS GIVEN ME TO SAVE A LIFE, ALL THANKS.

BUT IT MAY ALSO BE WITHIN MY POWER TO TAKE A LIFE.

THIS AWESOME RESPONSIBILITY MUST BE FACED WITH GREAT HUMILITY...

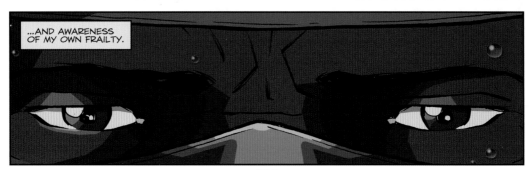

...AND AWARENESS OF MY OWN FRAILTY.

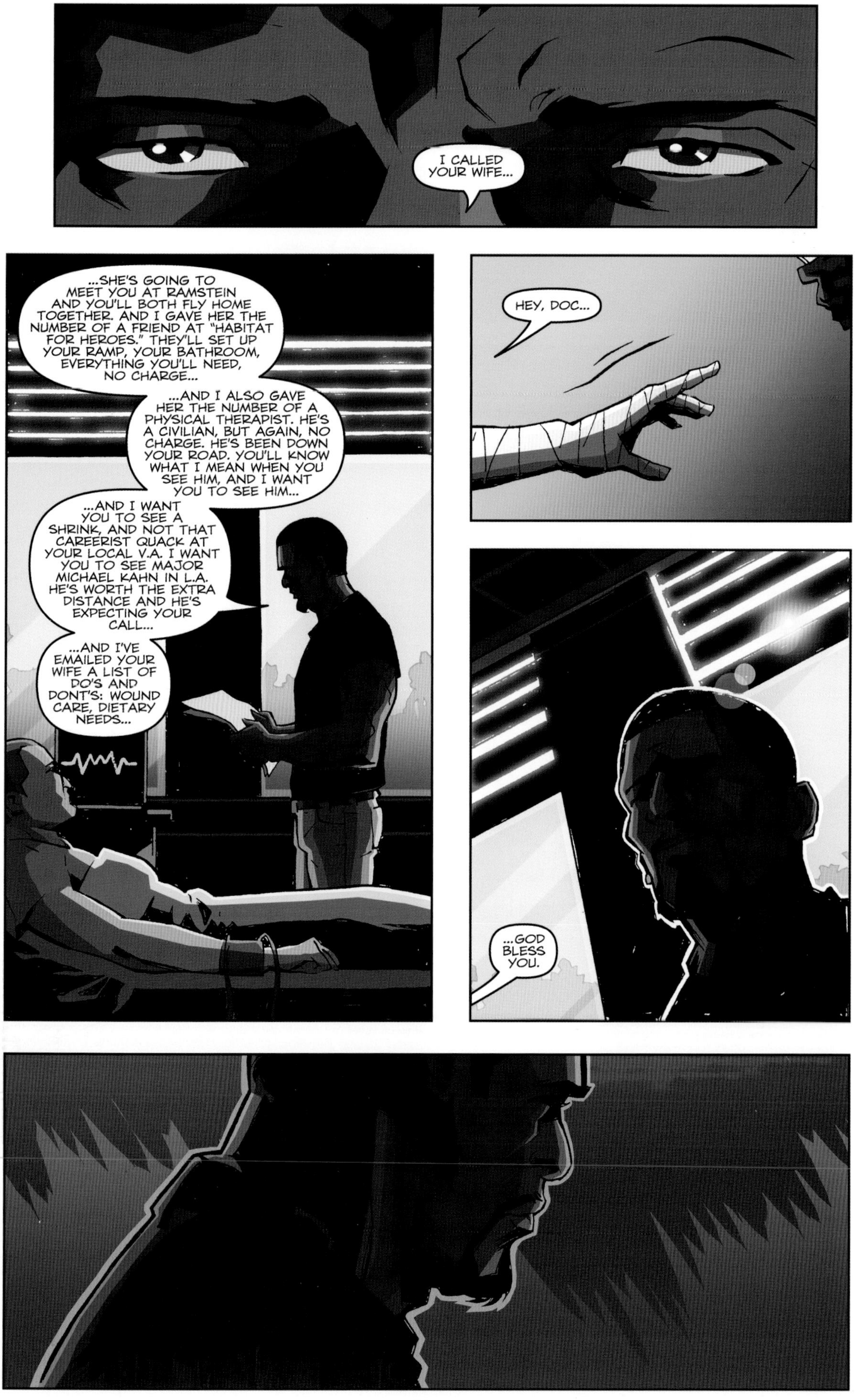
I CALLED YOUR WIFE...
...SHE'S GOING TO MEET YOU AT RAMSTEIN AND YOU'LL BOTH FLY HOME TOGETHER. AND I GAVE HER THE NUMBER OF A FRIEND AT "HABITAT FOR HEROES." THEY'LL SET UP YOUR RAMP, YOUR BATHROOM, EVERYTHING YOU'LL NEED, NO CHARGE...
...AND I ALSO GAVE HER THE NUMBER OF A PHYSICAL THERAPIST. HE'S A CIVILIAN, BUT AGAIN, NO CHARGE. HE'S BEEN DOWN YOUR ROAD. YOU'LL KNOW WHAT I MEAN WHEN YOU SEE HIM, AND I WANT YOU TO SEE HIM...
...AND I WANT YOU TO SEE A SHRINK, AND NOT THAT CAREERIST QUACK AT YOUR LOCAL V.A. I WANT YOU TO SEE MAJOR MICHAEL KAHN IN L.A. HE'S WORTH THE EXTRA DISTANCE AND HE'S EXPECTING YOUR CALL...
...AND I'VE EMAILED YOUR WIFE A LIST OF DO'S AND DONT'S: WOUND CARE, DIETARY NEEDS...
HEY, DOC...
...GOD BLESS YOU.

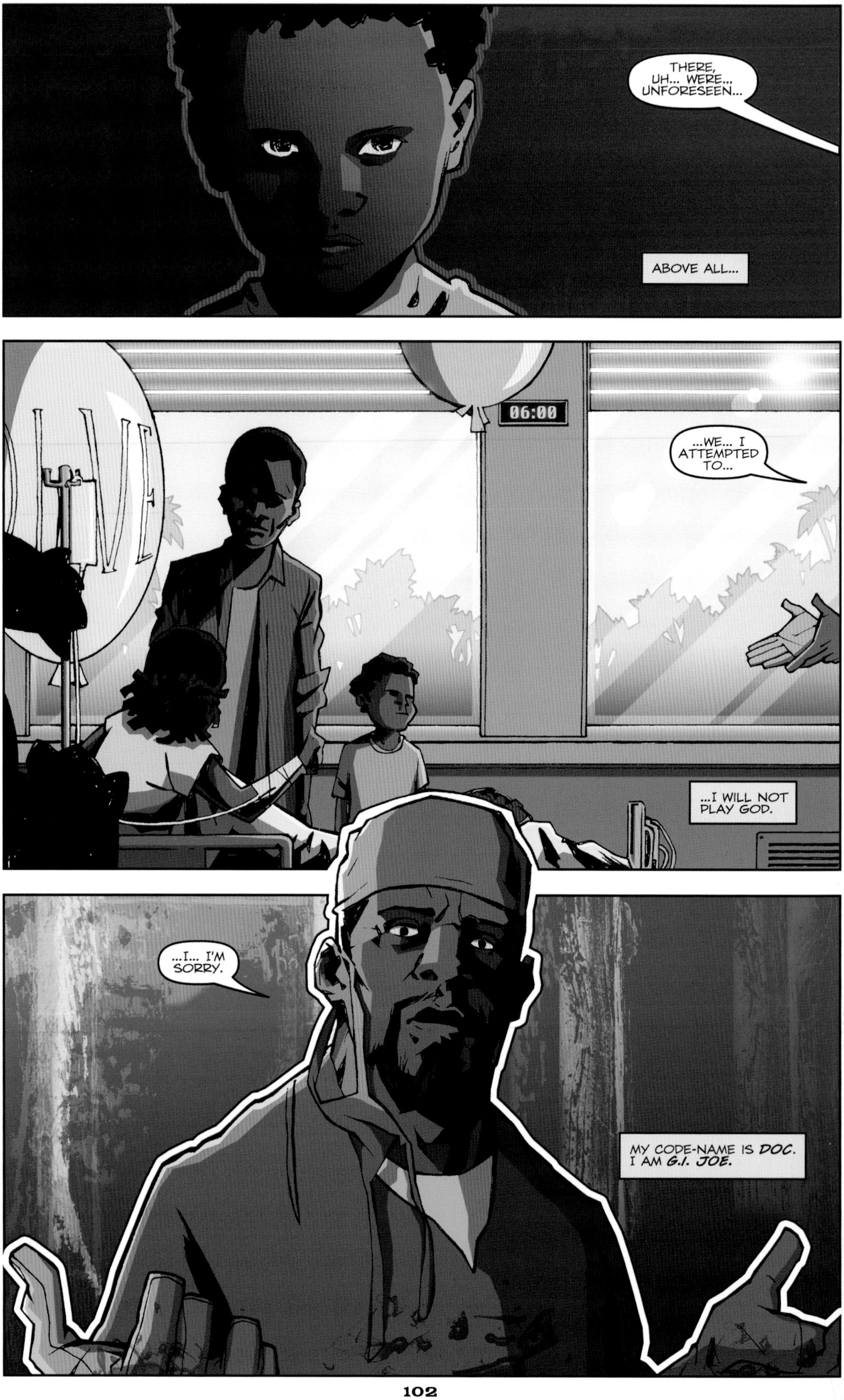
THERE, UH... WERE... UNFORESEEN...
ABOVE ALL...
06:00
...WE... I ATTEMPTED TO...
...I WILL NOT PLAY GOD.
...I... I'M SORRY.
MY CODE-NAME IS DOC. I AM G.I. JOE.

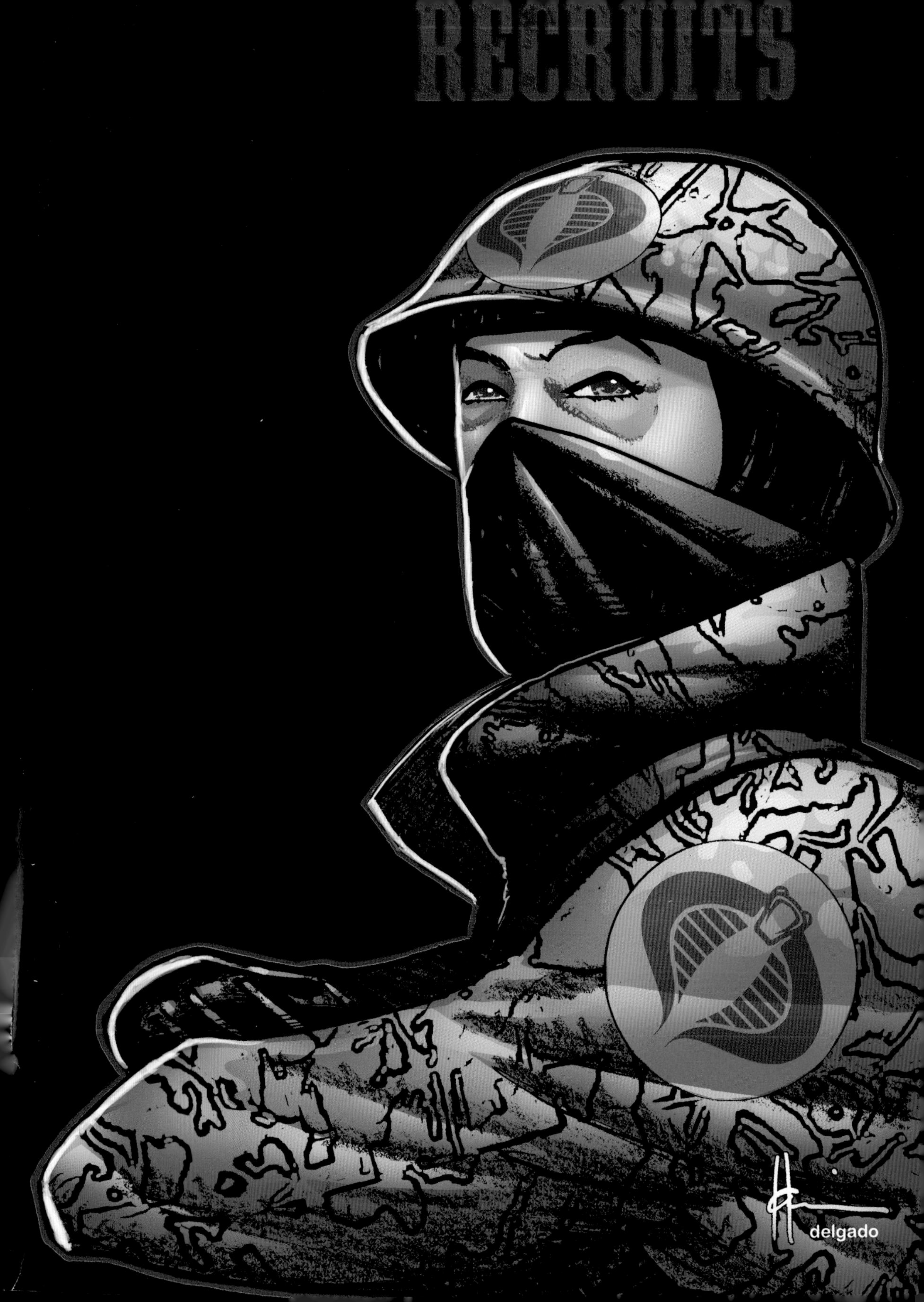
RECRUITS
delgado

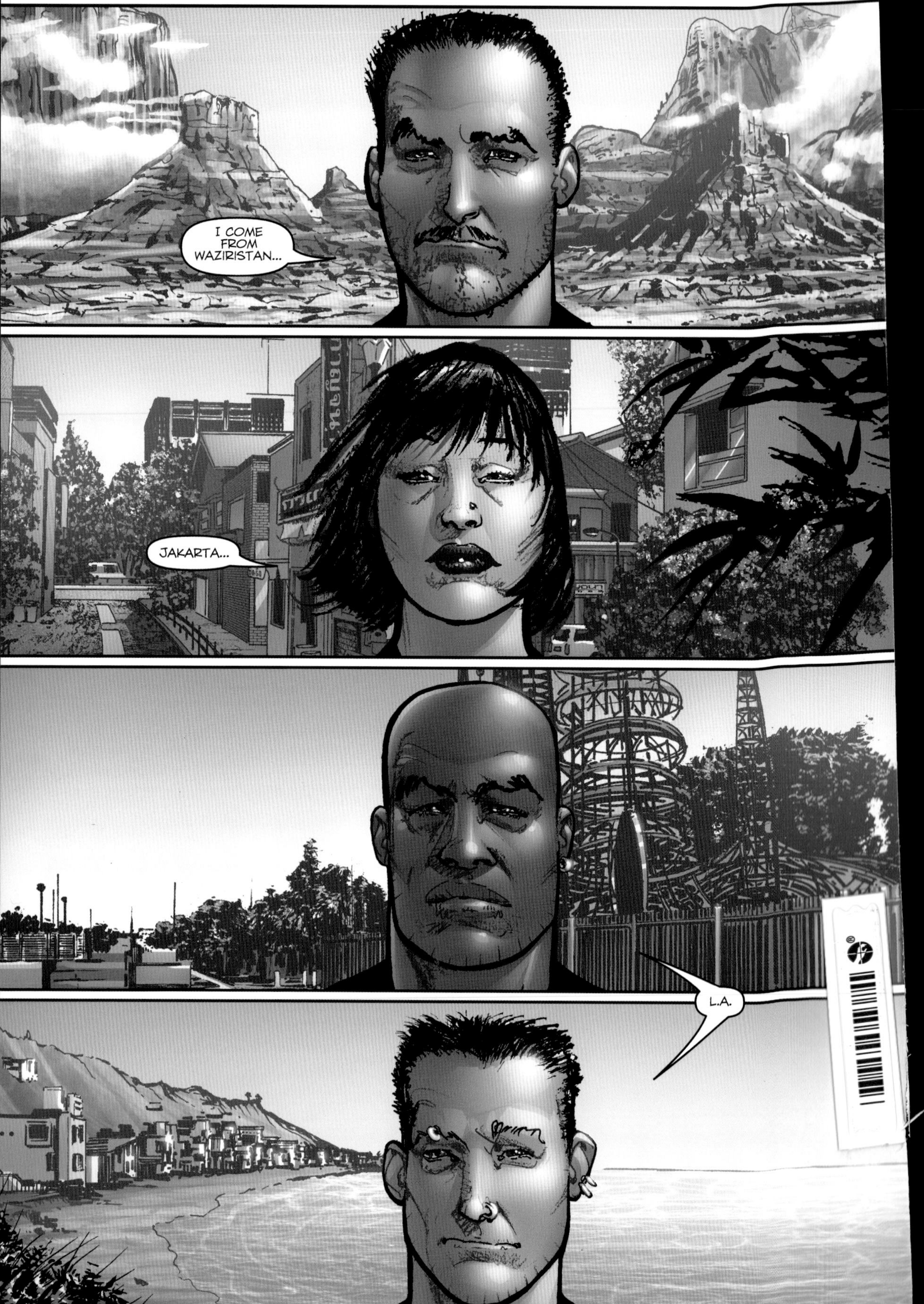
I COME FROM WAZIRISTAN...
JAKARTA...
L.A.

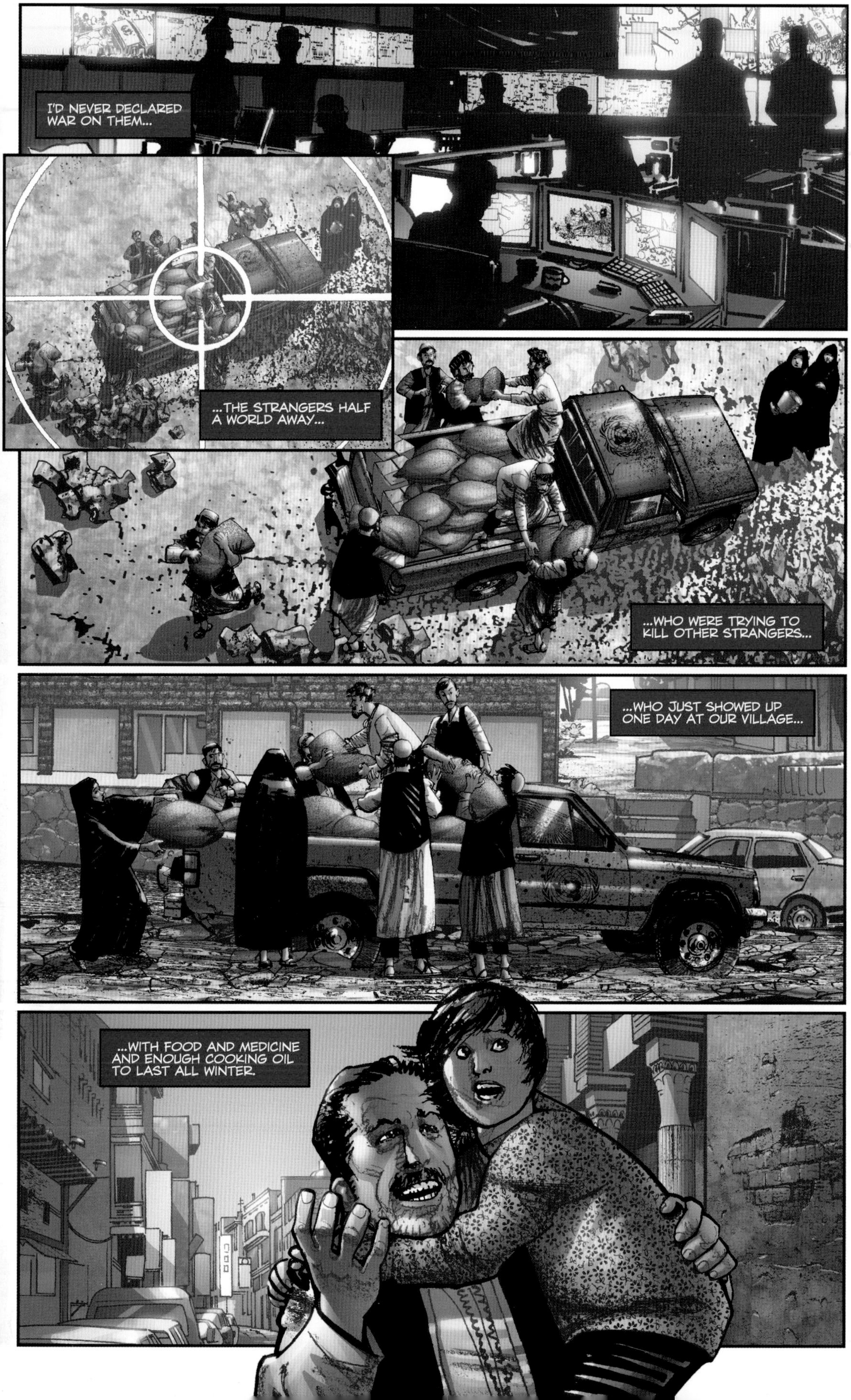
I'D NEVER DECLARED WAR ON THEM...
...THE STRANGERS HALF A WORLD AWAY...
...WHO WERE TRYING TO KILL OTHER STRANGERS...
...WHO JUST SHOWED UP ONE DAY AT OUR VILLAGE...
...WITH FOOD AND MEDICINE AND ENOUGH COOKING OIL TO LAST ALL WINTER.

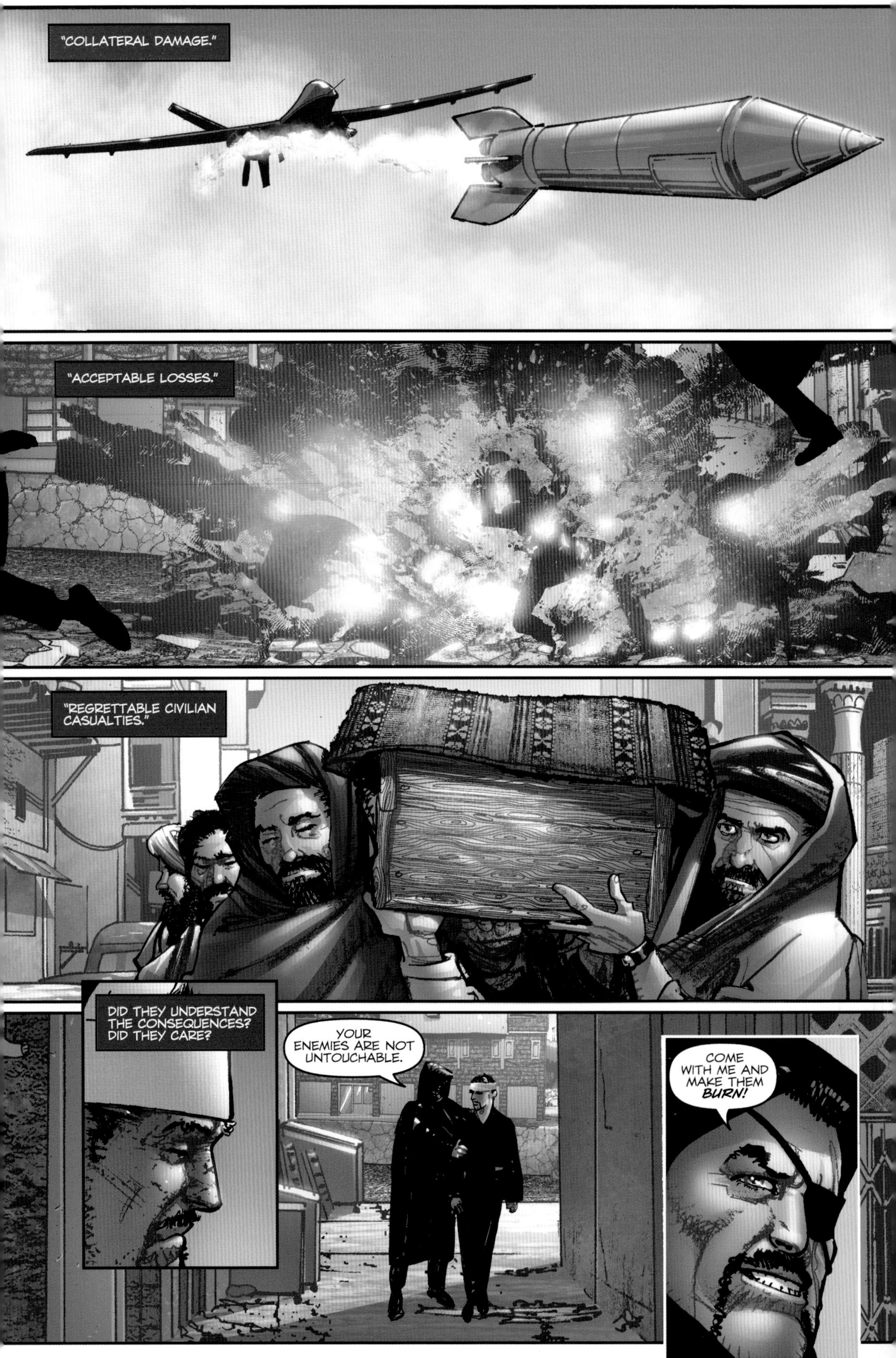
"COLLATERAL DAMAGE."
"ACCEPTABLE LOSSES."
"REGRETTABLE CIVILIAN CASUALTIES."
DID THEY UNDERSTAND THE CONSEQUENCES? DID THEY CARE?
YOUR ENEMIES ARE NOT UNTOUCHABLE.
COME WITH ME AND MAKE THEM *BURN!*

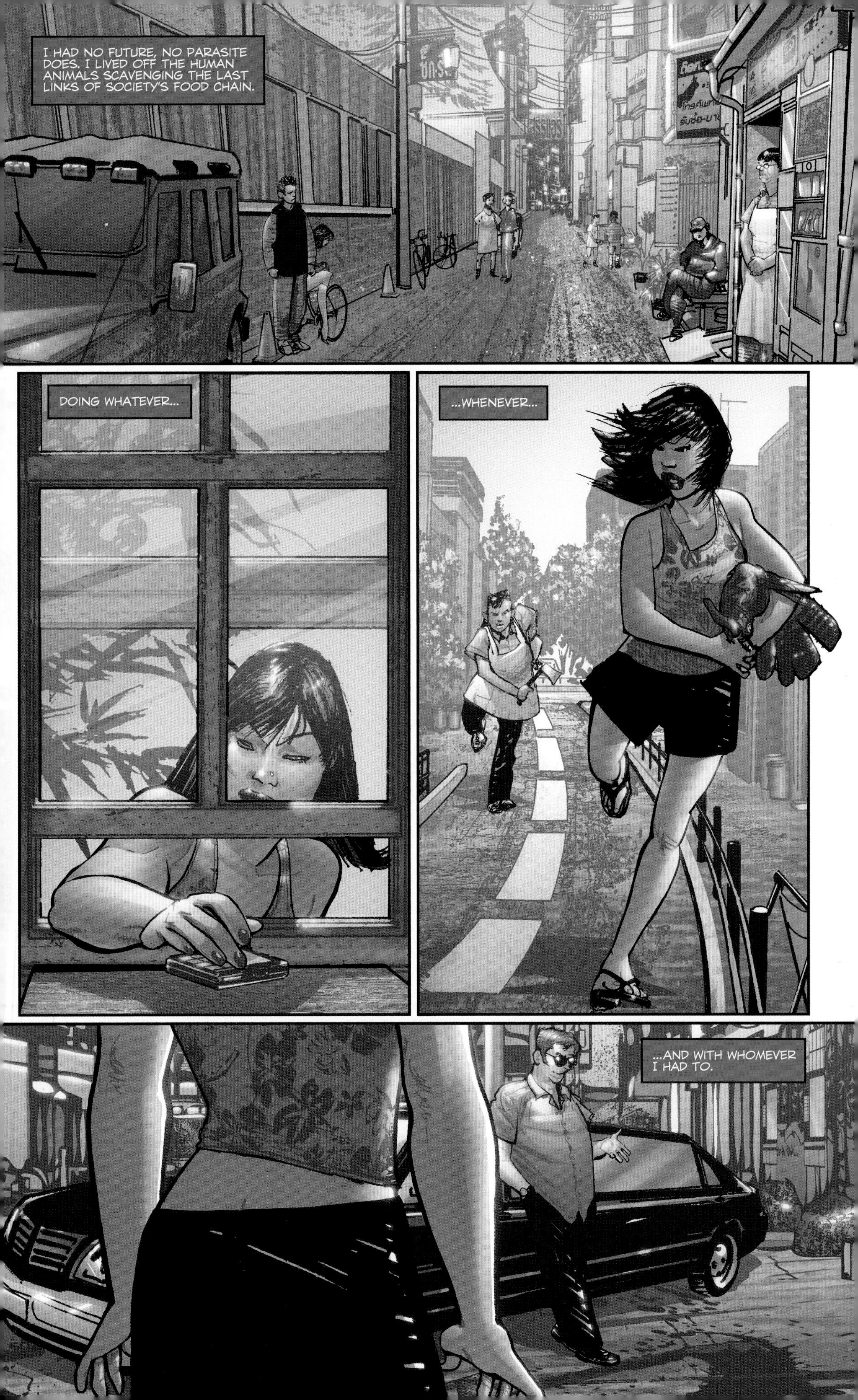
I HAD NO FUTURE, NO PARASITE DOES. I LIVED OFF THE HUMAN ANIMALS SCAVENGING THE LAST LINKS OF SOCIETY'S FOOD CHAIN.
DOING WHATEVER...
...WHENEVER...
...AND WITH WHOMEVER I HAD TO.

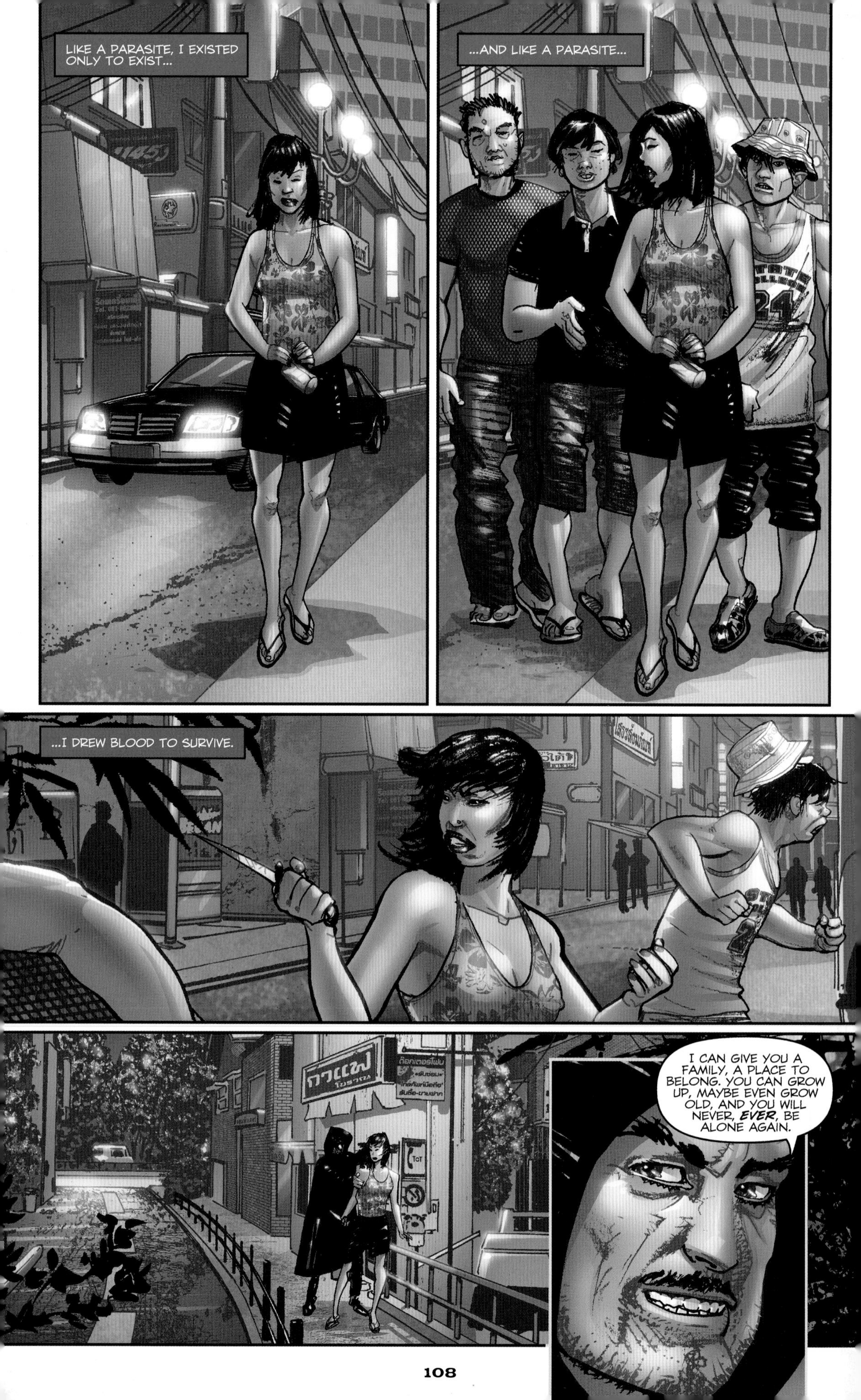
LIKE A PARASITE, I EXISTED ONLY TO EXIST...
...AND LIKE A PARASITE...
...I DREW BLOOD TO SURVIVE.
I CAN GIVE YOU A FAMILY, A PLACE TO BELONG. YOU CAN GROW UP, MAYBE EVEN GROW OLD, AND YOU WILL NEVER, *EVER*, BE ALONE AGAIN.

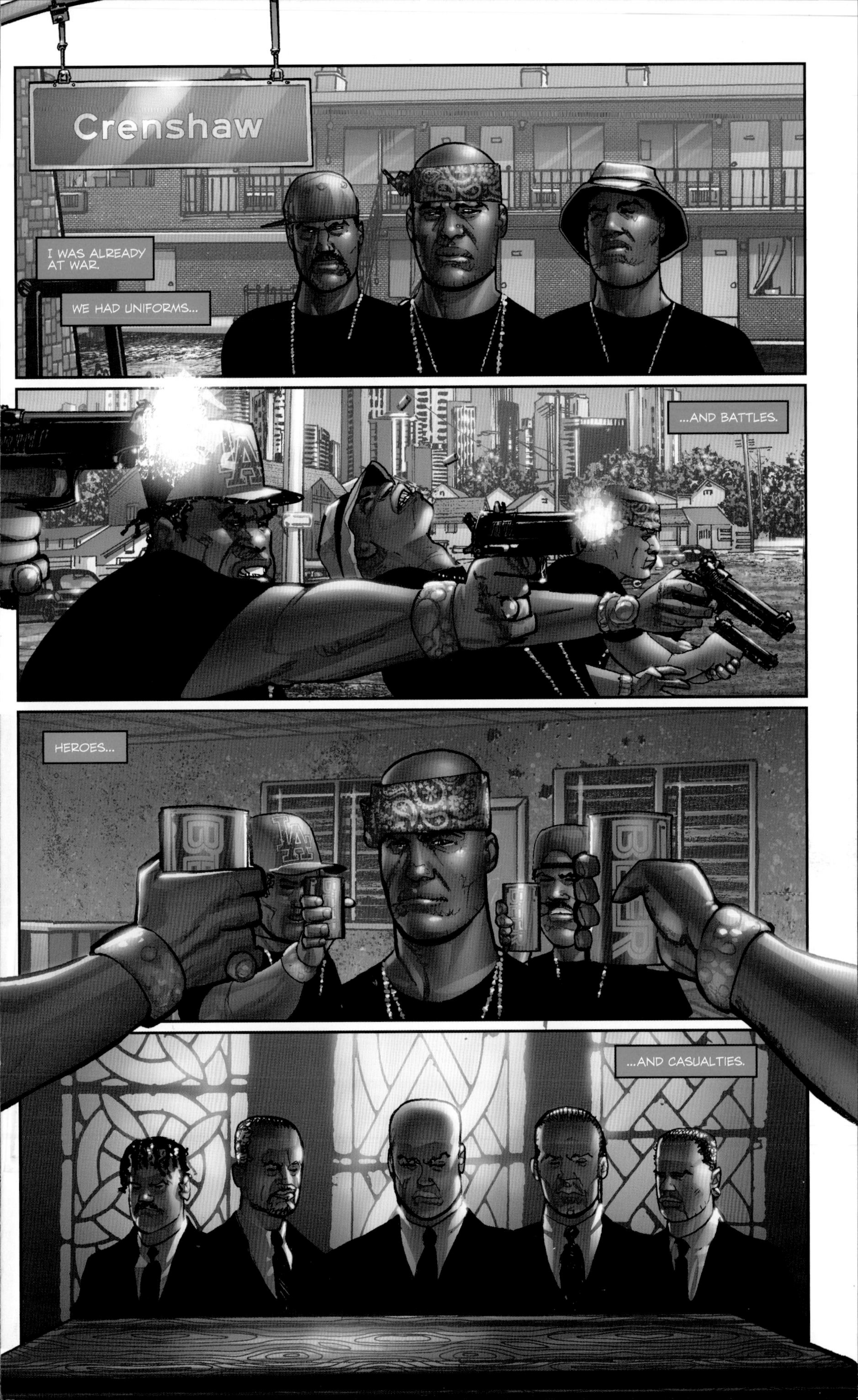
Crenshaw
I WAS ALREADY AT WAR.
WE HAD UNIFORMS...
...AND BATTLES.
HEROES...
...AND CASUALTIES.

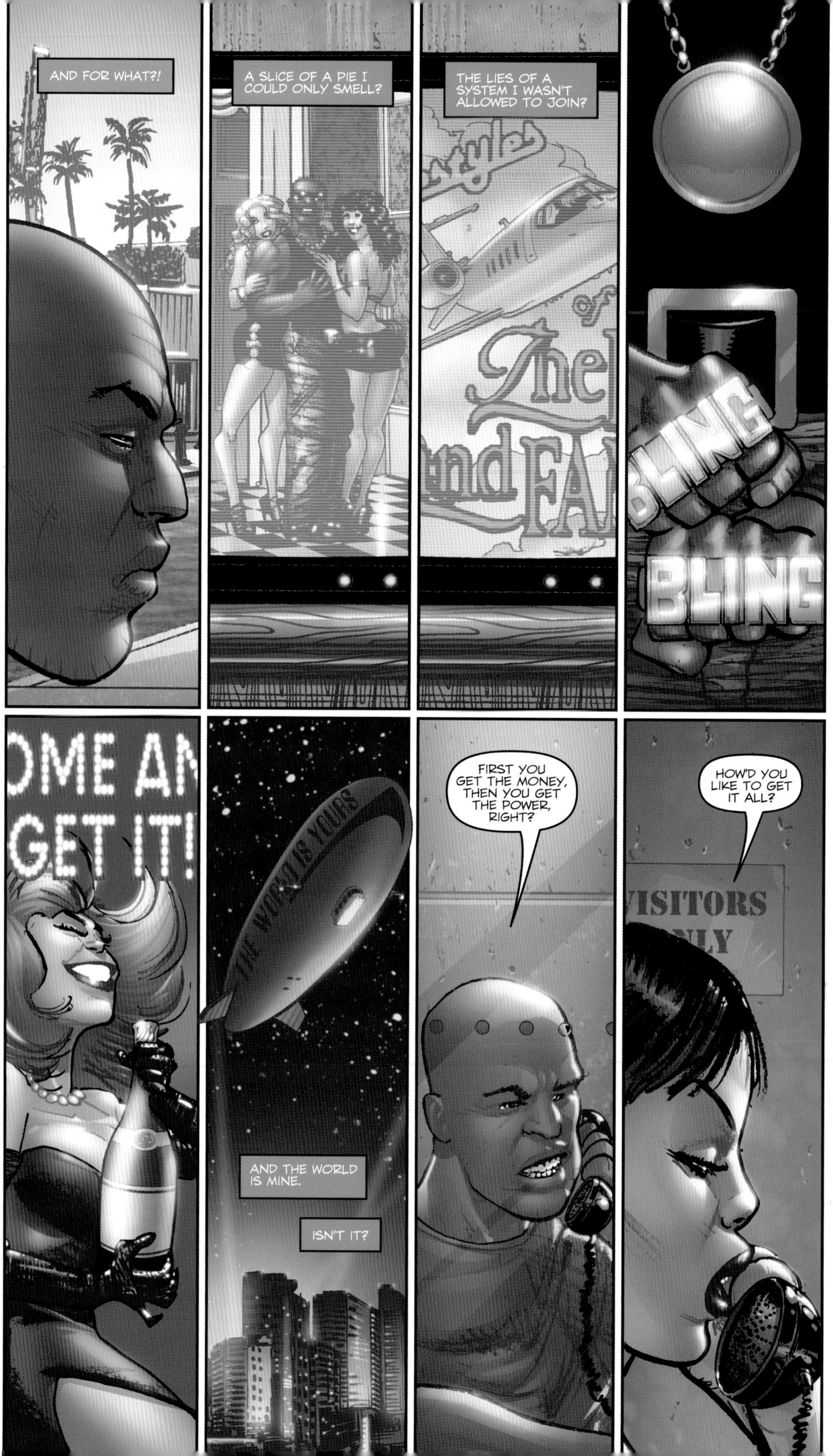

AND FOR WHAT?!
A SLICE OF A PIE I COULD ONLY SMELL?
THE LIES OF A SYSTEM I WASN'T ALLOWED TO JOIN?
BLING
BLING
OME AN
GET IT!
THE WORLD IS YOURS
AND THE WORLD IS MINE.
ISN'T IT?
FIRST YOU GET THE MONEY, THEN YOU GET THE POWER, RIGHT?
HOW'D YOU LIKE TO GET IT ALL?
VISITORS
NLY

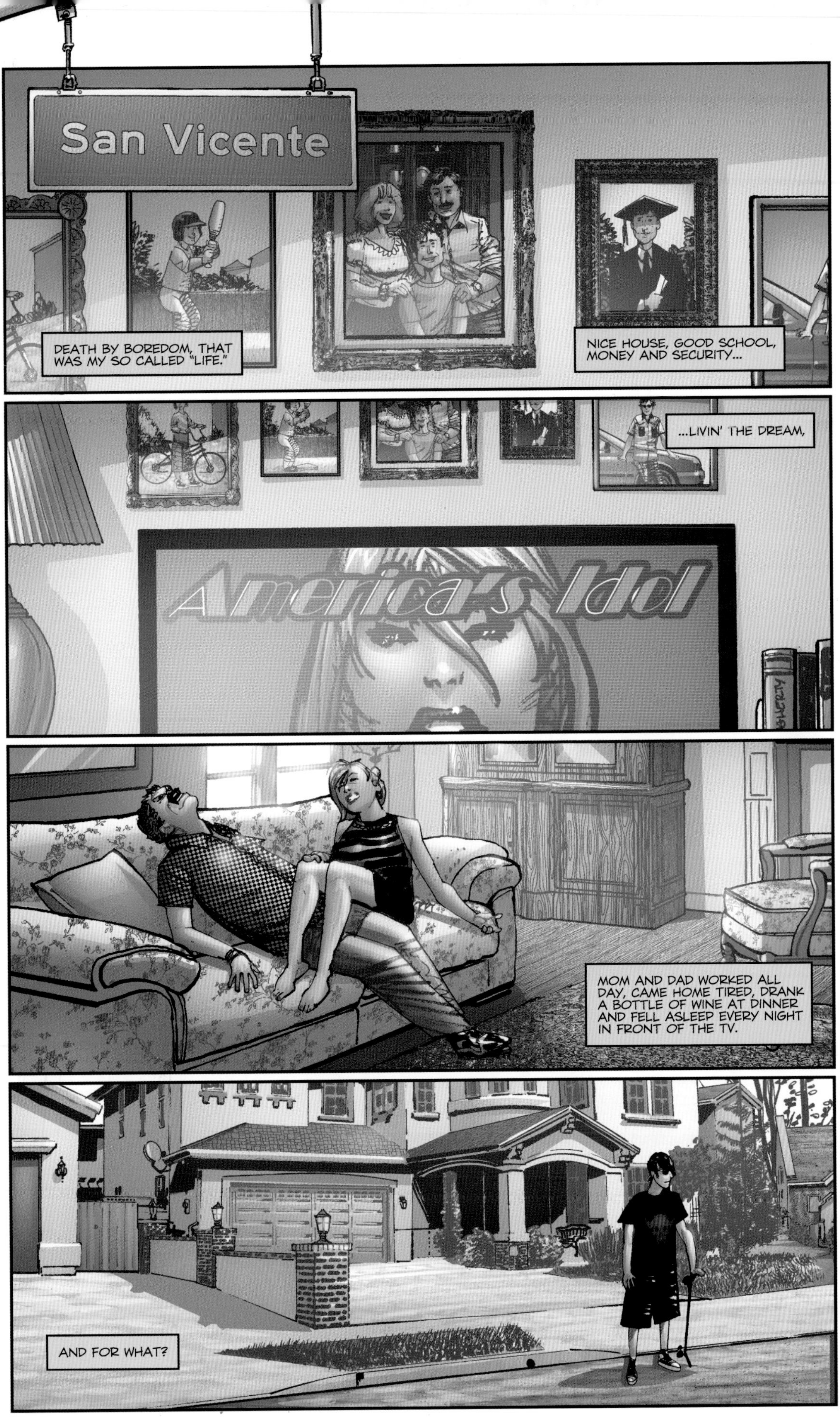
San Vicente
DEATH BY BOREDOM, THAT WAS MY SO CALLED "LIFE."
NICE HOUSE, GOOD SCHOOL, MONEY AND SECURITY...
...LIVIN' THE DREAM,
America's Idol
MOM AND DAD WORKED ALL DAY, CAME HOME TIRED, DRANK A BOTTLE OF WINE AT DINNER AND FELL ASLEEP EVERY NIGHT IN FRONT OF THE TV.
AND FOR WHAT?

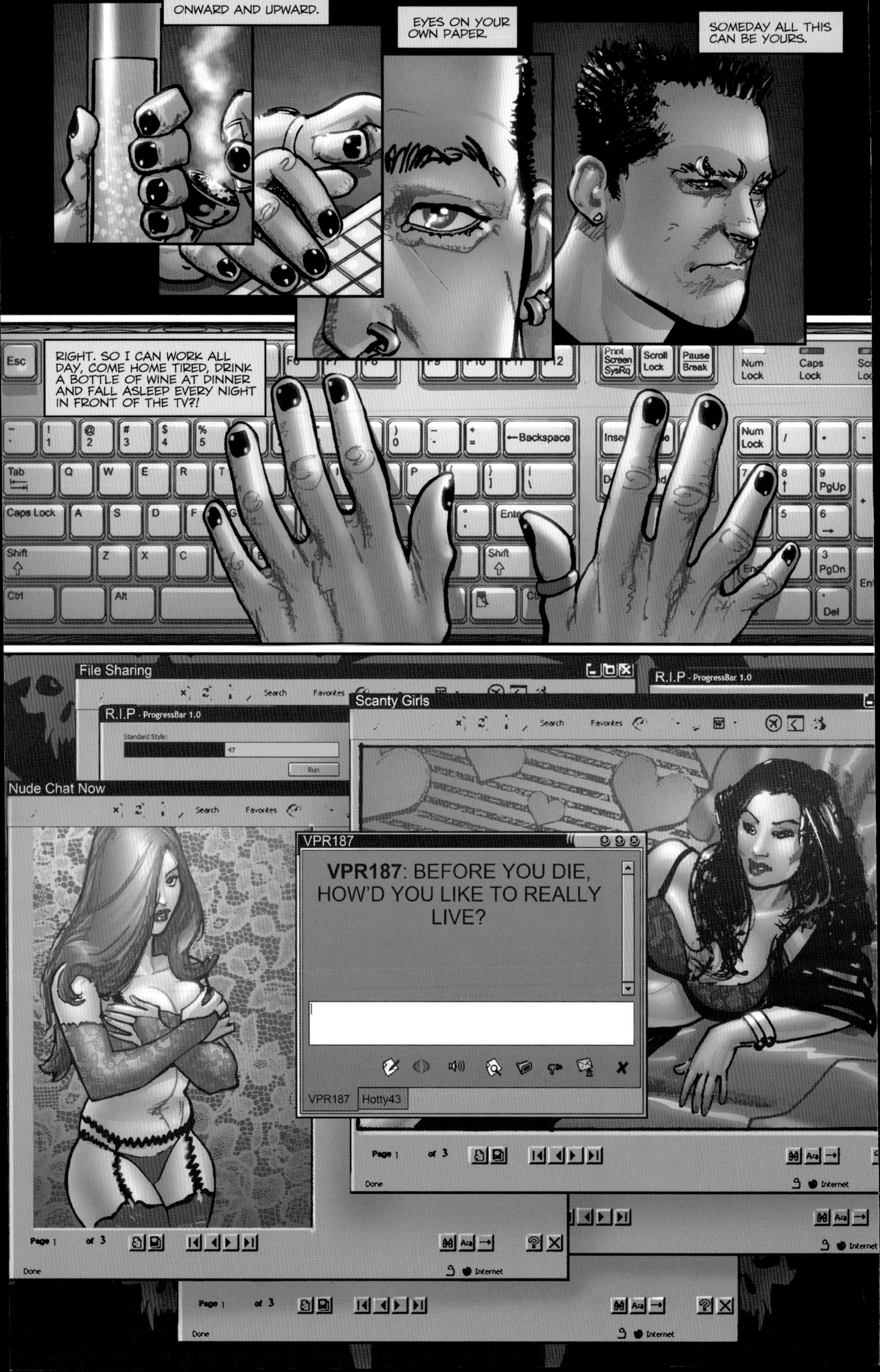

ONWARD AND UPWARD.
EYES ON YOUR OWN PAPER.
SOMEDAY ALL THIS CAN BE YOURS.
RIGHT. SO I CAN WORK ALL DAY, COME HOME TIRED, DRINK A BOTTLE OF WINE AT DINNER AND FALL ASLEEP EVERY NIGHT IN FRONT OF THE TV?!
File Sharing
R.I.P - ProgressBar 1.0
Scanty Girls
Nude Chat Now
VPR187
VPR187: BEFORE YOU DIE, HOW'D YOU LIKE TO REALLY LIVE?
VPR187
Hotty43

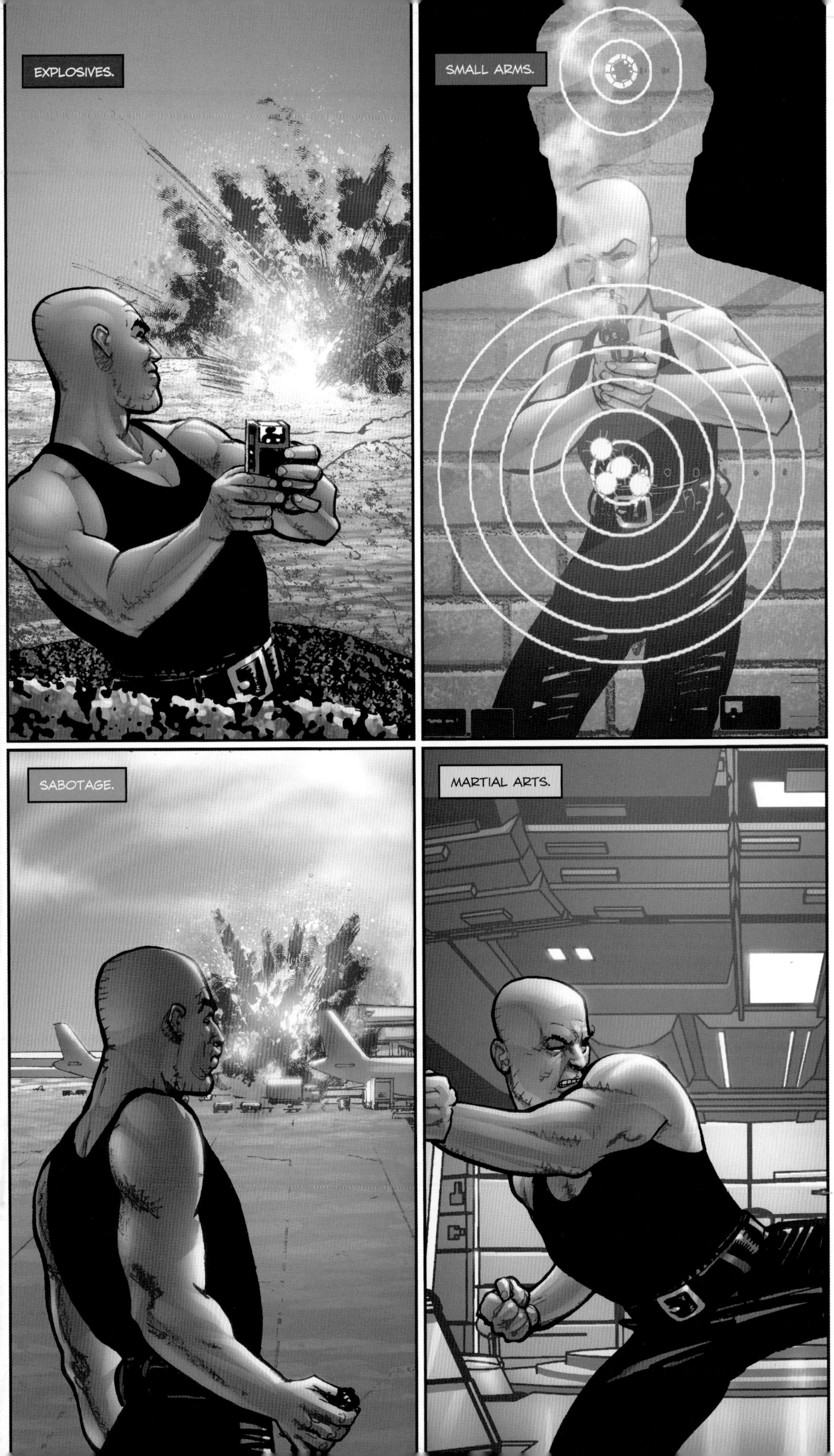
EXPLOSIVES.
SMALL ARMS.
SABOTAGE.
MARTIAL ARTS.

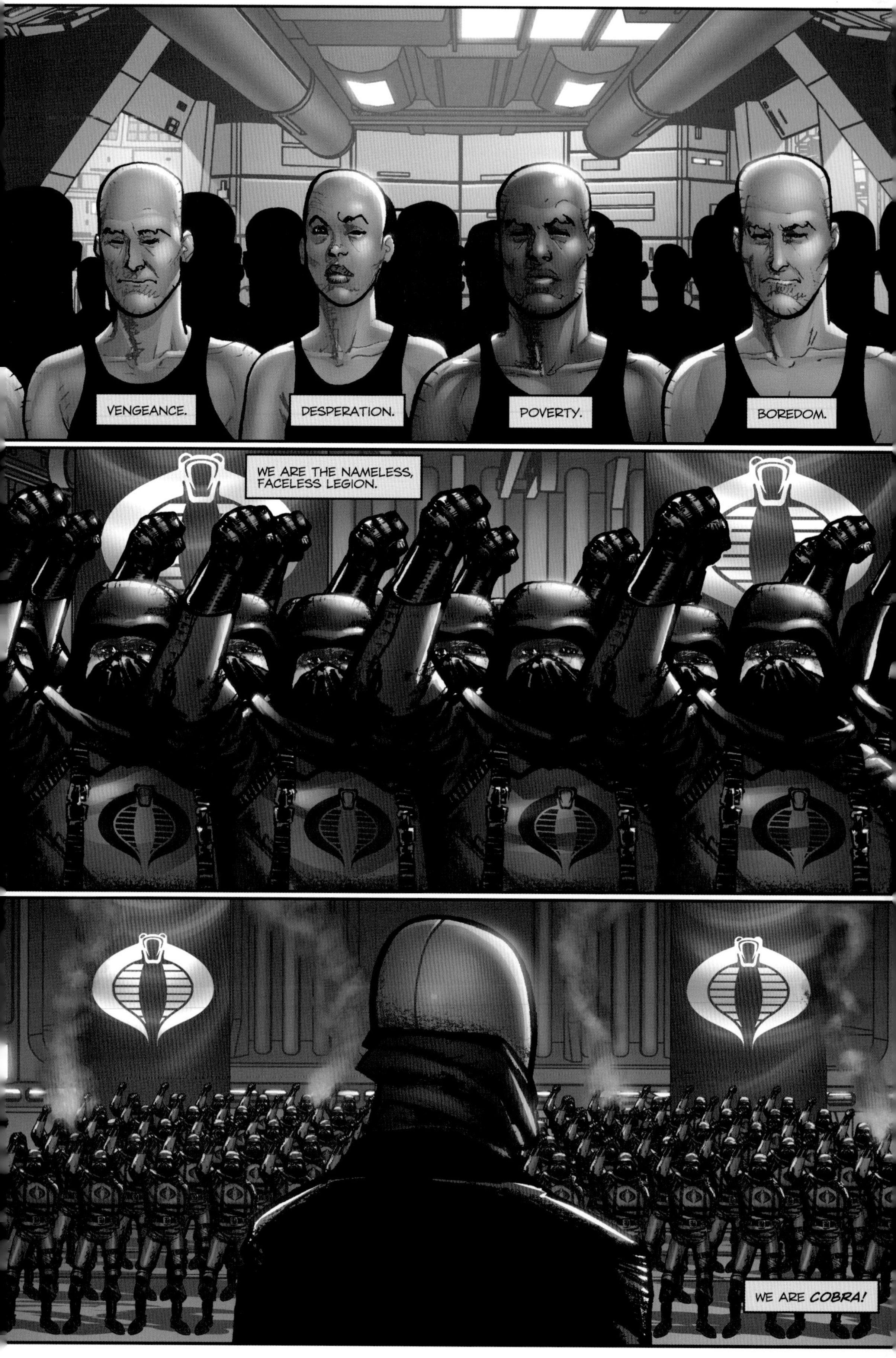
VENGEANCE.
DESPERATION.
POVERTY.
BOREDOM.
WE ARE THE NAMELESS, FACELESS LEGION.
WE ARE *COBRA!*

BLOWTORCH

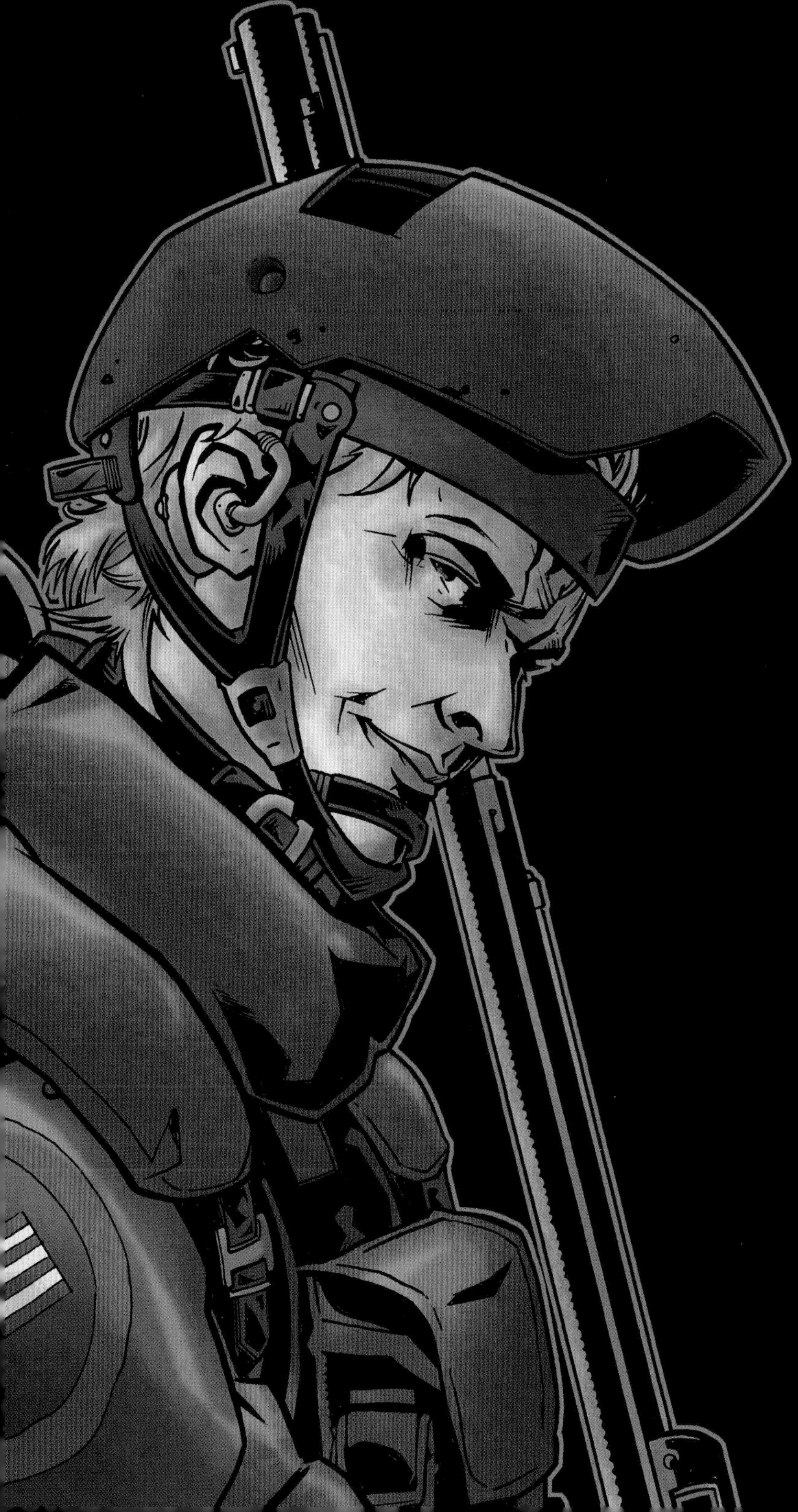

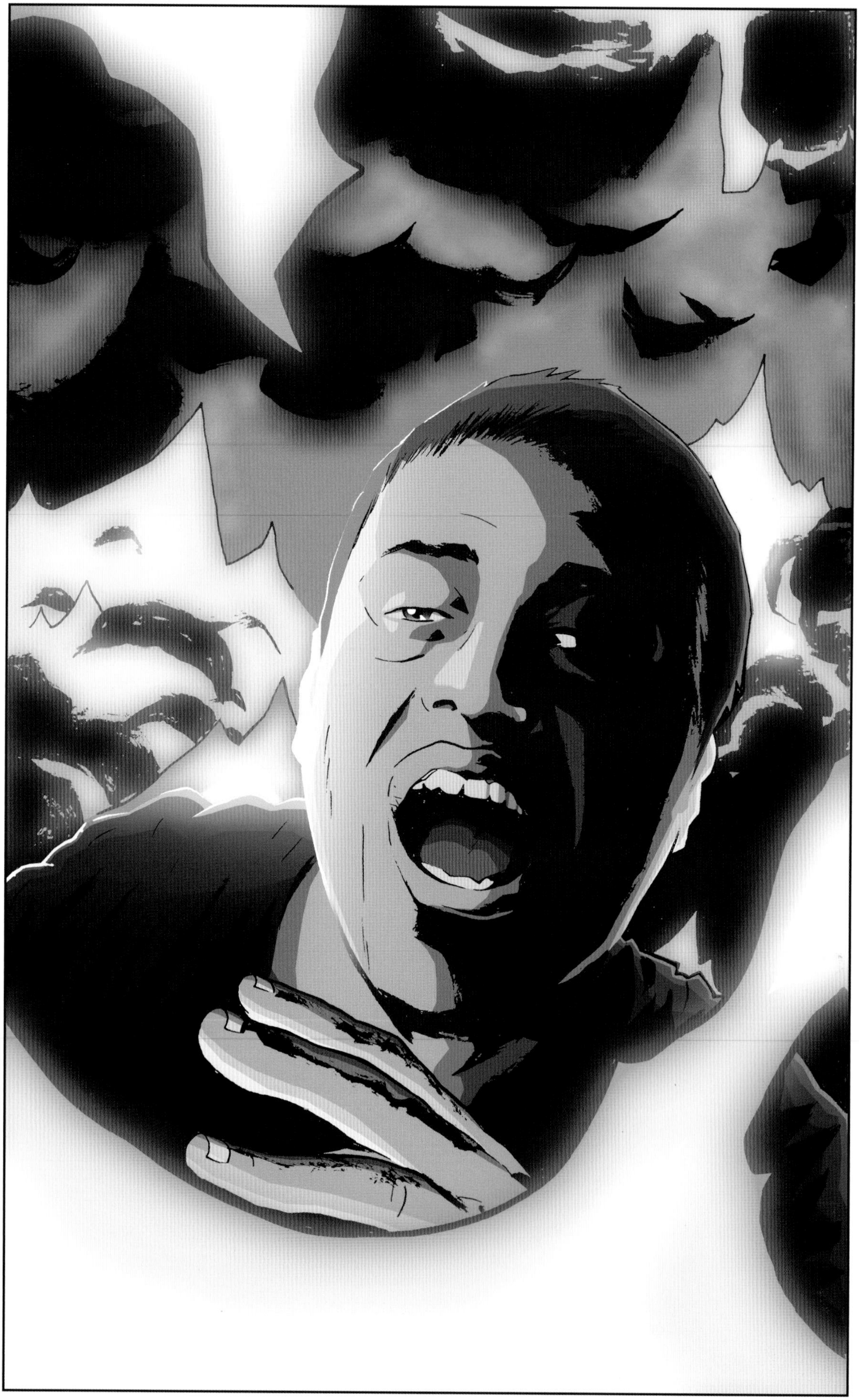

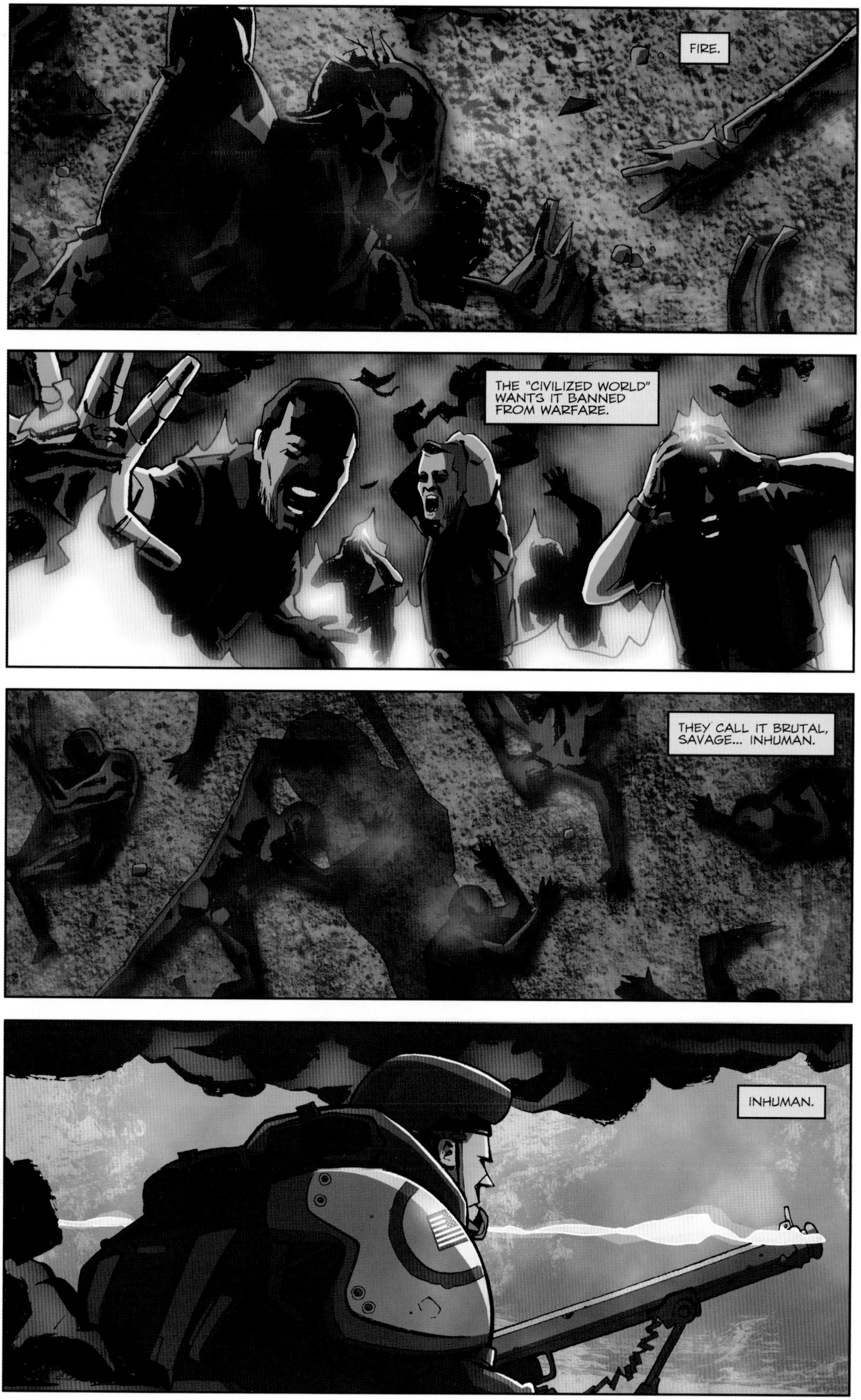
FIRE.
THE "CIVILIZED WORLD" WANTS IT BANNED FROM WARFARE.
THEY CALL IT BRUTAL, SAVAGE... INHUMAN.
INHUMAN.

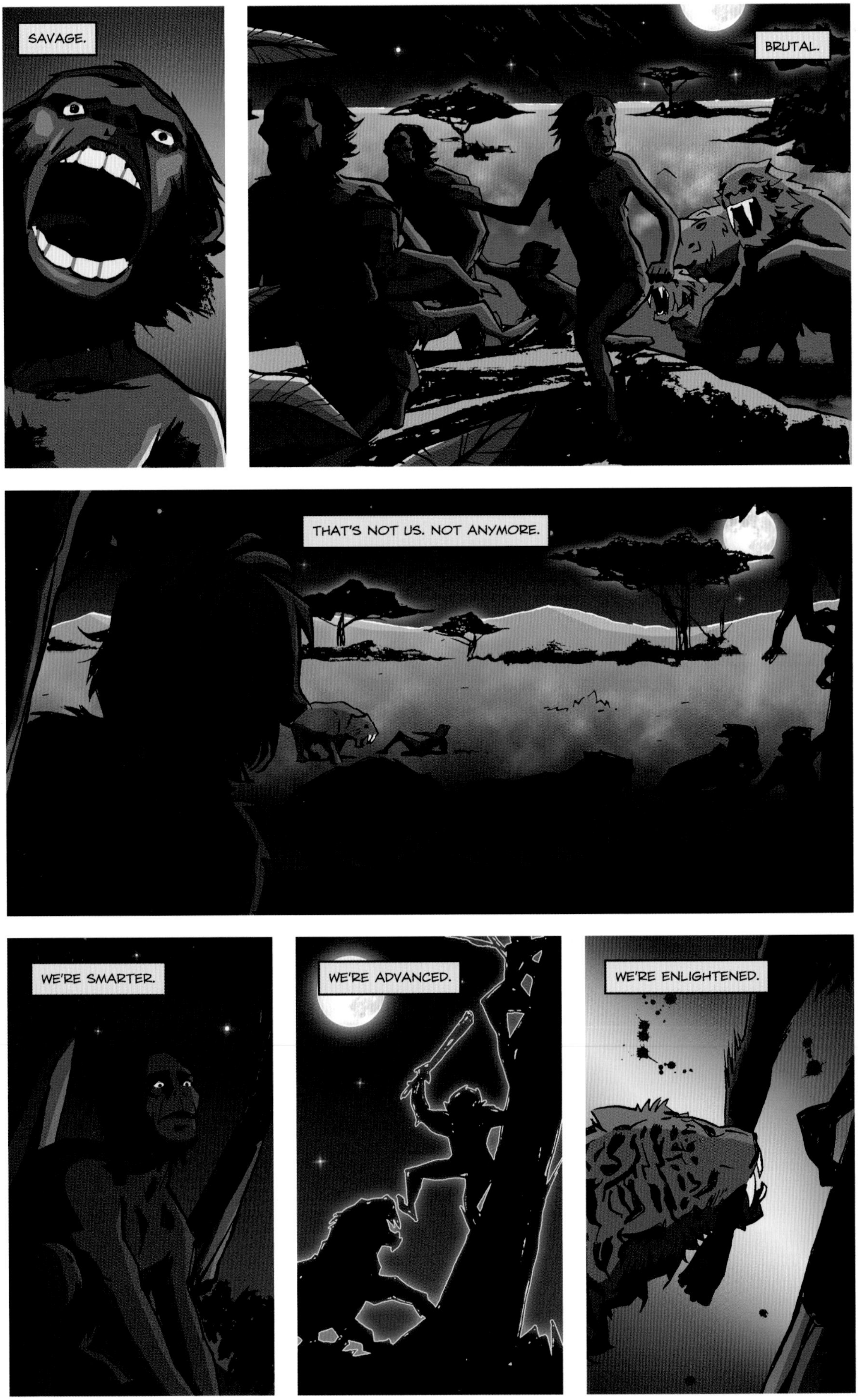
SAVAGE.
BRUTAL.
THAT'S NOT US. NOT ANYMORE.
WE'RE SMARTER.
WE'RE ADVANCED.
WE'RE ENLIGHTENED.

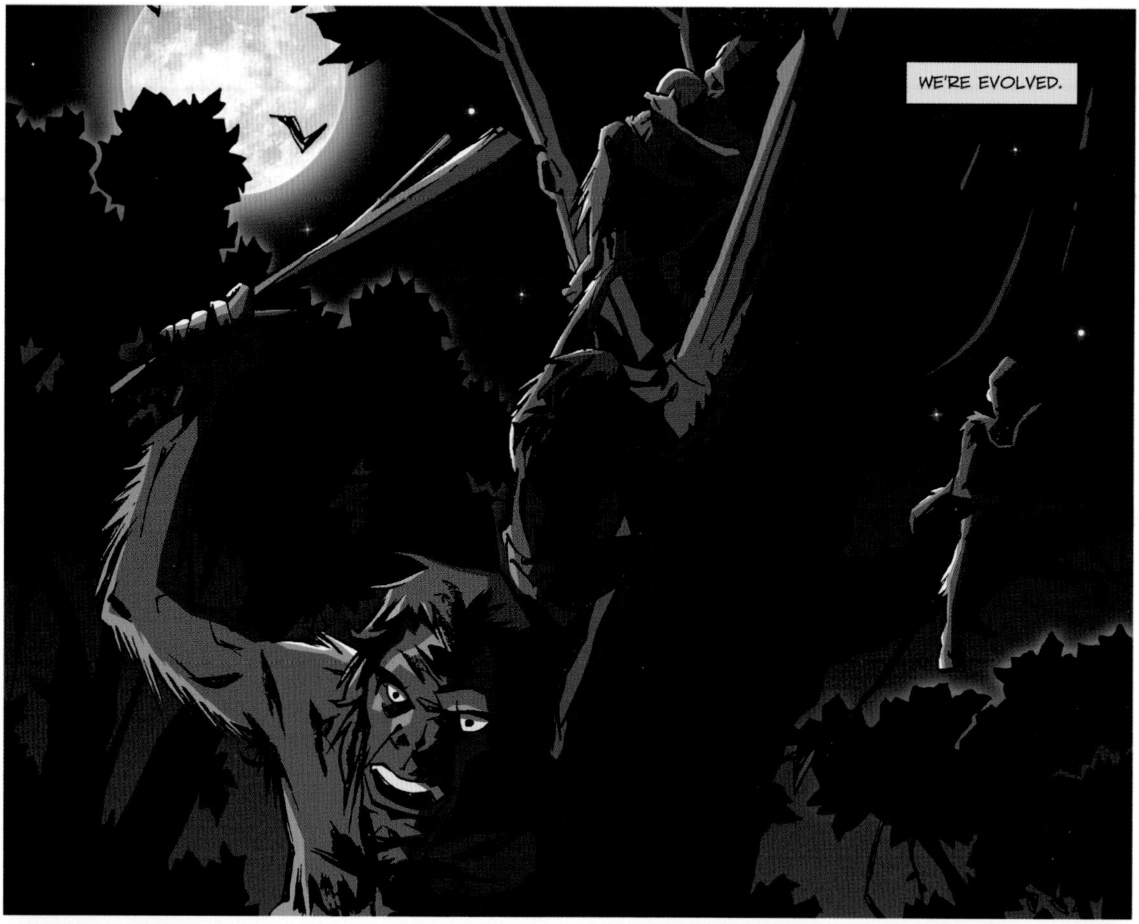
WE'RE EVOLVED.

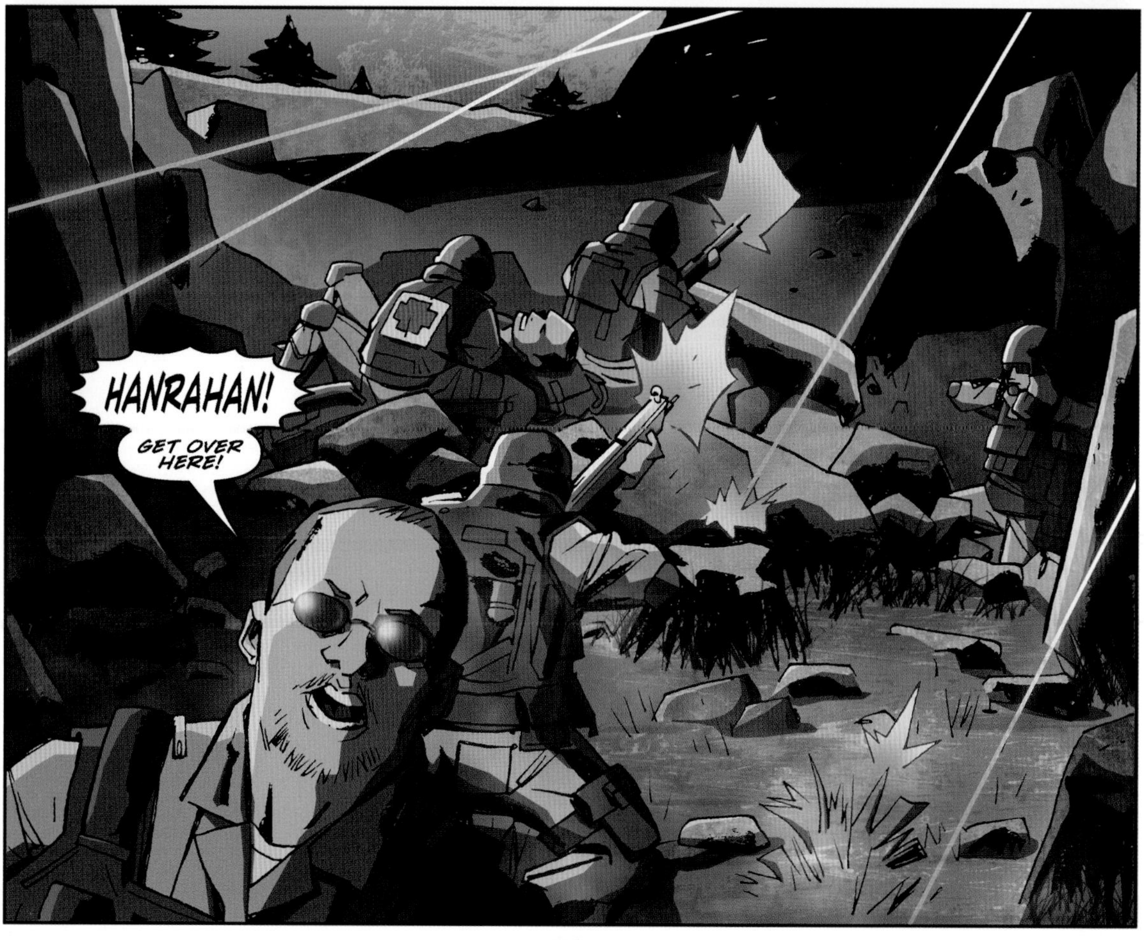
HANRAHAN!
GET OVER HERE!

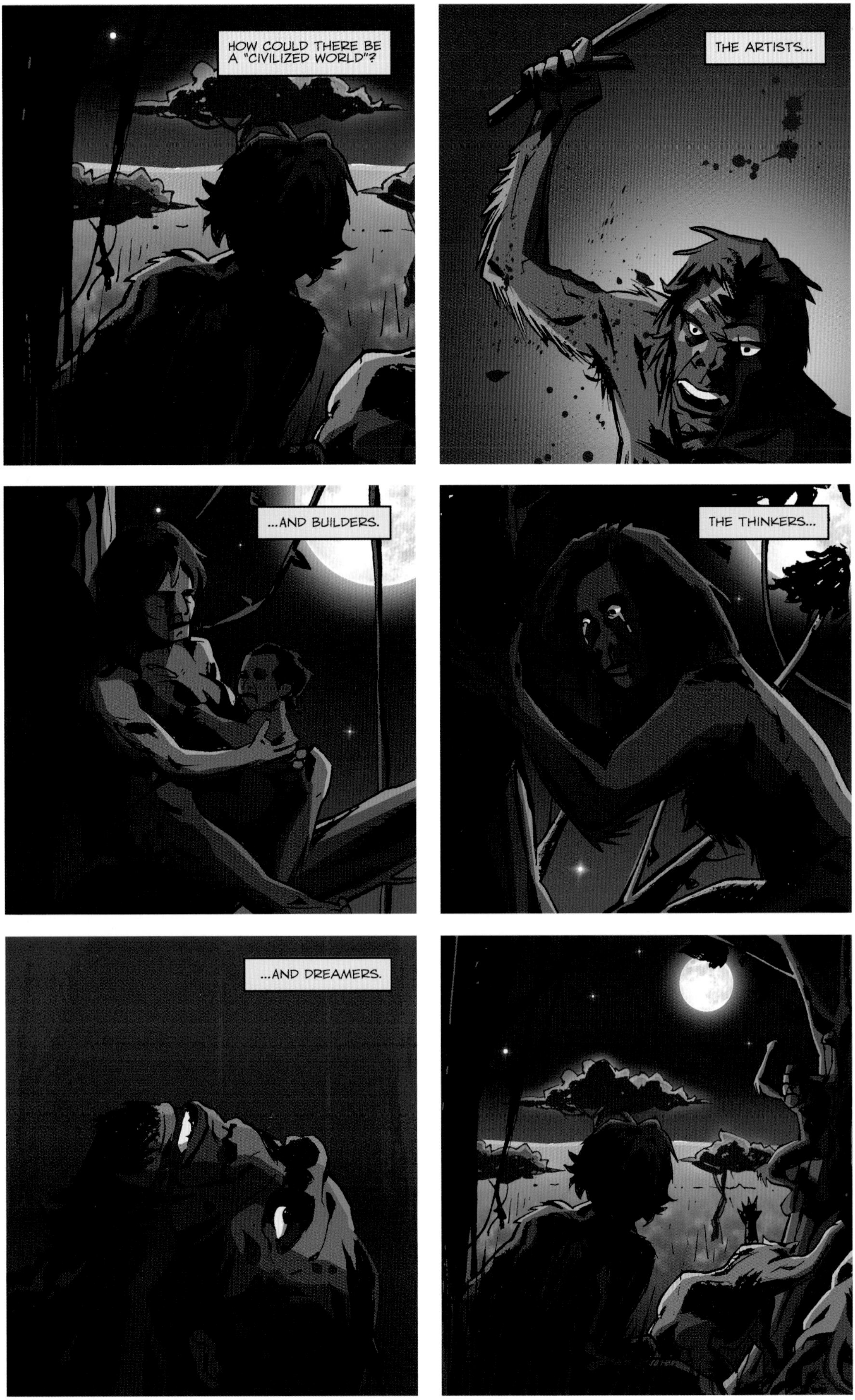
HOW COULD THERE BE A "CIVILIZED WORLD"?
THE ARTISTS...
...AND BUILDERS.
THE THINKERS...
...AND DREAMERS.

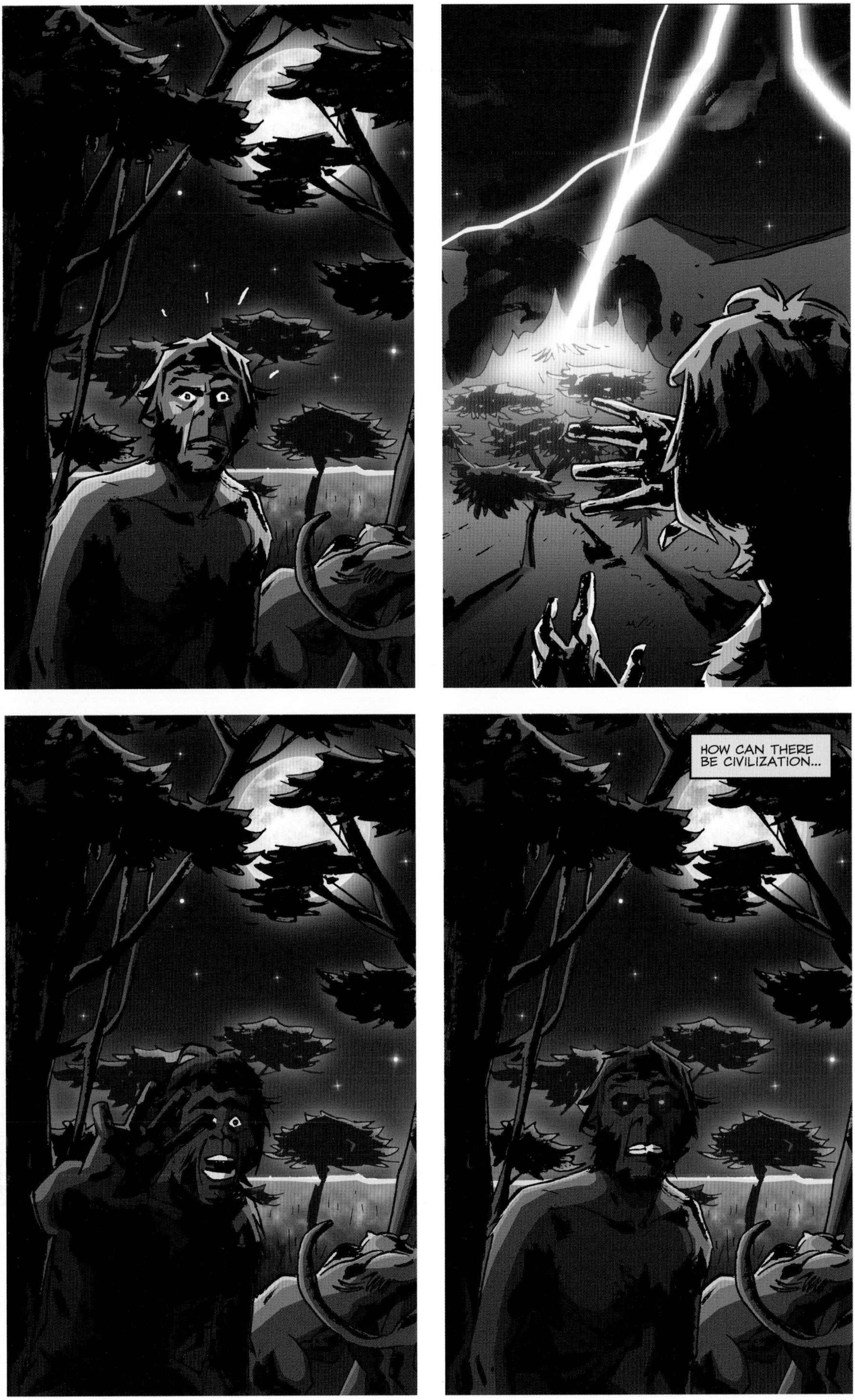
HOW CAN THERE
BE CIVILIZATION...

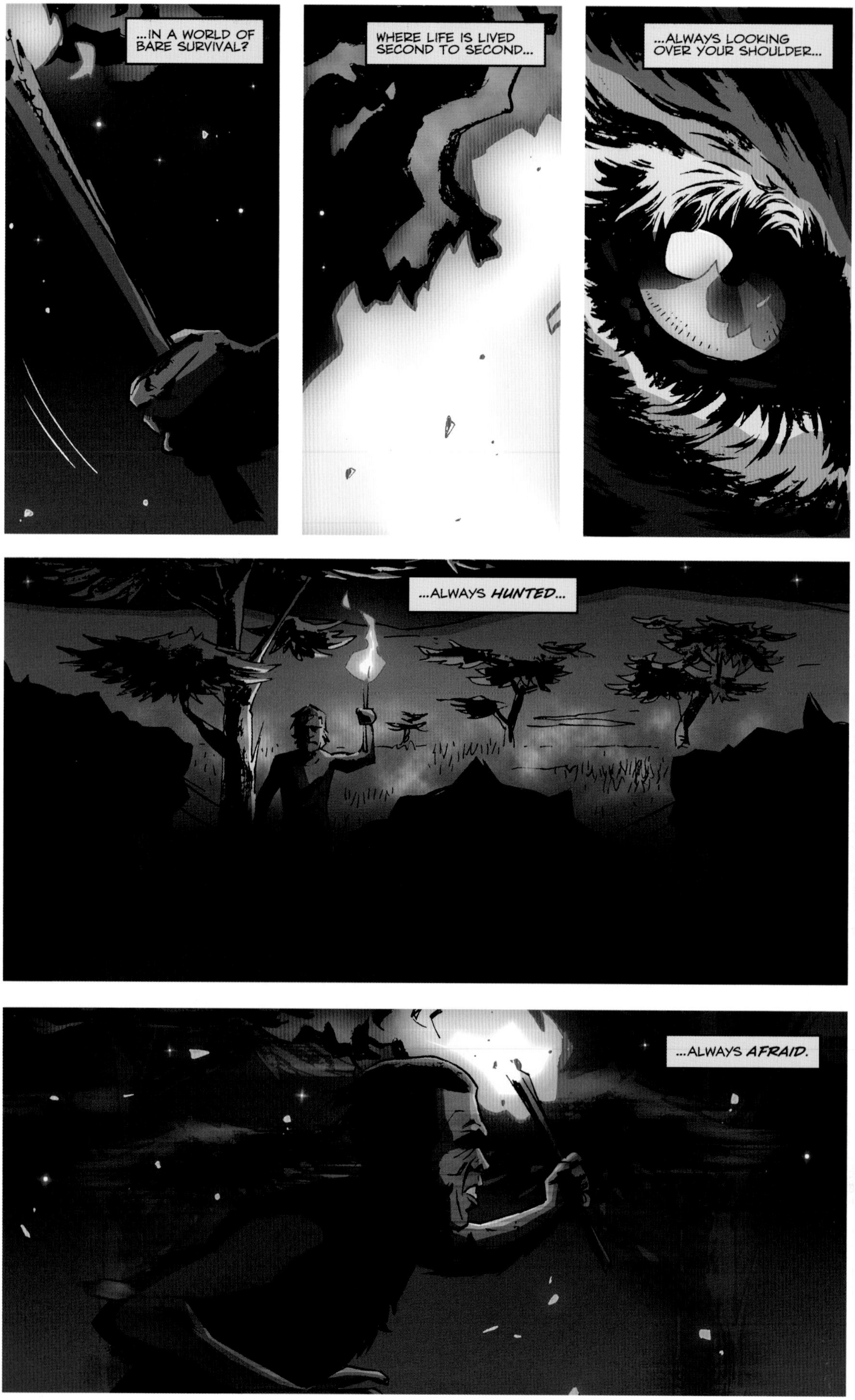
...IN A WORLD OF BARE SURVIVAL?
WHERE LIFE IS LIVED SECOND TO SECOND...
...ALWAYS LOOKING OVER YOUR SHOULDER...
...ALWAYS *HUNTED*...
...ALWAYS *AFRAID*.

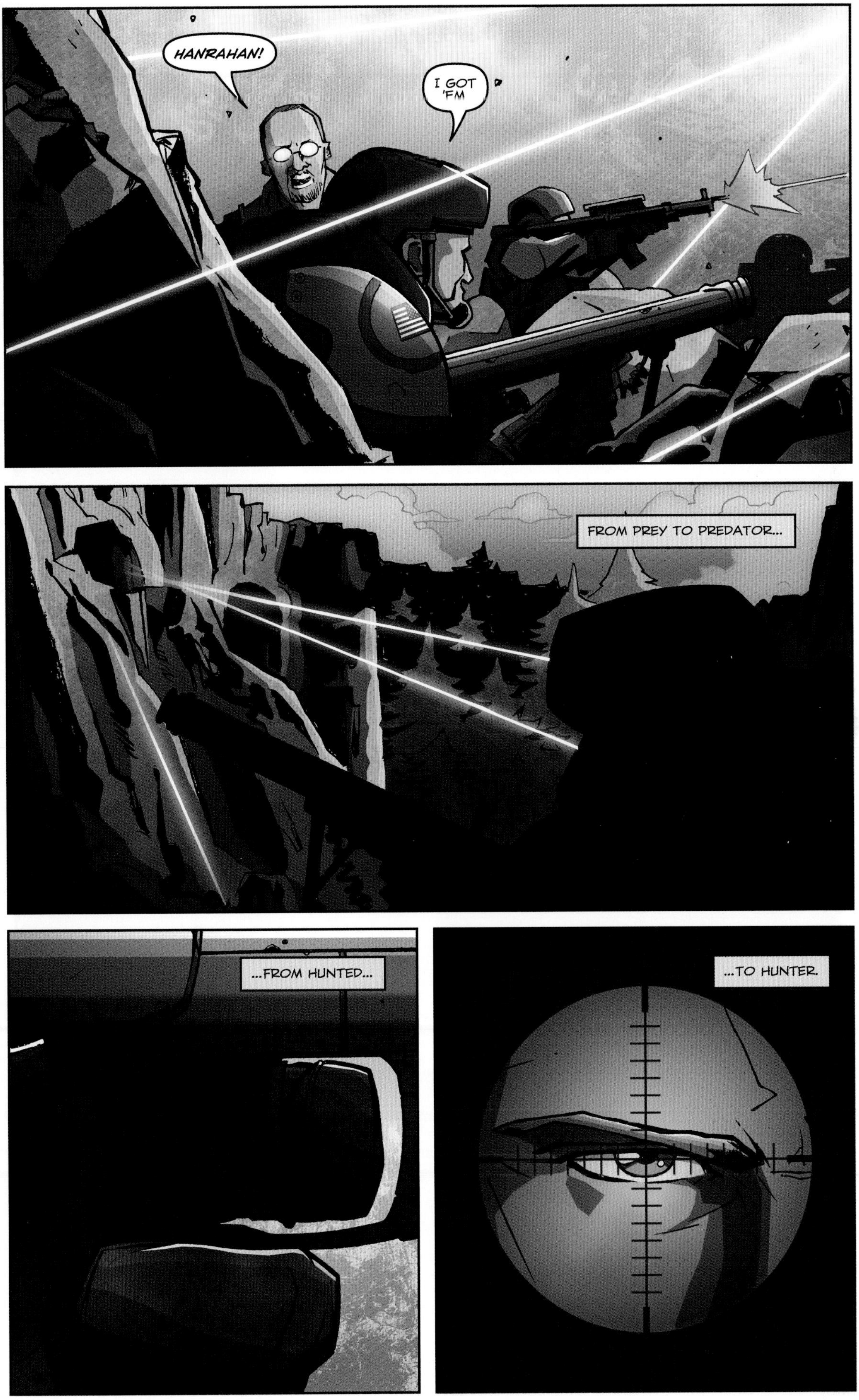
HANRAHAN!
I GOT 'EM
FROM PREY TO PREDATOR...
...FROM HUNTED...
...TO HUNTER.

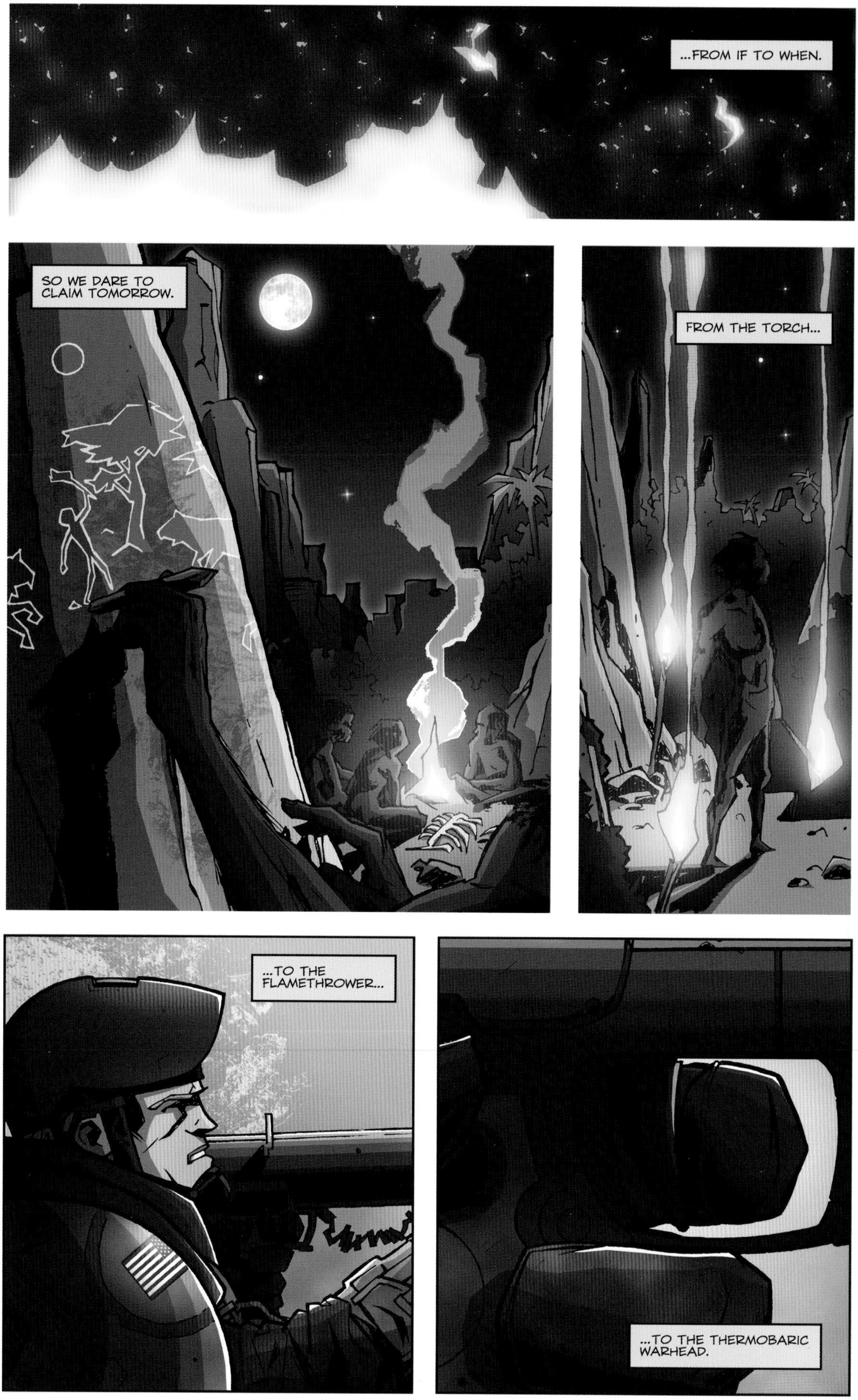
...FROM IF TO WHEN.
SO WE DARE TO CLAIM TOMORROW.
FROM THE TORCH...
...TO THE FLAMETHROWER...
...TO THE THERMOBARIC WARHEAD.

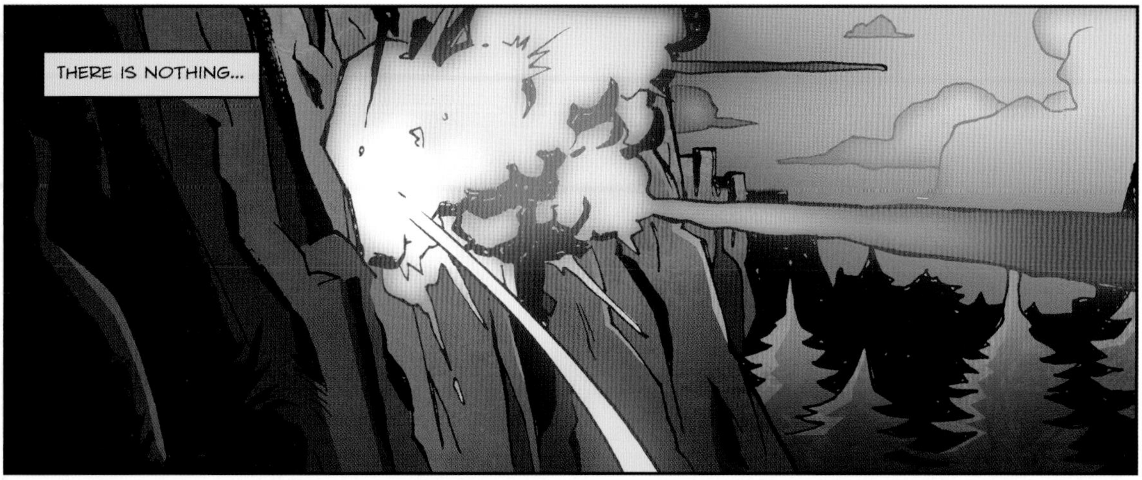
THERE IS NOTHING...

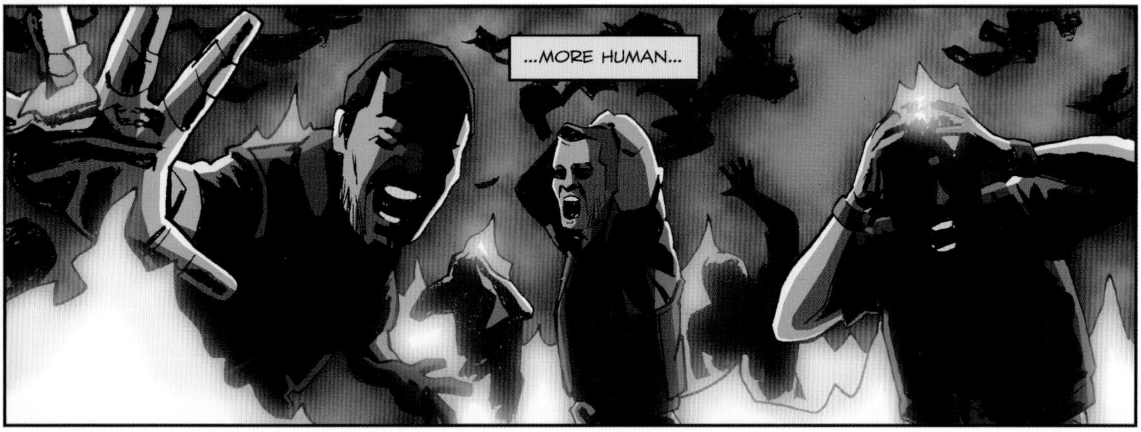
...MORE HUMAN...

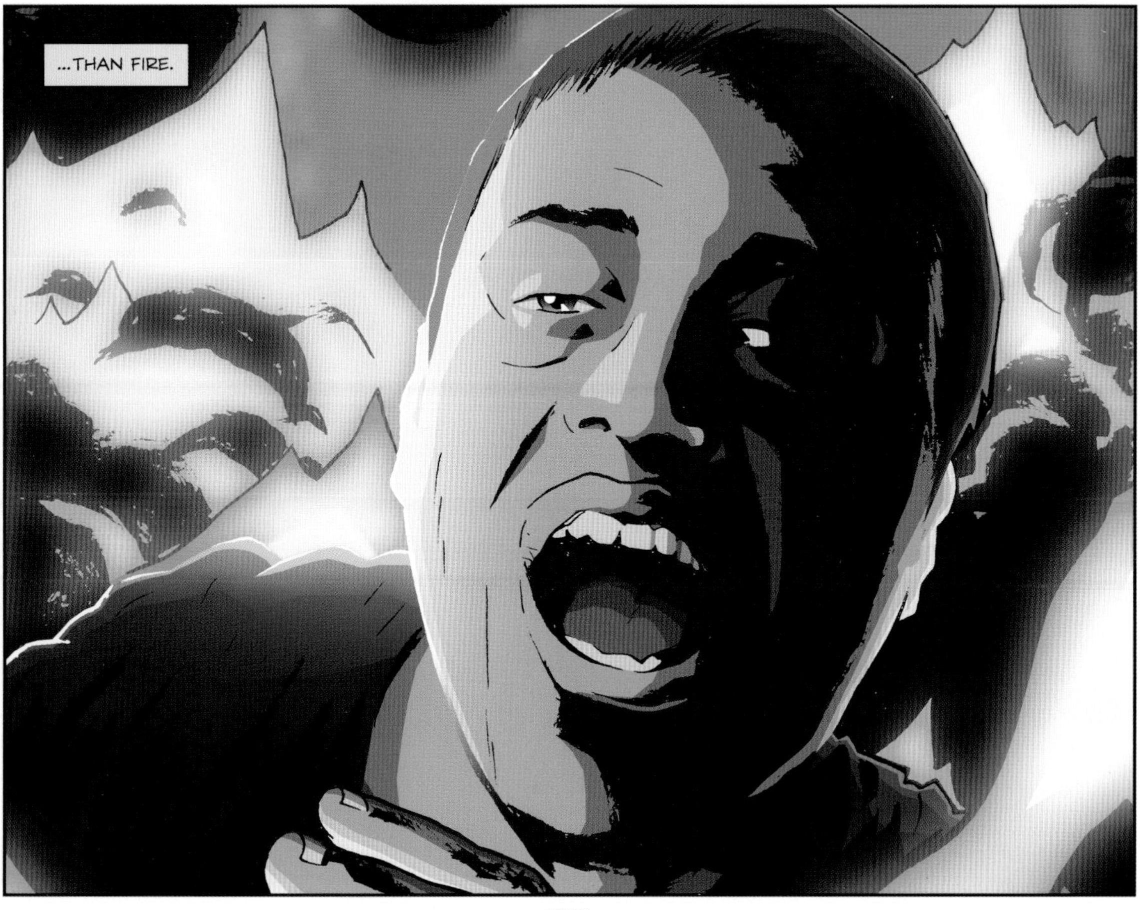
...THAN FIRE.

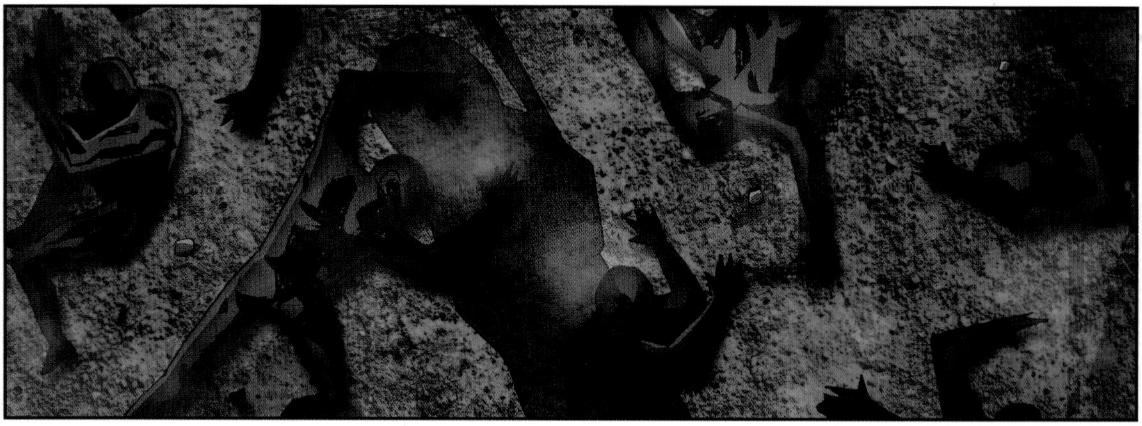

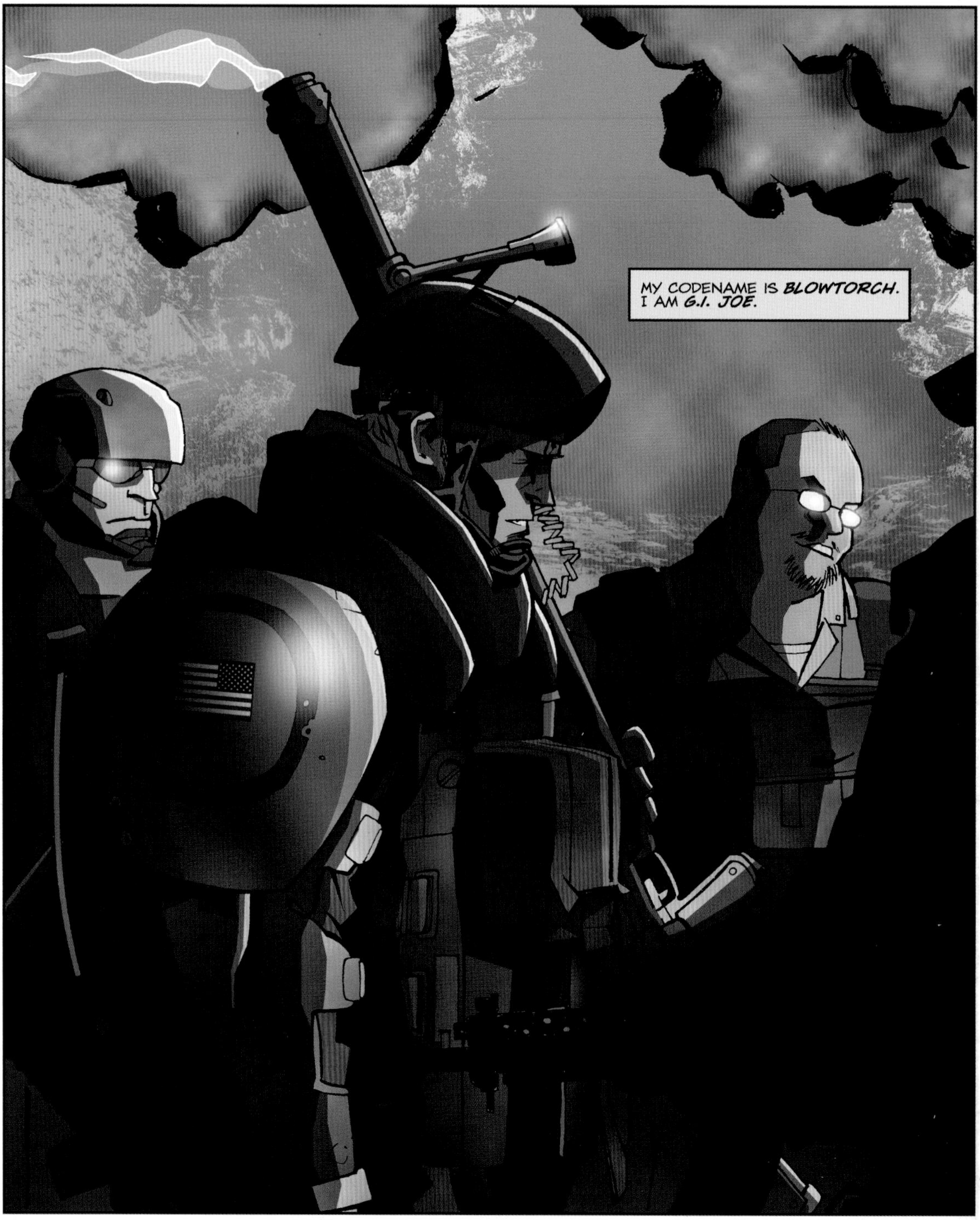
MY CODENAME IS BLOWTORCH.
I AM G.I. JOE.

HEARTS & MINDS

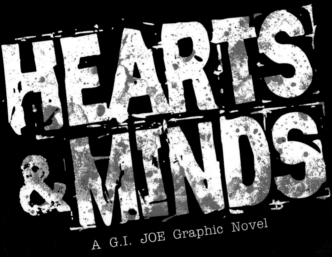

A G.I. JOE Graphic Novel

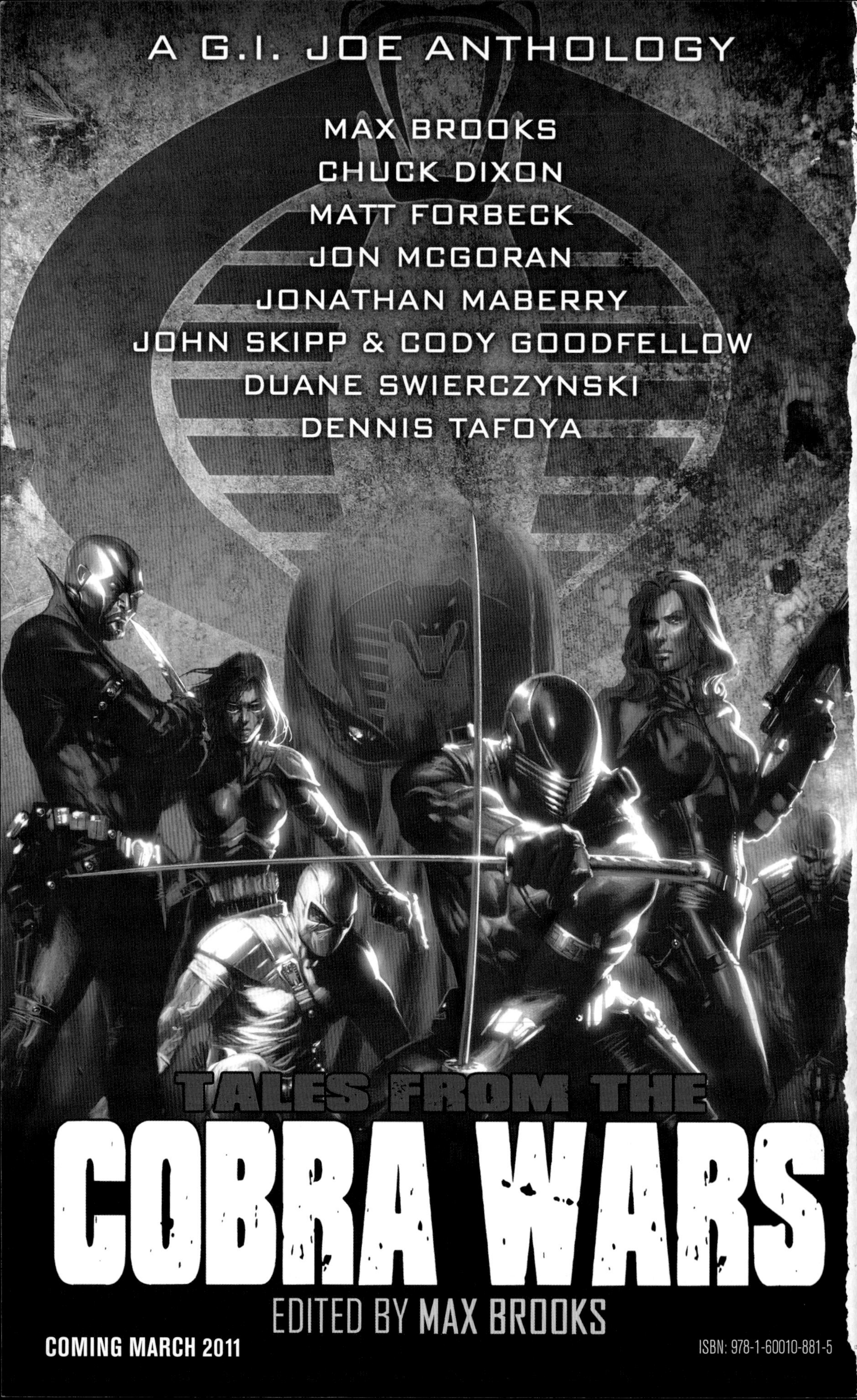
A G.I. JOE ANTHOLOGY
MAX BROOKS
CHUCK DIXON
MATT FORBECK
JON MCGORAN
JONATHAN MABERRY
JOHN SKIPP & CODY GOODFELLOW
DUANE SWIERCZYNSKI
DENNIS TAFOYA
TALES FROM THE
COBRA WARS
EDITED BY MAX BROOKS
COMING MARCH 2011
ISBN: 978-1-60010-881-5